E.D. Perle

BRITISH TOWNS

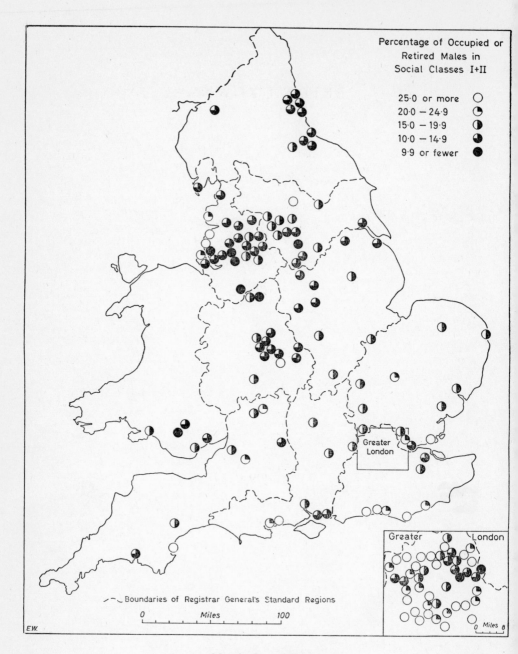

Greater
London

Greater   London

Boundaries of Registrar General's Standard Regions

0   Miles   100

0   Miles 8

E.W.

MAP 1. SOCIAL CLASS

Towns with populations of 50,000 or over
England and Wales, 1951

BRITISH TOWNS

*A statistical study of their
social and economic differences*

C. A. MOSER

and

WOLF SCOTT

OLIVER AND BOYD

EDINBURGH AND LONDON

OLIVER AND BOYD LTD

Tweeddale Court
Edinburgh 1

39a Welbeck Street
London W.1

First published 1961

Printed in Great Britain by
Robert Cunningham and Sons Ltd., Alva

Centre for Urban Studies

The Centre was established at University College London in January 1958. It is its object to contribute to the systematic knowledge of towns, and in particular of British towns; to study urban development, structure and society; and to link academic social research with social policy.

The Centre undertakes and assists a variety of relevant studies in this country; it also keeps in touch with comparable research in other countries. In its work, the Centre attempts to bring together the interests of the social sciences and those of allied fields, such as public health and town planning.

The members of the Committee which governs the Centre for Urban Studies are listed below.

Preface

WHEN the Committee for Urban Studies, as it was then called, was formed in 1957, its research programme gave top priority to a study of the economic and social features of the present urban scene in Britain. For easy reference the study was called 'Urban Typology' since it aimed at identifying and relating urban characteristics in such a way that towns, and perhaps regions, could be 'typed' into fairly distinct groups. Now that the main results are published in this volume, a new short title has been selected and amplified by a longer sub-title. The original plan of the project has been followed very closely by Mr Moser and Mr Scott, who began their analysis early in 1959 and worked on it until the end of 1960.

The urban features examined, in all British towns with populations over 50,000 in 1951, are of several kinds. Some of them are demographic and concerned with population structure and change. Others are economic, having mainly to do with people's jobs. A good many are social, in the fields of housing, health and education. The figures derived from voting at national and local elections have a political content. Many features which are clearly worth study—earnings, employment, land use, entertainment and leisure activities are instances—could not be included in the analysis because of the lack of accessible or comparable data in the period since 1951. Even so, the number of variables related in the study is large, sixty in all. It was only by the use of modern resources for computation that the handling of relationships within such a large complex of variables was feasible. The basic material for this analysis is the set of 1,653 coefficients shown in Table 26, calculated in less than an hour by the high-speed digital computer Mercury. If desk machines had been used, the job could have been done within a month only if forty skilled operators had been employed, and if it had been possible to organise them appropriately.

One object of the study, and the simpler one, is to provide a description of towns of various kinds—metropolitan centres, suburbs and dormitory towns, seaside resorts, country market towns, and so forth. The statistics presented in the early chapters of the book show up the great diversity of urban living in Britain, while also illustrating the similarities between towns such as Bristol and York which are geographically so far apart. The other object, involving both refined analysis and a great mass of computations, is to trace the interdependence of the characteristics of various towns in all its complexity. In attacking this problem, the authors have laid stress on the methodological aspect of their study. It is a pioneering piece of work, at least in this respect, and a full exploitation of the method will only be achieved when it is repeated and developed by others and for other times and places.

The two lines of approach come together in the classification of British towns which the authors suggest in Chapter VI. Most of us have a classificatory urge and there can be few who look upon the 14 groups to which the 157 towns in England and Wales are allotted without a quickening of interest—and without a feeling that they can do better than the authors. There is the fascinating list of 'normal' towns ranging from Cardiff and Darlington to Watford and Worcester. These are the places whose characteristics cluster neatly around the average with few extreme variations. There is the group of towns classified as 'commercial centres with some industry' which include so many of the up and coming universities: Bristol, Reading and Southampton on the one hand, and York, Norwich and Lancaster on the other.

Quite apart from the exploitation of the techniques, this study is directly relevant both to social research and to social policy. The results should have an immediate use as a valuable background for empirical studies in Britain. Future sampling designs cannot fail to be influenced by them. Further studies following up this first approach suggest themselves very readily, and indeed some of them have already been taken up by the Centre.

But this analysis is not only of academic interest. As it reveals more clearly than has been done before the great differences which still exist between the conditions of the towns and regions of Britain, it will have to be taken into account in many considerations of social policy.

R. G. D. ALLEN

17th May 1961

Acknowledgments

OUR thanks are due to a number of departments for supplying us with statistical material, and we would like in particular to mention the General Register Office, the Department of Health for Scotland, the Ministry of Labour and National Service and the Ministry of Education. We are grateful to the Controller of Her Majesty's Stationery Office for permission to use extracts from the Social Survey (Central Office of Information) publication *Some useful data when sampling the population of England and Wales*. The Executive Officers of the 157 towns included in the study supplied us with copies of town guides and other background material for which we are most grateful.

The statistical analysis was done on the Mercury Digital Computer of the University of London Computer Unit, and we are grateful to Mr W. L. B. Nixon and Mr E. Nixon and to their assistant, Mrs Gallagher, for their technical help with programming and machining, and also for their advice. At another stage of the processing we employed Hollerith cards, and wish in this connection to acknowledge the help both of Mrs Pat Mooney and of Mr J. G. Pritchard of the Tabulating Research Centre. We thank Professor M. G. Kendall, Director of the Research Techniques Division at the London School of Economics, for a grant of £100 to finance part of the analysis, and Miss J. M. May and her staff in the Division for carrying out computational work. A good deal of work of this kind was also done by the staff of the Centre for Urban Studies.

For the drawing of the maps we are indebted to Mrs E. Wilson of the Geography Department of the London School of Economics, and for help with diagrams to Mrs J. P. Mandeville. Mr I. C. Cannon gave us advice on typographical matters. We also thank Miss F. H. Johnson and Miss P. M. Smith, both of the London School of Economics, and, especially, Mrs J. M. Forbes, of the Centre for Urban Studies, for a great deal of typing and secretarial assistance throughout the production of the book.

In conclusion, we have great pleasure in recording our debt to a number of experts who gave us technical advice and comments on an earlier draft: Professor R. G. D. Allen, Dr B. Benjamin, Miss A. Doig, Miss K. E. Gales, Professor D. V. Glass, Professor E. Jones, Professor M. G. Kendall and Professor Ramkrishna Mukherjee. Above all, we want to thank Mrs Ruth Glass for having suggested the idea of the study and for her invaluable guidance.

C. A. M.
W. S.

Contents

List of Tables

xii

Part One

I

Outline and Main Results

THE study reported in these pages is designed to fill a gap in our knowledge of British towns. Hitherto in this country no systematic and general research has been done into the ways in which British towns differ from or resemble one another. One is all too ready to speak of *the* urban dweller, *the* urban pattern, *the* urban way of life, without appreciating the variations found both within and between cities. Many studies have investigated differences between towns for one particular factor, such as infant mortality, in terms of other features like social class or housing conditions. The central idea of this study has been to unravel the relationships between a great number of urban characteristics, and measure them precisely, rather than to study in detail any single feature. Our approach has been made possible by modern computing machines which can readily assimilate greater masses of material than would have been conceivable in the past.

The two main objectives were, first to assemble and collate material, pointing out the similarities and contrasts, and secondly to classify towns on the basis of their social, economic and demographic characteristics.

This opening chapter describes how we went about our task. It also summarises our findings for the benefit of the reader who is primarily interested in aims and results, and wants to avoid the more technical sections.

Chapters II and III are concerned with our first objective. They demonstrate the striking diversity of British towns. In the course of this descriptive section attention is directed to suburban, as well as urban, areas. Here too our data emphasise the remarkable range of variation.

This brings us to the second and more important objective of our study. In spite of the notable diversity between the towns, it is obvious that many of them have features in common and that they could be grouped into rough categories. Indeed any one of the indices of urban structure covered in the analysis could be used for grouping the towns—according to industrial structure, to demographic pattern, to levels of health or education, and so forth. Such classifications have their individual uses, and we would not argue that the grouping derived below is necessarily to be preferred to them. We have in fact attempted something more ambitious and in a sense more general. It is obvious that the many series used to describe the towns

2

are not independent, that they overlap in the story they tell. Towns with a high proportion of heavy industry tend, on the whole, to have 'low social class' proportions, to have a substantial Labour vote, high infant mortality, and so on. A study of the interrelationships between all the pairs of variables (in Chapter IV) suggests that there may be certain common threads running through these individual variables, and that, if this be so, the towns could usefully be classified according to these common threads. This is what we have tried to do. Chapter V contains the component analysis through which the common factors are extracted, and these factors are then used, in Chapter VI, to form the basis for classifying the towns.

Finally, the study is intended to supply reference material. Appendix A discusses the sources of statistics available for local authority areas and explains the nature and sources of the sixty variables used in the text. Appendix B gives the full data for each of the 157 towns in England and Wales included in the study.

In Appendix C we have tried to make up for the omission from the main body of the analysis of the Scottish towns,[1] of which there were in 1951 seven with populations of over 50,000. This Appendix sets out the data for the Scottish towns, and shows their position with respect to the major social and economic features, as compared with the English and Welsh towns. Appendix D explains the derivation of a useful new index of public health in local authority areas: the expectation of life at year One. Appendix E, finally, contains some notes on previous research into urban differentiation.

'Towns' and local authority areas

Comparative studies of British towns in the past have in the main been confined to County Boroughs. We decided to go beyond these, and to cover all the 157 towns in England and Wales with populations in 1951 of 50,000 or more. These include all except three of the 80 County Boroughs (the exceptions being Canterbury, Chester and Burton-on-Trent which had fewer than 50,000 inhabitants) as well as 64 Municipal Boroughs and 12 Urban Districts. The 157th town is the Administrative County of London.

The inclusion of towns other than County Boroughs has restricted the amount of data available to us, particularly in such fields as education, health and crime. It has however greatly widened the range of *types* of town embraced by the study, which now includes such diverse places as Bexley, a London dormitory, the cotton town of Burnley, Rhondda, a mining area in South Wales, the spa of Harrogate, and Willesden, which

[1] The Scottish General Registry Office, which is the counterpart of the General Register Office in England and Wales, publishes data in a form closely resembling that for England and Wales, but the differences are large enough to make it impossible to obtain matching series on many topics.

is in the very heart of North London. Such diversity is very desirable in what is essentially a pilot study.

The 157 towns, which are listed in Appendix B, contained in 1951 slightly over half the population of England and Wales. A further 30 per cent. lived in smaller towns and 20 per cent. in rural districts.[1] The size distribution is shown in Table 1.

TABLE 1

SIZE DISTRIBUTION OF LOCAL AUTHORITY AREAS IN ENGLAND AND WALES, 1951

	Size group	Population		Local authorities	
		Number	Per cent.	Number	Per cent.
Urban areas					
(County Boroughs,	1,000,000 +	4,460,667	10·2	2	0·1
Municipal Boroughs	500,000-	2,509,810	5·7	4	0·3
and Urban Districts)	250,000-	2,450,822	5·6	8	0·6
	100,000-	7,393,093	16·9	52	3·6
	75,000-	2,122,710	4·9	25	1·7
	50,000-	4,100,435	9·4	66	4·6
Sub-total: Urban areas 50,000 or over		23,037,537	52·7	157	10·9
	25,000-	5,809,070	13·3	163	11·3
	10,000-	4,568,309	10·4	277	19·2
	0-	1,920,805	4·4	368	25·5
Total urban areas		35,335,721	80·8	965	66·9
Total rural districts		8,422,167	19·2	477	33·1
Grand total for England and Wales		43,757,888	100·0	1,442	100·0

Source: General Register Office, Census 1951, England and Wales, *General Tables*, London: H.M.S.O., 1956.

One critical feature of this study is that it is conducted in terms of local authority areas, rather than of towns in the more popular conception of distinct self-contained, built-up areas surrounded by open country.[2]

[1] The distinction between urban and rural areas is often artificial. Some rural areas, for example the mining areas of Durham, are urban in character but do not have urban status; the same applies to some of the growing outer suburbs of London, such as Watford R.D. and Eton R.D. Easington Rural District in Durham County, another example, in 1951 had a population of 82,170 and a density of 2·4 persons per acre, as compared, for example, with Lydd, which is a Municipal Borough but in 1951 had a population of 2,774 and a density of 0·2 persons per acre. Even County Boroughs can be quite small. Canterbury in 1951 had a population of 27,795 and a density of only 5·9 persons per acre.

[2] The distinction is illustrated in quantitative terms by an analysis undertaken by the General Register Office in connection with the 1951 Census of Population. A count was made of the number and size of areas with continuous urban development, ignoring local authority boundaries. An area was said to be built up if its density was 10 persons to the acre or more, but this definition was modified by reference to ordnance survey maps and aerial photographs.. (*Continued opposite*)

In fact, this latter concept hardly corresponds to the reality of urban distribution in Britain, where towns are generally found in clusters, as around London, in the textile areas of South-East Lancashire or in West Yorkshire. One town begins where the last leaves off and the countryside starts only at the extremes of the clusters. In these conditions, the definition of a town as a continuous built-up area makes little sense, for two towns may be physically adjacent, as are Brighton and Hove, yet each retain its distinct characteristics.

Nor would the Census conurbations, each consisting of a cluster of towns, be satisfactory units of analysis. Their boundaries are disputed and become quickly out of date.[1] The Northern conurbations, in particular, are only loosely linked conglomerations of towns whose boundaries happen to touch, but which are in every other respect quite independent. Few people would care to describe a cluster of towns including Leeds, Huddersfield, Bradford, Wakefield and Keighley, all contained in the West Yorkshire conurbation, as a single town in any meaningful sense of the term.

A positive argument in favour of the administrative local authorities as units of analysis is the association of the statistics which we have collected with local government administration. Housing conditions, for example, including overcrowding and the building of new municipal housing, are the responsibility, within the limits imposed by central government, of the Borough or Urban District Council. The councils are also directly concerned with various aspects of health and, in some cases, education and town planning. In a wider sense indeed there is no aspect of urban life, as described in our data, which is not in some way affected by local administration.

[1] Note a few definitions of Greater London in current use:

	Population in 1958 ('000)	Number of local authority areas in 1958
Census conurbation, 1951	8,222	95
Royal Commission Review Area, 1957	8,790	104
Abercrombie Greater London Plan, 1944	10,641 (approx.)	142
Ministry of Housing and Local Government Greater London Region, 1959	12,072	216

(Continued from p. 4)

1951 population in size group	Urban clusters	Local authority areas
	Number of areas	
500,000 or over	7	6
100,000 –	40	60
25,000 –	101	254
Total 25,000 or over	148	320

Altogether 320 local authority areas were therefore contained in 148 urban clusters, a little over two areas per cluster. Most clusters in fact contain only one entire local authority area, the remainder of the surplus being absorbed by a few large conurbations.

B

A functional redefinition of towns

The reasons given for the use of local authority areas as units of analysis do not preclude the possibility of alternative solutions. At the moment we lack the information essential for distinguishing other types of area. Where a town overflows its boundaries to include parts of the surrounding countryside, the analysis might be improved by including these new additions. But in Britain the process is usually more complicated. There is, for example, little if any open country between the adjacent conurbations of South-East Lancashire and Merseyside. Should we therefore combine the two into one single super-conurbation, and treat the whole as a single unit for analysis?

Between the extremes of the country town overflowing into the adjacent rural districts, on the one hand, and the gradual physical merger of giant complexes of towns, on the other, lie every variety of urban species, both simple and complex. No single formula could describe them all. Continuity of bricks, lime and playing fields is irrelevant for any meaningful definition of a town. The better approach is one of functional analysis, treating one complex at a time. To this end a start has been made both in Greater London and in South-East Lancashire by Westergaard[1] and Green[2] respectively, who attempt to analyse the functional inter-relationships between the separate units contained in their respective conurbations.

Also needed are new indices expressing such inter-relationships in quantitative terms. We have in the present study suggested two indices, both based on 1951 census statistics, which touch upon one aspect of functional relationships, namely the demand for, and supply of, labour. The job ratio measures the daily *net* flow of labour into, or out of, an area; the commuting ratio measures both total inflow *and* total outflow. Thus the two indices describe the extent to which an area is dependent for the placing of its labour and/or the filling of its own vacancies on other local authority areas. Where the ratios indicate considerable commuting, one could further study its direction and on this basis delineate the spheres of influence of employment centres.

The choice of data

Urban life can be described in terms of an endless number of demographic, economic and social attributes. Population structure, housing conditions, economic activity, health, education, social life, administration, voting behaviour, are but a few of the many facets of town life which could be included, and each of these contains many sub-divisions. In practice, one is limited by the statistics available. Absence of data for small areas is

---

[1] Westergaard, J., 'The Growth and Structure of Greater London', in Centre for Urban Studies, *Statement of Evidence to the Royal Commission on Local Government in Greater London*, London, 1959.

[2] Green, L. P., *Provincial metropolis: the future of Local Government in south-east Lancashire: a study in metropolitan analysis*, Allen and Unwin, London, 1959.

a familiar lament among statisticians (just as the multitude of data is sometimes a cause of lament among laymen), which we need not enlarge on. Equally serious is the fact that such local statistics as do exist often refer to differing sets of areas. Employment statistics are based on labour exchange areas, national assistance board data on N.A.B. areas, television and sound licence data on Post Office areas, election data on parliamentary constituencies, and so forth. Such variations make comparative studies troublesome, and we have been forced to confine ourselves to statistics classifiable according to local authority areas.[1]

In consequence, we have covered only the following areas of enquiry:

1. Population size and structure
2. Population change
3. Households and housing
4. Economic character
5. Social class
6. Voting
7. Health
8. Education

The Census of Population for England and Wales 1951 is our main source. It yields a wide range of data on population structure, including age and marital status; education; occupation and industry, including the classifications into social classes; housing structure; and the journey to work. Its main disadvantage is that the data are now a decade out of date. This has not, however, worried us, since this is in any case only a pilot study. If it is thought sufficiently fruitful, it can be repeated when the results of the next census are available.

The Registrar-General for England and Wales publishes a wide range of statistics relating *inter alia* to population size, fertility, mortality, and notifications of infectious diseases. We have used certain of these in the analysis.

Various other sources have been utilised. The Board of Trade Census of Distribution 1950 yielded the data on retail sales; statistics of new housing have been taken from the quarterly returns of the Ministry of Housing and Local Government; election statistics from *The Times Guide to the House of Commons* for 1951 and 1955; the J-index from a Government Social Survey publication; and so forth.

It might be thought that the financial and administrative statistics of local authorities would have been a fruitful source. In fact we decided

---

[1] Exceptions are the four sets of data on the general elections of 1951 and 1955, showing participation in the elections and votes cast for the left-wing candidates. The figures are for Parliamentary Constituencies which in the great majority of cases correspond to local authority areas.

not to use them since they need specialist knowledge and a more detailed treatment than we had time to give.

Another general source of data, the results of sample surveys, has also had to be passed over. There are, of course, many sets of survey results dealing with relevant topics, but any one of them would cover only a few of the 157 towns and, even in these, would contain too small a sample to yield reliable results.

The sixty variables used in the study are listed in Appendix A together with their sources. Three of them, numbered S.1, S.2 and S.3, were added after the analysis was begun, and are included only in Chapter II and in Appendices B and C.

We could add to this list another quite as long of variables that were considered but had, for one reason or another, to be ruled out. It would have been desirable to include figures relating to the physical characteristics of towns, such as smoke pollution, parks and open spaces, factory building and land use generally, but none of these proved feasible. Nor did we manage to include an index of city 'sprawl'. We should have liked to give indicators of cultural activities, but data on radio and T.V. licences, cinema attendance, membership of youth clubs and of other social organisations, public houses, newspaper readership and the like, were each too patchy to merit inclusion. On religious activities no reliable information exists. Crime is a field we would like to have covered, but no suitable data were available for areas other than County Boroughs.

An even more serious gap is in the field of employment and income. Figures on employment and unemployment are available only for Ministry of Labour areas, which are not comparable to those in our study. In the case of income, there is no source of statistics for the towns available to us. The same applies to ownership of durables, such as cars and refrigerators, and to home ownership. In the field of population structure, we have no index of population replacement, nor of internal migration. The Census provides data bearing on internal migration (in the analyses of area of origin), but these can only be used to study movement between counties, not between towns.

Some of the above topics, and many others, could have been brought into the analysis had we had more time or resources. As it is, we have preferred to press ahead with a limited coverage, on the supposition that the study may be repeated on up-to-date figures and a wider selection of variables.

The diversity of British towns

The tremendous variation between the towns for almost each one of the primary variables became apparent as soon as we began the analysis. The details are given in Chapter II and are summarised in Table 2. Consideration of the averages and measures of dispersion suggests that, even if the population of the northern towns 'never had it so good', they could still do considerably better by attaining the standards of their southern neighbours. In 1951 one household in five in Gateshead lived in overcrowded conditions as against one in sixty in Coulsdon & Purley; over one third of the households of Dewsbury (living in unshared accommodation) were without exclusive use of a water closet, as compared with one per cent. of households in Ilford. Voting participation varied by as much as 18 per cent. in the General Election of 1955 (from 67 to 85 per cent.), and 48 per cent. (votes cast as per cent. of total electorate) in the local elections of 1956 to 1958 (from 3 to 51 per cent.). Infant mortality rates in the years 1950-52 were over three times as high in Rochdale or the Rhondda as in Merton and Morden. Five years later different towns were at the extreme ends of the scale and the average level of infant mortality had declined, but the differential between extremes, relative to the average, had actually increased.

The differences between towns of the north and the south are not consistent; Lancashire has its Blackpool and Yorkshire its Harrogate, where conditions approximate to those of the southern seaside resorts; London, on the other hand, trails in its wake areas such as West Ham, which is similar in many characteristics to the industrial towns of north-east England. For a large range of characteristics, however, it appears almost as if there were two universes of towns within the narrow confines of this country, divided by a line running approximately from the Wash in the east to the Bristol Channel in the west, leaving the industrial towns of Durham, Yorkshire and Lancashire on one side, and the market towns, London suburbs and seaside resorts of southern England on the other.

Differences between four broad regions of England and Wales (the North; Midlands and Wales; Greater London and the South-East; and the remainder of the South and South-West) are shown in Chapter III. Reference should also be made to Appendix C, where Scotland is shown to have had in 1951 even more appalling housing conditions—and tuberculosis rates—than the North of England.

Chapter III also distinguishes towns according to three other groupings —by size, by social class, and by population change—so that we can compare, for example, large, small and medium towns, or those of high and low social class, with respect to each of the remaining variables.

Finding a pattern of variation

The rest of the study is devoted to reducing the mass of data contained in the primary variables to manageable proportions, by extracting a small number of underlying factors, and using them as a basis for a classification of towns. A pair of towns like Eastbourne and Hove, for example, have many common features distinguishing them from other towns, such as high social class, an elderly population, low birth rates, a high proportion

TABLE 2

SUMMARY TABLE SHOWING THE DIVERSITY OF THE 157 LARGEST TOWNS IN ENGLAND AND WALES, IN 1951, FOR EACH OF 60 VARIABLES

Variable[1]	Median	Inter-quartile range	Extreme towns and their values				Range
POPULATION SIZE AND STRUCTURE							
1. Population ('000)	84	65	London A.C.	(3348)	Harrogate	(50)	3298
2. % of population aged 0-14	21·8	3·1	Hove	(15·8)	Huyton with Roby	(31·1)	15·3
3. % of population aged 15-64	67·3	1·9	Worthing	(58·8)	Wembley	(71·3)	12·5
4. % of population aged 65 or over	10·4	2·8	Dagenham	(4·9)	Worthing	(24·6)	19·7
5. Females per 1000 males	1108	91	Gosport	(939)	Worthing	(1507)	568
6. Females per 1000 males, age 25-44	1042	84	Barnsley	(917)	Worthing	(1306)	389
7. % of females aged 20-24 ever married	48·1	6·7	Coulsdon & Purley	(31·3)	Scunthorpe	(59·1)	27·8
POPULATION CHANGE							
8. 1931-51—total (%)	11·0	44·5	West Ham	(−41·9)	Huyton with Roby	(973·2)	1015·1
9. 1931-51—births and deaths (%)	9·0	9·1	Hove	(−13·2)	Huyton with Roby	(170·4)	183·6
10. 1931-51—balance of change (%)	2·5	33·9	West Ham	(−48·8)	Huyton with Roby	(802·8)	851·6
11. 1951-58 (%)	−0·2	7·1	Wolverhampton	(−9·1)	Romford	(29·2)	38·3
12. Birth rate ratio, 1950-52	96	19	Epsom & Ewell, Wembley	(70)	Middlesbrough	(139)	69
13. Birth rate ratio, 1955-57	94	19	Merton & Morden, Epsom & Ewell	(71)	Huyton with Roby	(139)	68
14. % illegitimate births, 1950-52	4·9	1·9	Beckenham	(2·3)	Brighton	(8·3)	6·0
15. % illegitimate births, 1955-57	4·7	1·9	Wigan	(2·0)	Willesden	(8·8)	6·8
HOUSEHOLDS AND HOUSING							
16. % persons in private h/hlds	97·5	2·1	Colchester	(85·1)	Bexley, Wembley, Barking	(99·7)	14·6
17. % one-person h/hlds	9·9	4·6	Dagenham	(3·7)	Hove	(20·3)	16·6
18. % six- or more person h/hlds	7·2	3·0	Southgate	(4·0)	Huyton with Roby	(17·4)	13·4
19. % 1-3-room dwellings	10·6	7·5	Doncaster	(3·6)	Gateshead	(50·1)	46·5
20. Persons per room	0·74	0·14	Gt. Yarmouth, Worthing	(0·60)	Dagenham	(0·97)	0·37
21. % overcrowded h/hlds (composite)	5·9	3·3	Coulsdon & Purley	(1·7)	Gateshead	(20·9)	19·2
22. % h/hlds at over 1½ persons per room	4·3	2·3	Coulsdon & Purley	(1·2)	Gateshead	(16·5)	15·3
23. % h/hlds in shared dwellings	12·2	12·4	Dewsbury	(1·5)	Hornsey	(63·5)	62·0
24. % h/hlds with piped water	94	4	Sunderland	(75)	St. Helens, Coulsdon & Purley, Rotherham, Wakefield	(98)	23
25. % h/hlds with W.C.	97	4	Dewsbury	(66)	(15 towns)	(99)	33
26. % h/hlds with 5 amenities	65	22	Rhondda	(20)	Ruislip-Northwood	(96)	76
27. % h/hlds with all 5, or only bath missing	91	7	Dewsbury	(61)	Ruislip-Northwood, Huyton with Roby, Coulsdon & Purley, Ilford, Epsom & Ewell	(97)	36
28. New-housing rate 1945-58—total	48	33	Willesden	(8)	Solihull	(129)	121
29. New-housing rate 1945-58—L.A.s	32	24	Willesden	(4)	Scunthorpe	(90)	86
30. % L.A. of total houses 1945-58	72·8	24·7	Hornchurch	(23·8)	Bootle	(97·7)	73·9

ECONOMIC CHARACTER							
31. Occupied as % of total population	59·7	7·2	Worthing	(43·6) —	Oldham	(69·1)	25·5
32. % of women in labour force	32·6	5·7	Gosport	(20·9) —	Blackburn	(41·2)	20·3
33. % in manufacture etc.	41·6	27·8	Gillingham	(10·3) —	Oldbury	(78·4)	68·1
34. % in all service industries	37·4	23·8	Oldbury	(14·4) —	Gillingham	(75·4)	61·0
35. % in retail	10·3	4·0	Stretford, Oldbury	(3·7) —	Crosby	(23·9)	20·7
36. % in finance, etc.	1·4	0·9	Oldbury, Hayes & Harlington, Dagenham	(0·4) —	Harrogate	(7·1)	6·2
37. % in professional services	6·8	3·7	Stretford	(2·0) —	Carshalton	(35·0)	33·0
38. Job ratio	99	32	Huyton with Roby	(28) —	Acton	(182)	154
39. Commuting ratio	51	56	Hastings, Sheffield	(16) —	Acton	(177)	161
40. Per capita retail sales, 1950 (£)	125	53	Huyton with Roby	(38) —	Worcester	(244)	206
SOCIAL CLASS							
41. % in social classes I+II	15·8	94	Dagenham	(7·7) —	Coulsdon & Purley	(45·4)	37·7
42. % in social classes IV+V	26·0	8·2	Southgate	(10·1) —	Bootle	(43·6)	33·5
43. Social class index	99	46	Bootle	(55) —	Southgate	(252)	197
44. Social Survey J-index, 1954	5·5	6·5	Hayes & Harlington	(·3) —	Coulsdon & Purley	(20·2)	19·9
VOTING							
General elections:							
45. 1951 poll	83·7	3·5	Blackpool	(74·0) —	Blackburn	(89·0)	15·0
46. 1955 poll	78·0	5·3	West Ham	(66·7) —	Lincoln	(85·1)	18·4
47. 1951 % voting left	49·6	14·9	Southgate	(22·6) —	Rhondda	(85·5)	62·9
48. 1955 % voting left	48·8	14·8	Southgate	(20·0) —	Rhondda	(80·9)	60·9
Local elections, 1956-58:							
49. % voting in contested elections	41	10	Wigan	(19) —	Blackburn	(56)	37
S.1 % uncontested seats	11	31	(49 towns)	(0) —	Merthyr Tydfil	(92)	92
S.2 Votes as % of total electorate	34	16	Merthyr Tydfil	(3) —	Lincoln, York	(51)	48
HEALTH							
50. Infant mortality rate, 1950-52	28	10	Merton & Morden	(15) —	Rochdale	(47)	32
51. Infant mortality rate, 1955-57	23	8	Wimbledon	(12) —	West Hartlepool	(43)	31
S.3 Expectation of life at year One, 1950-52	70·1	1·8	Carlisle	(66·2) —	Chigwell	(75·7)	9·5
52. T.B. notification rate, 1957	88	58	Dewsbury	(19) —	Southall	(197)	178
53. Mortality rate 1957—lung cancer	116	41	Coulsdon & Purley	(47) —	Barking	(243)	196
54. Mortality rate 1957—other cancer	106	16	Colchester	(75) —	Barking	(145)	70
55. Mortality rate 1957—bronchitis	106	64	Esher	(23) —	Salford	(277)	254
EDUCATION							
56. % with terminal edn. age under 15	67·8	16·5	Beckenham	(33·6) —	Stoke on Trent	(86·2)	52·6
57. % aged 15-24 in full-time education	8·1	5·4	Dagenham	(4·4) —	Coulsdon & Purley	(25·0)	20·6

[1] In this and subsequent tables only summary titles of variables are given. Full titles appear in Appendix A. All data refer to 1951 unless otherwise stated.

of single-person households, an insignificant degree of overcrowding; they differ from each other *inter alia* with respect to stage of development (Eastbourne declined between 1931 and 1951, while Hove added 25 per cent. to its population), housing structure, local election participation and tuberculosis notification rates.

The objective we set ourselves is to see to what extent one can discern a systematic pattern for all, or groups of, towns both in the common and contrasting elements. A multivariate technique known as component analysis is used to deal with this, and is described in Chapter V. Here we outline only the basic approach and summarise the results of the analysis.

The starting-point is the study of urban differentials, taking one variable at a time. This at once suggests some systematic variation, since certain towns, distinguished by abnormally favourable or unfavourable characteristics, keep on appearing at the extremes of the classifications. In order to study the pattern, we go on to construct indices of simultaneous variation; first, taking two variables at a time, and then continuing with an analysis of the joint movement of many variables.

The first computational step is the construction of a product moment correlation matrix (shown in Chapter IV) which gives the 1,653 relationships between the variables, taken two at a time. This serves not only as raw material for the more complex analysis to come, but is of interest in itself.[1] It throws light on the nature of many statistical series commonly used in urban differentiation: the sex ratio, for example, is seen to be largely a reflection of age distribution (the correlation coefficient between the sex ratio for all ages and the proportion of persons aged 65 or over is 0·834); the proportion of females aged 20-24 who were or had been married is found to be closely linked with the social class structure of the area—the lower the social class, the higher the proportion married. Other relationships are more surprising, such as the low correlations of population size with the other variables. For these large towns at least, size seems to play only a minor role in urban differentiation, compared, for example, with social class, which is highly related to many other variables.

Common factors

The idea of common factors underlying a large number of variables can be explained by means of Figure 1. This is purely illustrative and greatly simplifies the situation:

[1] A telling comment on modern methods of analysis is provided by the speed of computing the matrix. By desk calculator the 1,653 coefficients in the matrix would have required upwards of 6,612 hours or 165 weeks to compute. On the Mercury digital computer the calculations were completed in 40 minutes.

FIGURE 1

AN EXAMPLE SHOWING THE RELATIONSHIP OF COMPONENTS TO PRIMARY VARIABLES

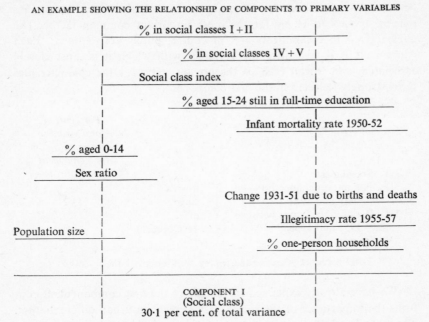

We can think of the variance (or spread) of each of the 57 variables as bars of various size which, put end to end, would add up to the total variance on all the variables. But the variables are correlated with each other; in other words, they overlap, as shown in the diagram. Component analysis can be thought of as a technique for studying the degree of overlapping and for measuring the common segments in an 'area of overlap'. For example, the diagram shows a hypothetical section, marked by dotted lines, to denote one of the components. We can make two sorts of statements about this. First, adding up all the 57 segments cut off by the component (i.e. lying inside the dotted lines) and expressing the sum as a fraction of the total distance obtained by putting all the bars end to end, would give the proportion of the total variance accounted for by that component. The higher the proportion, the more important is the component as a common factor in urban differentiation. Secondly, some kind of sociological meaning can be given to the components by noting which of the bars have a substantial part of their lengths inside the dotted lines.

In the illustration, the following bars are to a large extent inside the sector: per cent. in social classes I+II; per cent. in social classes IV+V; the social class index; the infant mortality rate; per cent. in full-time education. All of these variables are related to 'social class', or more precisely to the occupational structure of the population which is generally referred to as 'social class'. The component with a large social class content was found in the analysis to contain almost a third of the total between-towns variance for all variables. In fact, this 'social class component' proved to be by far the most important common factor. The names given to components are, of course, purely conventional. Each component is named after the variables with which it is most closely associated, and 'social class' is the obvious term for the characteristics most strongly reflected in the first component.

We extracted four major components:

			Per cent. of total variance accounted for by the component
I	Social class		30·1
II	Population change between 1931 and 1951	town's	13·2
III	Population change between 1951 and 1958	stage of	9·8
IV	Overcrowding	development	7·3
	Total percentage accounted for by components I-IV		60·4

We have already explained the nature of the first component. It confirms the importance of the social class element in urban differentiation. The second and third components are linked with the 'age' of a town or its stage of development, as reflected in the change in population for the periods for which such figures are available. Dagenham, for example, which increased its population between 1931 and 1951 by 28 per cent., can be described as a town of recent vintage, whereas at the other extreme, London (the administrative county of London) reached its population peak over 60 years ago and has been losing population ever since; between 1931 and 1951 it lost as much as 24 per cent. Between these extremes, we find every possible variation, with the Yorkshire and Lancashire towns generally having gained least, if at all, in population, and the London suburbs having gained most. The change of population between 1931 and 1951 is, on the whole, an inadequate index of the age of a town, but we could not delve further back into history.

The importance of the growth or decline of a town is clearly apparent when we consider the number of characteristics associated with it, which are described in Chapter V. As a town grows older, and space becomes cramped, the younger people tend to move out to new housing estates in the suburbs, or to adjacent towns, leaving behind them a surplus of older people. This movement is characterised by various features, such as low average size of household, a preponderance of the elderly, low birth rates, houses lacking in modern conveniences, and relatively high per capita retail sales. (The latter characteristic is attributable to the fact that shopping facilities are seldom transferred to the new areas to an extent proportionate to the movement of population.)

The real pattern is of course not as simple as this picture may suggest. The older towns do not have a monopoly of the elderly, nor the more recent towns of children. The differences in the age composition of old and new towns are differences of degree, not of kind.

The third component is associated with changes between 1951 and 1958, the last year for which statistics were available to us. Factors associated with this period again reflect aspects of the ages of towns, and of their stages of development. Thus this component draws attention to the fact that the development which we have described, for example in Dagenham, had come to an end some time before 1951, and that it was the turn of a new set of towns, such as Romford and Thurrock in Essex, to start the cycle of growth.

Above all, this component is important because it stresses the dynamic nature of our analysis. Almost as soon as the data are collected, they are in need of revision; in the case of rapidly growing towns, they may even be out of date. We did not, therefore, adhere to our original intention to exclude data collected after 1951: if that had been done, we should have obtained not only a less topical, but also an incomplete, picture of urban differentiation. The point to note is that an analysis such as the present one should be repeated periodically as differentials between towns are subject to change. And this may be so particularly at periods, such as the recent and current ones, when both urban reconstruction and new expansions take place, with consequent shifts in the demographic and economic characteristics of towns, or parts of towns, old and new.

The fourth component is associated with housing density. The variables with which it is most closely associated are the proportion of households living at over $1\frac{1}{2}$ persons per room; the (rather similar) overcrowding index; the proportion of 1-3-room dwellings (overcrowding tends to be worst where the basic type of house or flat is small); the number of persons per room; the proportion of households without exclusive use of internal piped water supply.

The extent to which the components account for differences between the towns varies greatly between the variables, as is shown in the table overleaf. The components are, for example, closely related to the age structure of the population, in the sense that variations in the latter are very largely accounted for by the components. The opposite is true of such variables as T.B. notifications and population size. If we regard the components as substitutes for the primary variables, they are clearly less efficient substitutes for population size than for the age structure.

The use to which the components may be put will be seen in the next section. One important consideration should however be briefly mentioned, namely that the 'output' of a component analysis depends partly on the

TABLE 3

VARIABLES WITH RESPECTIVELY THE HIGHEST AND LOWEST PROPORTIONS OF THEIR VARIANCE
ACCOUNTED FOR BY COMPONENTS I TO IV COMBINED

Highest	%	Lowest	%
% in social classes I & II	88·81	Tuberculosis notification rate, 1957	12·24
Social class index	86·21	Population size	17·44
% population aged 0-14	85·95	Mortality rate, 1957—bronchitis	20·20
Persons per room	83·60	Mortality rate, 1957—cancer,	
% households at over 1½		other than lung or bronchial	27·99
persons per room	83·56	% households with W.C.	28·35
% in social classes IV & V	83·51	% poll in local elections,	
Birth rate ratio, 1950-52	83·47	1956-58	31·92
% one-person households	82·48	% households in shared dwellings	32·79
Females per 1000 males,		% households with piped	
age group 25-44	81·23	water	35·28
Females per 1000 males,		% 1-3 room dwellings	35·85
all ages	81·09	% poll 1951 general election	44·33

'input'. If we had fed into the machine nothing but social class variables, we would have emerged with the conclusion that social class is in fact not only the most important, but the only factor of any consequence in urban differentiation. This point is also illustrated by the post-1951 data which we discussed above. Had we included no statistics relating to events after 1951, the third component would have disappeared altogether.

This is inevitable, and all we can claim is that the selection of series was determined by the data available, not by the desire to produce impressive components. We consider that the range of statistics is broadly representative of urban characteristics in the fields chosen and that the picture has not been seriously distorted by the selection procedure.

The classification of towns

The chief point of the components is that they make possible a generalised classification of the 157 towns. Instead of having to classify the towns, in turn, by each of the 57 variables, we need now only do so according to the four components. The classification groups together towns possessing roughly the same component scores.

The process is explained in Chapter VI and reference should be made to Figure 2 facing p. 80, which shows the towns plotted, not in geographical terms, but in relation to their positions on the first two components. The circles indicate the approximate preliminary grouping of towns adjacent to each other. In fact the process is much more complicated since the classification also takes into consideration the third and fourth components. (For example, towns not included in a circle, such as Brighton, were later allocated to the nearest groups by reference to the other two component values. Similarly, towns originally included in one group might as a result of the computations be found to belong to another. Wood Green is an example.) The classification is given below.

MAINLY RESORTS, ADMINISTRATIVE AND COMMERCIAL TOWNS

Group 1 (mainly *seaside* resorts):
Worthing; Hove; Hastings; Eastbourne; Bournemouth; Torquay; Southport; Harrogate; Brighton; Blackpool.

Group 2 (mainly *spas, professional and administrative* centres):
Bath; Cheltenham; Poole; Oxford; Cambridge; Exeter; Maidstone; Bedford; Colchester; Southend-on-Sea.

Group 3 (mainly *commercial* centres with some industry):
Southampton; Portsmouth; Plymouth; Bristol; Gloucester; Great Yarmouth; Norwich; Ipswich; Lincoln; Peterborough; Reading; Northampton; Lancaster; Worcester; York; Cardiff.

MAINLY INDUSTRIAL TOWNS

Group 4 (including most of the traditional *railway* centres):
Crewe; Darlington; Swindon; Doncaster; Derby; Carlisle; Chesterfield; Barrow in Furness; Mansfield; Coventry; Sheffield; Wakefield; Stockport; Newcastle under Lyme.

Group 5 (including many of the large *ports* as well as two Black Country towns):
Birkenhead; Liverpool; Grimsby; Hull; Tynemouth; Newport; Swansea; Newcastle upon Tyne; Wolverhampton; Birmingham.

Group 6 (mainly *textile* centres in Yorkshire and Lancashire):
Huddersfield; Halifax; Leeds; Dewsbury; Bradford; Keighley; Bolton; Burnley; Blackburn; Bury; Manchester; Oldham; Preston; Rochdale; Leicester; Nottingham.

Group 7 (including the industrial towns of the *north-east seaboard* and *mining* towns of Wales):
Gateshead; South Shields; Sunderland; West Hartlepool; Barnsley; West Ham; West Bromwich; Salford; Warrington; Merthyr Tydfil; Rhondda.

Group 8 (including the more recent *metal manufacturing* towns):
Stockton-on-Tees; Scunthorpe; Middlesbrough; Thurrock; Nuneaton; Rotherham; Bootle; Dudley; Walsall; Stoke-on-Trent; St. Helens; Wigan; Smethwick; Oldbury.

SUBURBS AND SUBURBAN TYPE TOWNS

Group 9 (mainly '*exclusive*' *residential* suburbs):
Coulsdon & Purley; Epsom & Ewell; Esher; Bromley; Sutton & Cheam; Wanstead & Woodford; Beckenham; Finchley; Southgate.

Group 10 (mainly *older mixed residential* suburbs):
Wood Green; Hornsey; Ealing; Hendon; Wimbledon; Ilford; Heston & Isleworth; Twickenham; Croydon; Surbiton; Crosby; Wallasey.

Group 11 (mainly *newer mixed residential* suburbs):
Chigwell; Orpington; Solihull; Hornchurch; Chislehurst & Sidcup; Ruislip-Northwood; Bexley; Harrow; Carshalton; Wembley; Merton & Morden.

Group 12 (including *light industry* suburbs, *national defence* centres and towns within the sphere of influence of large conurbations):
Gosport; Gillingham; Romford; Luton; Uxbridge; Watford; Slough; Enfield; Mitcham.

Group 13 (mainly *older working-class* and *industrial* suburbs):
Willesden; Tottenham; East Ham; Leyton; Brentford & Chiswick; Southall; Edmonton; Walthamstow; Acton; Stretford (Lancs.).

Group 14 (mainly *newer industrial* suburbs):
    Hayes & Harlington; Barking; Dagenham.
Not allocated to any group:
    London A.C.; Huyton with Roby.

This classification is to be regarded as illustrative; both the number of groups and the allocation of marginal towns are arbitrary and can be adjusted to meet differing needs. Only a few of the groups, those on the periphery of the diagram, are reasonably self-contained; examples are the group of seaside resorts and the middle-class suburbs of group 9. Two towns stand apart from the remainder: London, on the left-hand side of the diagram, surely deserves its description as the 'unique city' at least among the large towns of England and Wales; Huyton with Roby, on the right-hand side of the diagram, owes its singularity to the fact that it increased its population tenfold between 1931 and 1951. None of the New Towns were included in the analysis, since they had fewer than 50,000 inhabitants in 1951, but they would presumably have shown characteristics similar to Huyton in respect of population increase, age distribution, birth rates, etc.

The remaining towns form a continuum, with the suburban types of town occupying the right-hand part of the diagram, and the non-suburban towns the left. Each major division is sub-divided according to the social class structure of the town and its associated elements. The chiefly commercial and 'professional' towns are distinct from the industrial towns (note, for example, the distance between Bath and Cambridge on the one hand, and Gateshead and Bootle on the other). Similarly, the industrial suburbs of Dagenham and Hayes & Harlington, are set well apart from mainly middle-class dormitories like Coulsdon & Purley and Southgate; or the more recently built-up areas like Solihull and Chigwell, from Croydon and Wimbledon whose period of expansion reached their peak some considerable time ago.

The industrial groups lie perhaps more closely together than the grouping indicates. There is little distinction between the marginal towns of groups 3 and 4, or 4 and 5. The extremes, however, are well apart; for example, the older textile centres of Leeds, Halifax and Dewsbury from the 'metal' towns of Oldham and Scunthorpe; or the railway towns of Darlington, Swindon and Doncaster from the Durham towns of South Shields, West Hartlepool and Sunderland.

The final classification, which was obtained through a purely statistical process, provides a grouping in close accordance with our background knowledge of British towns. The distinction between our process of classification and one which makes use of simpler methods, such as dividing towns according to their chief industry, is that we have taken into account a very much wider set of characteristics and. that the criteria of classification emerged from the analysis itself.

Further research

The present study may be looked upon chiefly as providing raw material for further research in the field of urban differentiation. It should help with the selection of relevant statistics for 'explanatory' analyses, in studying infant mortality rates, election results and the like, which from time to time receive attention from sociologists. The correlation matrix (facing p. 58), for example, shows the relationship of each variable to the other 56, besides providing the raw material for other types of multivariate analysis. This in itself should prove of value.

More directly arising from this study is the need to extend the analyses to other towns, perhaps those in the size range 25,000 to 50,000. It should in any case be repeated when the results of the 1961 census are available.

Part Two

II

The Diversity of British Towns

THE main object of our analysis is to classify the towns into a few relatively homogeneous categories or, to put it more modestly, to see whether such a classification makes sense in terms of the 60 variables covered. The approach to this lies in analysing the relationships between variables, rather than in observing any one or other of them singly. This analysis of relationships will occupy Chapter IV, where it is tackled simply, and Chapter V, where we approach it in a more sophisticated manner.

The study of single variables is of greatest interest for conveying the sheer diversity of the towns. Whether we look at population structure and growth, industrial specialisation, housing conditions, health, or any of the other fields touched on, the range of conditions shown in the large British towns is astonishing. The present chapter aims to illustrate this. We need hardly stress that this one-variable approach is to be regarded merely as an introduction to a more searching analysis. Time and again, we are tempted to explain the variation and spread in one variable in terms of another; this, however, must remain the task of later chapters.

Five items of information will be given about each variable, corresponding to five evenly spaced points on the distribution of the 157 towns.[1]

1st-5th town	—	Highest values
Mid-point of 39th and 40th ,,	—	Upper quartile (Q3)
79th ,,	—	Median (Mi)
Mid-point of 118th and 119th ,,	—	Lower quartile (Q1)
153rd-157th ,,	—	Lowest values

These are conventional measures for describing distributions. We have preferred them to others, such as the mean and the standard deviation, largely because of the relative insensitivity of medians and quartiles to extremes. Most of the figures speak for themselves, and we have confined our comments to the minimum.

Population size

As a preliminary, we need to recall that the towns included in the following tables vary from relatively small towns comprising 50,000 people

---

[1] The order is occasionally reversed to accord with the subject matter of the variables.

to the metropolis of London A.C., with over 3 million. Table I showed the complete size distribution, and there is no point in summarising it by averages or measures of dispersion. The five largest and smallest towns, with their respective populations, in 1951, are listed below:

Largest		Smallest	
London A.C.	3,347,982	Harrogate	50,465
Birmingham	1,112,685	Gt. Yarmouth	51,105
Liverpool	788,659	Mansfield	51,352
Manchester	703,082	Esher	51,432
Sheffield	512,850	Chigwell	51,802

On 1959 population figures, Leeds would replace Sheffield as the fifth of the largest towns; the five smallest towns would of course be quite different.

Population structure

TABLE 4[1]

AGE COMPOSITION, 1951

		Percentage of population aged			
0-14		15-64		65 or over	
Lowest		*Lowest*		*Highest*	
Hove	15·8	Worthing	58·8	Worthing	24·6
Blackpool	16·4	Hastings	60·7	Hove	21·3
Worthing	16·6	Chigwell	62·9	Hastings	19·7
Southport	16·7	Hove	62·9	Eastbourne	19·0
Bournemouth	17·2	Eastbourne	63·2	Bournemouth	18·9
Q1	20·5	Q1	66·2	Q3	12·1
Mi	21·8	Mi	67·3	Mi	10·4
Q3	23·6	Q3	68·1	Q1	9·3
Liverpool	26·0	Carshalton	70·2	Chigwell	7·0
Middlesbrough	26·4	Hendon	70·3	Barking	6·9
Bootle	27·7	Heston	70·5	Hayes	5·8
Chigwell	30·1	Merton	70·9	Huyton	5·5
Huyton	31·1	Wembley	71·3	Dagenham	4·9
Highest		*Highest*		*Lowest*	

The agedness of the seaside towns is clearly brought out in Table 4, as is the youthfulness of recently developed towns like Huyton and Chigwell. None of the figures need occasion surprise, yet is it worth noting that there are towns in which a fifth or more of the population are 65 or

[1] We have abbreviated some of the names of towns in the tables. Huyton with Roby becomes Huyton; Hayes & Harlington becomes Hayes; etc. The full names are given in Appendix B. The variables also have been abbreviated: full titles are given in Appendix A.

over, and others, like Dagenham, in which the old, so defined, account for only one in twenty. Conversely there are towns in which almost one in three of the population are under twenty. The practical importance of such variations to the social worker and town planner is obvious.

TABLE 5

SEX RATIOS AND MARITAL STATUS, 1951

Females per 1000 males				Per cent. of females aged 20-24 ever married	
All ages		Aged 25-44			
Lowest		Lowest		Lowest	
Gosport	939	Barnsley	917	Coulsdon	31·3
Gillingham	957	Coventry	931	Finchley	33·8
Scunthorpe	967	Scunthorpe	935	Epsom	33·9
Thurrock	978	Thurrock	944	Crosby	34·0
Coventry	995	Nuneaton	950	Hendon	35·2
Q1	1057	Q1	1007	Q1	44·5
Mi	1108	Mi	1042	Mi	48·1
Q3	1148	Q3	1091	Q3	51·2
Eastbourne	1385	Eastbourne	1246	Barnsley	58·6
Hastings	1391	Southport	1248	Rotherham	58·6
Bournemouth	1396	Bournemouth	1257	Gosport	58·7
Hove	1481	Hove	1264	Nuneaton	58·9
Worthing	1507	Worthing	1306	Scunthorpe	59·1
Highest		Highest		Highest	

There is not much variation between the sex ratios and marriage rates, although a handful of towns with very high and very low rates stand out. The seaside resorts contain the largest surplus of women (which is not due only to the presence of the elderly), while the most severe shortage of women appears to be in the naval base of Gosport! Since middle-class girls tend to marry later than working-class girls, typical middle-class suburbs such as Coulsdon & Purley and Finchley contain the largest proportion of unmarried women aged 20-24. The highest marriage rates among young women appear also in the towns with the lowest sex ratios, such as Scunthorpe, Nuneaton and Barnsley.

Population change

The first column of Table 6 suffices to show the vast differences in population growth between towns. But we should at this point remind ourselves that these towns are local authority areas and not urban agglomerations in a geographical sense. When we see in Table 6 that the population of London fell by about a quarter between 1931 and 1951, we know this fact to refer to the administrative county of London, not to the

TABLE 6
POPULATION CHANGE, 1931-51 AND 1951-58

Per cent. change in population 1931-51						Per cent. change in population 1951-58	
Total		Due to births and deaths		Due to other causes			
Lowest		*Lowest*		*Lowest*		*Lowest*	
West Ham	−41·9	Hove	−13·2	West Ham	−48·8	Wolverhampton	−9·1
London A.C.	−23·9	Worthing	−12·3	London A.C.	−27·8	Edmonton	−8·7
Rhondda	−21·2	Southport	− 7·8	Rhondda	−26·4	Salford }	−8·2
Salford	−20·2	Blackpool	− 7·5	Tottenham	−26·1	East Ham }	
Tottenham	−19·5	Hastings	− 6·0	Salford	−25·7	Tottenham	−7·3
Q1	− 1·0	Q1	5·5	Q1	− 8·5	Q1	−3·1
Mi	11·0	Mi	9·0	Mi	2·5	Mi	−0·2
Q3	34·5	Q3	14·6	Q3	26·0	Q3	4·0
Hayes	185·6	Bexley	35·7	Bexley	136·5	Swindon	16·4
Chislehurst	208·8	Solihull	37·7	Chislehurst	177·7	Chigwell	18·0
Chigwell	217·1	Hayes	51·0	Chigwell	195·6	Solihull	25·2
Ruislip	325·9	Ruislip	53·4	Ruislip	272·5	Thurrock	28·6
Huyton	973·2	Huyton	170·4	Huyton	802·8	Romford	29·2
Highest		*Highest*		*Highest*		*Highest*	

Greater London region.[1] At the other extreme, Huyton with Roby, the suburb of Liverpool, has no equal among the larger towns, having multiplied its population almost tenfold in the intercensal period.

The major part of the average increase in population was clearly accounted for by births and deaths, which is also the more stable of the two components of population change. The second and third columns of Table 6, which summarise these figures, are treated independently of one another, and of the first: for example, West Ham, which had the largest population decline between 1931 and 1951, did not figure among the first five as regards 'natural' change which indeed was positive. All the towns among the extremes owe their presence there to gain or loss by migration. The two towns at the bottom of the table, Ruislip-Northwood and Huyton with Roby, are extremes both in terms of natural growth and of internal migration.

The population change between 1951 and 1958 naturally shows less variation. Even so, there are towns whose populations declined by nearly a tenth in these years, and others whose populations rose by a quarter or more. A handful of the towns which had shown the greatest change between 1931 and 1951 again appear here, Salford and Tottenham at the bottom end, Chigwell at the top.[2]

[1] The population of the Greater London Conurbation increased only very slightly in this period (1·6 per cent. as compared with a national increase of 9·5 per cent.) and actually fell by 1·5 per cent. in the period 1951 to 1958. This merely indicates that the new suburbs into which population moved on leaving the inner areas are outside the boundary of the Census conurbation. In terms of population movement, the boundaries of the conurbation are of even less use than those of the administrative county which at least roughly demarcate the older and declining areas.

[2] But see comments in Appendix A, item 11.

TABLE 7
Birth rates and illegitimacy, 1950-52 and 1955-57

Local birth-rate (standardised) as per cent. of national rate				Per cent. of live births which were illegitimate			
1950-52		1955-57		1950-52		1955-57	
Lowest		*Lowest*		*Lowest*		*Lowest*	
Epsom	70	Merton }	71	Beckenham	2·3	Wigan	2·0
Wembley }		Epsom }	72	Coulsdon	2·6	Hornchurch	2·2
Southgate }	71	Leyton }		Wigan }	2·7	Coulsdon	2·3
Hove }		Wembley }	73	Southgate }		Orpington }	2·6
Southport }		Eastbourne }		Barking }		Dudley }	
Heston }	72			Hornchurch }	2·8		
Worthing }				Dudley			
Q1	87	Q1	84	Q1	3·8	Q1	3·6
Mi	96	Mi	94	Mi	4·9	Mi	4·7
Q3	106	Q3	103	Q3	5·7	Q3	5·7
						Gt. Yarmouth }	7·9
Liverpool	126	Sunderland	124	Bournemouth }	7·4	Bournemouth }	
Sunderland	127	W. Hartlepool	129	Halifax }		Blackpool }	8·0
W. Hartlepool	128	Middlesbrough	133	Cheltenham	7·7	Oxford }	
Bootle	134	Bootle	137	Hove	8·1	London A.C.	8·4
Middlesbrough	137	Huyton	139	Brighton	8·3	Willesden	8·8
Highest		*Highest*		*Highest*		*Highest*	

In Table 7, it is once again the extremes that command attention, some towns, notably the London middle-class suburbs, having birth rate ratios of 70, others in the North of England having ratios about twice as high.

The scatter about the average of illegitimate births is very considerable. We may note the prominence at the upper extreme of the seaside resorts and spas such as Brighton, Hove, as well as of Willesden and London A.C. To quote the County Medical Officer of Health for London: 'With a greater proportion of women of child-bearing age and fewer of them married in London than in the country generally, there is a greater exposure to the risk of illegitimacy. Nevertheless, this does not account for the illegitimacy rate being nearly double that of England and Wales. Some part of the London excess is due to unmarried mothers making their way to London to bear their children in the shelter of the anonymity of a large city and to take advantages of the facilities therein. . . .'[1] Similar considerations may apply to the seaside resorts which, though they lack the 'anonymity of a large city', possess all the other attributes of impersonal privacy.

Households and housing

It is but a short step from this demographic summary to a study of the households into which the population is grouped. Table 8 shows little variation in the proportions living in private households. Only a handful

---

[1] *Report of the County Medical Officer of Health and Principal School Medical Officer for the Year 1957*, London County Council, 1958.

of towns have substantial proportions living in institutional households; among these is Colchester with its military establishments, Epsom & Ewell with a large number of hospitals and seaside resorts like Torquay, Bournemouth and Blackpool.

TABLE 8

PRIVATE HOUSEHOLDS: HOUSEHOLD AND DWELLING SIZE, 1951

Per cent. of persons living in dwellings occupied by private households		Per cent. of private households with				Per cent. of dwellings with 1-3 rooms	
		1 person		6 or more persons			
Highest		*Lowest*		*Highest*		*Lowest*	
Bexley ⎫		Dagenham	3·7	Huyton	17·4	Doncaster	3·6
Wembley ⎬ 99·7		Hayes	4·2	Bootle	16·2	Solihull	4·7
Barking ⎭		Scunthorpe	4·5	St. Helens	15·1	Scunthorpe	5·0
Merton		Chigwell ⎱ 5·2		Liverpool	13·2	Gloucester ⎫	
Walthamstow ⎬ 99·6		Huyton ⎰		Dagenham	12·9	Leicester ⎬ 5·1	
Wood Green						Coulsdon ⎭	
Smethwick ⎭							
Q3 —⎪—	98·3	Q1 —⎪—	7·6	Q3 —⎪—	8·9	Q1 —⎪—	8·0
Mi —⎪—	97·5	Mi —⎪—	9·9	Mi —⎪—	7·2	Mi —⎪—	10·6
Q1 —⎪—	96·3	Q3 —⎪—	12·1	Q1 —⎪—	5·8	Q3 —⎪—	15·6
				Leyton ⎱ 4·8			
Blackpool	88·9	Bournemouth	16·5	Blackburn ⎰		Newcastle-on-Tyne	40·6
Bournemouth	88·7	Hornsey	17·1	Beckenham	4·7	Dewsbury	43·4
Torquay	87·2	Hastings	17·5	Hornsey	4·5	South Shields ⎱ 44·7	
Epsom	86·2	London A.C.	19·7	Hove	4·4	Halifax ⎰	
Colchester	85·1	Hove	20·3	Southgate	4·0	Gateshead	50·1
Lowest		*Highest*		*Lowest*		*Highest*	

More remarkable is the large variation in dwelling size, as expressed by the proportion of dwellings with 1-3 rooms. The range is from a mere 4 per cent. in Doncaster to 50 per cent. in Gateshead. But this is partly a reflection of regional differences in the structure of housing, illustrated in the following figures:

Registrar-General's Standard Region	*Percentage of occupied dwellings with 1-3 rooms*
Northern	31·9
East and West Ridings	24·0
North Western	12·4
North Midland	9·8
Midland	12·6
Eastern	11·2
London and South Eastern	17·3
Southern	12·2
South Western	12·1
Wales	10·3

Source: General Register Office, Census 1951, England and Wales, *Housing Report*, London: H.M.S.O., 1956, which also contains a note on the contents of the standard regions.

Variations in household size are considerable, in keeping with differences in housing and population structure. The seaside resorts cater for old people living by themselves, while London A.C. and Hornsey have large areas of old residential property, suitable for conversion into single-room lodging houses. At the other extreme are the newer suburbs with their three- to five-room houses and young families.

Housing density and sharing of dwellings

Overcrowding is greatest in the north-eastern seaboard towns and in Liverpool, and least in the middle-class London suburbs. It is a sad reflection on the state of some northern towns that every fifth, sixth or seventh household should live below a standard which represents the least that might be expected in a civilised community.[1] It is to be hoped that the 1961 Census will show the extent of overcrowding in the north to have been reduced.

TABLE 9

PERSONS PER ROOM, OVERCROWDING AND SHARING, 1951

Average number of persons per room		Per cent. of households living at				Per cent. of households in shared dwellings	
		over 1½ persons per room		In overcrowded conditions —composite index			
Lowest		*Lowest*		*Lowest*		*Lowest*	
Yarmouth } Worthing }	·60	Coulsdon	1·2	Coulsdon	1·7	Dewsbury	1·5
Coulsdon	·62	Beckenham	1·4	Beckenham	2·4	Keighley	2·3
Beckenham } Eastbourne }	·63	Solihull	1·8	Worthing	2·5	Bury	2·7
		Worthing } Wanstead }	1·9	Yarmouth } Solihull }	2·6	Halifax	2·9
						Burnley	3·1
Q1 -|-	0·64	Q1 -|-	3·4	Q1 -|-	4·7	Q1 -|-	7·6
Mi -|-	0·74	Mi -|-	4·3	Mi -|-	5·9	Mi -|-	12·2
Q3 -|-	0·78	Q3 -|-	5·7	Q3 -|-	7·9	Q3 -|-	20·0
Huyton } Barking }	·90	Liverpool } South Shields }	10·2	Liverpool	12·5	Plymouth	47·6
Sunderland	·95	Huyton	10·3	South Shields	14·7	London A.C.	47·8
Gateshead } Dagenham }	·97	Newcastle-on-Tyne	12·9	Newcastle-on-Tyne	16·3	Acton	48·0
		Sunderland	13·7	Sunderland	17·7	Willesden	57·8
		Gateshead	16·5	Gateshead	20·9	Hornsey	63·5
Highest		*Highest*		*Highest*		*Highest*	

Unlike overcrowding, sharing is not primarily an index of poor housing. It is defined in terms of access from the dwelling to a common staircase or passage, as might be expected in a badly converted, though possibly otherwise adequate, house. It is also a reflection of the amount of subletting.

Household amenities

The picture of housing amenities covers only households living in undivided dwellings. Sharing of amenities therefore points not so much

[1] Appendix C shows that overcrowding in Scotland is considerably worse than even in the Durham towns.

to an imperfect conversion or to the presence of lodging houses as to the structural defect of a house. In Sunderland, for example, where 25 per cent. of all undivided households are without the exclusive use of piped water laid on inside the house, the water is often obtained from a tap in the back yard.

TABLE 10

HOUSEHOLD AMENITIES, 1951

Per cent. of private households in undivided dwellings with exclusive use of

Internal piped water supply		W.C.		All five standard household arrangements[1]		All five arrangements or only bath shared or missing	
Lowest		*Lowest*		*Lowest*		*Lowest*	
Sunderland	75	Dewsbury	66	Rhondda	20	Dewsbury	61
Grimsby	79	Warrington	69	Merthyr	30	Rhondda	63
South Shields } W. Bromwich }	81	South Shields } Leeds }	71	West Ham	35	Merthyr } South Shields }	64
Hull	83	Barnsley } Huddersfield }	74	Oldham	37	Warrington } Leeds }	66
↑				Rochdale	39		
				↑		↑	
Q1 –|–	91	Q1 –|–	94	Q1 –|–	57	Q1 –|–	87
Mi –|–	94	Mi –|–	97	Mi –|–	65	Mi –|–	91
Q3 –|–	95	Q3 –|–	98	Q3 –|–	79	Q3 –|–	94
↓		↓		Dagenham } Coulsdon }	93	Ruislip ⎫ Huyton ⎪	
(11 towns)	97	(15 towns)	99	Huyton	94	Coulsdon ⎬	97
St. Helens				Wembley	95	Ilford ⎪	
Coulsdon } Rotherham } Wakefield }	98			Ruislip	96	Epsom ⎭	
Highest		*Highest*		*Highest*		*Highest*	

The range of variation is relatively small except in the exclusive use of all five amenities, which is virtually an index of the possession of a fixed bath. This is common enough in the recently built suburbs, but in Rhondda only 22 per cent. of all households in undivided dwellings have a fixed bath inside the house for their own use.

New housing

Table 11 indicates that none of the towns which we had occasion to single out because of their poor housing conditions, with the exception of Sunderland, appear in the list of towns with the greatest amount of new building. As will be clear in Chapter IV, there is no simple relationship between poor housing conditions and building of new houses. In many parts of London, for example, the absence of any effective policy of re-development, involving the clearance of slum and quasi-slum property, has meant that little land was available for new building. Provision for new housing was made in the outer suburbs of London, and almost all the areas listed in the table as having built the smallest number of new houses have lost population since 1951. If housing will not come to the people,

[1] Piped water, W.C., cooking stove, kitchen sink, fixed bath.

TABLE 11
New housing, 1945-58

Houses built 1945-58 per 1000 population in 1951				Per cent. of houses built 1945-58 by Local Authorities	
Total		By Local Authorities			
Lowest		*Lowest*		*Highest*	
Willesden	8	Willesden	4	Bootle	97·7
Leyton	10	Southgate	7	Smethwick	96·8
Rhondda ⎫	13	Leyton	8	Rhondda	95·5
Tottenham ⎭		Wimbledon ⎫		Merthyr	94·5
Wood Green	14	Sutton ⎬	9	Gateshead	94·0
		Wood Green ⎭			
Q1 –⊢–	33	Q1 –⊢–	23	Q3 –⊢–	83·4
Mi –⊢–	48	Mi –⊢–	32	Mi –⊢–	72·8
Q3 –⊢–	66	Q3 –⊢–	47	Q1 –⊢–	58·7
		Cheltenham ⎫	64		
Swindon	101	Carlisle ⎭		Southgate	32·7
Orpington	105	Bootle	67	Sutton	28·3
Hornchurch	111	Sunderland	72	Worthing	27·9
Scunthorpe	113	Swindon	82	Solihull	24·7
Solihull	129	Scunthorpe	90	Hornchurch	23·8
Highest		*Highest*		*Lowest*	

the people must move to the houses, even if this means leaving the area where they like to live. The disadvantages of thus emptying the centre of a town are also felt in other ways, for example in the social and private costs of longer journeys to work.

Economic and industrial character

In this and the next section we present what information we have been able to assemble on the economic and industrial character of towns. Table 12 summarises the size of the labour force and the prominence of women in it. Table 14 (on p. 32) shows the distribution of the population working in the town in terms of five industrial classes. Labour force is interpreted according to the census meaning of the 'occupied population'.

The textile towns of the north, with substantial female employment, figure prominently among the most heavily occupied, the seaside towns, with their considerable retired populations, naturally being found at the opposite extreme. On average, about 60 per cent. of the population aged 15 and over in these towns are occupied, and the quartiles show relatively little variability around this average.

TABLE 12
LABOUR FORCE, 1951

Per cent. of total resident population aged 15 or over who were occupied		Per cent. of women in labour force	
Lowest		*Lowest*	
Worthing	43·6	Gosport	20·9
Hastings	48·2	Scunthorpe	21·6
Hove	48·4	Gillingham	22·4
Bournemouth	49·4	Rhondda	22·8
Epsom	49·6	Plymouth	23·0
Q1	56·9	Q1	29·5
Mi	59·7	Mi	32·6
Q3	64·0	Q3	35·2
Hayes } Burnley }	67·7	Eastbourne	38·7
Salford	68·5	Oldham	40·3
Rochdale	68·6	Rochdale	40·5
Stoke	68·7	Burnley	40·9
Oldham	69·1	Blackburn	41·2
Highest		*Highest*	

TABLE 13
JOB RATIO AND COMMUTING RATIO, 1951; RETAIL SALES, 1950

Job ratio		Commuting ratio		Retail sales per head (£)	
Lowest		*Lowest*		*Lowest*	
Huyton	28	Hastings } Sheffield }	16	Huyton	38
Bexley	29			Chigwell	61
Carshalton	30	Plymouth	17	Oldbury	63
Hornsey	42	Eastbourne }	18	Hornchurch	65
Hornchurch	44	Hull } Yarmouth }		Carshalton	66
Q1	79	Q1	30	Q1	106
Mi	99	Mi	51	Mi	125
Q3	111	Q3	86	Q3	159
Brentford	134	Wood Green } Wembley }	110	Eastbourne	200
London	146	Merton	114	Bedford } Oxford }	202
Derby	148	Brentford	139		
Stretford	166	Stretford	175	Bournemouth	236
Acton	182	Acton	177	Worcester	244
Highest		*Highest*		*Highest*	

TABLE 14

INDUSTRIAL DISTRIBUTION, 1951

Percentage of population working in the area in

Manufacture, agriculture, and mining	All service industries	Retail	Selected service industries — Finance, insurance, banking	Professional services
Highest	*Lowest*	*Lowest*	*Lowest*	*Lowest*
Oldbury 78·4	Oldbury 14·4	Stretford ⎱ 3·7	Oldbury ⎱	Stretford 2·0
Smethwick 75·1	Stretford 15·9	Oldbury ⎰	Hayes ⎰	Oldbury 2·1
Dagenham 73·7	Hayes 16·2	Hayes 4·0	Dagenham ⎱ 0·4	Acton 2·2
Stretford 73·1	Smethwick 17·9	Acton 4·1	Thurrock ⎰	Hayes 2·3
Coventry 69·4	Dagenham 18·5	Dagenham 5·3	Mitcham	Smethwick 2·6
			Barking ⎱	
			Smethwick ⎰ 0·6	
			Stretford	
Q3 56·4	Q1 28·5	Q1 8·6	Q1 1·1	Q1 5·5
Mi 41·6	Mi 37·4	Mi 10·3	Mi 1·4	Mi 6·8
Q1 28·6	Q3 52·3	Q3 12·6	Q3 2·0	Q3 9·2
Huyton 12·8	Huyton 69·3	Bournemouth 17·6	Bournemouth 3·6	Oxford 17·4
Crosby 12·1	Epsom 71·2	Worthing 17·8	Brighton 3·9	Cambridge 19·2
Hastings 11·8	Carshalton 71·6	Sutton 18·9	Norwich 4·0	Coulsdon 21·7
Eastbourne 11·4	Gosport 74·6	Bexley 22·6	London 6·3	Epsom 29·7
Gillingham 10·3	Gillingham 75·4	Crosby 23·9	Harrogate 7·1	Carshalton 35·0
Lowest	*Highest*	*Highest*	*Highest*	*Highest*

Table 14 demonstrates clearly the substantial differences, well known from general observation, in the industrial character of the major cities.

The indices in Table 13 (on page 31) are a mixed bunch. The first is the job ratio, defined as the population working in the areas per 100 resident occupied population: the greater the net outflow from the area the smaller the ratio, and vice versa. Some towns, like Huyton, Bexley or Carshalton, may be thought of primarily as dormitories, where many sleep but few work. Typically, these are the fringe towns of conurbations. At the other extreme, there are the centres of conurbations, and areas like Brentford & Chiswick, Stretford and Acton, which have an enormous daily influx of workers.

The commuting ratio is somewhat similar, being the sum of the daily inflow and the daily outflow and not, like the job ratio, only the balance. It is a measure of the 'independence' or self-containedness of an area, in terms of labour supply and demand. Hastings, for example, fills most of its vacancies with local residents, whereas, at the other extreme, Acton not only has many of its residents working in other boroughs, but also fills its own vacancies with workers from adjacent areas.

Thirdly, we have a traditional economic index: retain sales per head of population. For want of anything better, this is the nearest we can get to the economic status of an area. The results speak for themselves. The range is vast, from Worcester (£244 per head) to Huyton with Roby (£38 per head).

Social class

The Census grouping of occupations into so-called social classes is described in Appendix A. This is, as we shall see, the most important among our variables for differentiating urban life, since it is associated with so many of the others. The range is considerable, from 7·7 per cent. in social classes I + II in Dagenham to 45·4 per cent. in Coulsdon & Purley; and from 10·1 per cent. in social classes IV + V to 43·6 per cent. Map 1 (facing the title page), shows the social class proportions (in I and II) for the 157 towns.

Voting

The voting figures showing left-wing support are closely associated with the social class distribution. Perhaps of greater interest to the psephologist are the considerable differentials in the proportions using their vote, shown in the first two columns of Table 16.

Local election participation is expressed in terms of the proportion of seats contested; voting turn-out in contested seats; and, thirdly, the combined effect on total participation of uncontested seats and abstentions.

TABLE 15

SOCIAL CLASS, 1951; AND J-INDEX, 1954

Per cent. of occupied and retired males in				Social class index		J-index	
Social class							
I+II		IV+V					
Lowest		*Highest*		*Lowest*		*Lowest*	
Dagenham	7·7	Bootle	43·6	Bootle	52	Hayes	·26
Warrington	7·8	Grimsby	42·9	St. Helens }		Rhondda	·49
Bootle	8·0	West Ham	41·8	Warrington }	55	Stoke	·72
Rhondda	8·4	St. Helens	41·6	West Ham }		Merthyr	·80
St. Helens	8·5	Merthyr } Barnsley }	40·4	Rhondda	56	Crewe	·88
Q1	13·1	Q3	32·0	Q1	78	Q1	2·5
Mi	15·8	Mi	26·0	Mi	94	Mi	5·5
Q3	22·5	Q1	21·8	Q3	121	Q3	9·0
Wanstead	36·5	Wanstead	13·1	Ruislip	197	Chigwell	17·0
Esher	37·4	Ruislip	12·1	Wanstead	199	Epsom	17·2
Southgate	40·0	Coulsdon	11·5	Beckenham }	237	Merton	17·7
Beckenham	41·2	Beckenham	10·5	Coulsdon }		Surbiton	17·9
Coulsdon	45·4	Southgate	10·1	Southgate	238	Coulsdon	20·2
Highest		*Lowest*		*Highest*		*Highest*	

TABLE 16

GENERAL ELECTIONS, 1951 AND 1955

Per cent. of electorate polling in general election in				Per cent. of votes cast for Labour or other left-wing parties in general election in			
1951		1955		1951		1955	
Lowest		*Lowest*		*Lowest*		*Lowest*	
Blackpool	74·0	West Ham	66·7	Southgate	22·6	Southgate	20·0
Brighton	76·3	Blackpool	67·2	Southport	24·8	Worthing	22·9
West Ham	76·9	Brighton	68·7	Worthing	25·4	Esher	24·8
Liverpool } Barnsley }	77·2	Southport	68·8	Hove	25·8	Coulsdon	25·2
		Dagenham	68·9	Coulsdon	27·0	Torquay	25·4
Q1	82·0	Q1	75·2	Q1	41·4	Q1	39·0
Mi	83·7	Mi	78·0	Mi	49·6	Mi	48·8
Q3	85·5	Q3	80·5	Q3	56·3	Q3	53·8
Bexley	87·8	Stockton	83·8	Mansfield	69·9	Barnsley	72·8
Stockton } Chislehurst }	88·0	Keighley	83·9	Dagenham	76·1	West Ham	73·8
Burnley	88·7	Reading	84·1	West Ham	77·4	Dagenham	73·9
Blackburn	89·0	Chislehurst	84·9	Merthyr	79·6	Merthyr	77·2
		Lincoln	85·1	Rhondda	85·5	Rhondda	80·9
Highest		*Highest*		*Highest*		*Highest*	

TABLE 17
LOCAL ELECTIONS, 1956-58

Votes cast as per cent. of electorate in contested seats		Per cent. of seats uncontested		Votes cast as per cent. of total electorate	
Lowest		*Lowest*		*Lowest*	
Wigan	19	(49 towns)	0	Merthyr	3
Dagenham }	21			Wigan	4
Edmonton }				Hove	9
West Ham	22			Sunderland	11
Tottenham }	25			Swansea	12
Thurrock }					
Q1 —|—	36	Q1 —|—	0	Q1 —|—	25
Mi —|—	41	Mi —|—	11	Mi —|—	34
Q3 —|—	46	Q3 —|—	30	Q3 —|—	41
				Brentford }	
Barnsley }				Stockport }	48
Great Yarmouth }	53	Swansea	65	Southampton }	
York }		Sunderland	74	Plymouth	49
Carlisle	54	Hove	81	Lancaster	50
Eastbourne	55	Wigan	90	York }	51
Blackburn	56	Merthyr	92	Lincoln }	
Highest		*Highest*		*Highest*	

Note: Most of the data in this table were obtained after the analysis of Chapters III and VI had been completed. Only data giving votes cast as per cent. of electorate in contested seats, 1956-58, are used in the later analysis.

The low overall figures of participation in local government elections have evoked a good deal of public comment. Recent correspondence in *The Times* discussed the reason for the lack of interest in local government affairs, and one correspondent suggested that it lay in the 'concentration of functions in remote large authorities and boards which are infected with the endemic intolerance of local initiative . . .' (letter to *The Times*, 20th May 1960).

Our figures indicate that the process is too complex to be explained by any single formula. Before the electorate can vote for a candidate the rival parties must decide to contest the seat. The figures show that only in 49 towns were all seats contested, whereas in others a large proportion of seats remained uncontested. This is partly, but by no means wholly, explained by the estimate which the local parties form of their chance of winning a seat. This varies with the social class composition of the area, and also with the enthusiasm and tenacity of local party headquarters.

In the second place, it is clearly not enough to ascribe abstentions to

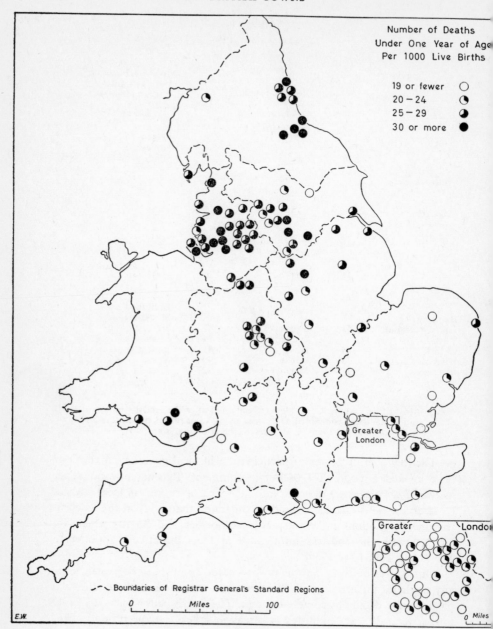

Number of Deaths
Under One Year of Age
Per 1000 Live Births

19 or fewer   ○
20 — 24   ◑
25 — 29   ◕
30 or more   ●

‒ ˜ ˷ Boundaries of Registrar General's Standard Regions

0   Miles   100

E.W.

Greater
London

Greater   London

0 Miles

MAP 2. INFANT MORTALITY, 1955 TO 1957

Towns with populations of 50,000 or over
England and Wales, 1951

general lack of interest when the degree of abstention in contested elections varies from as much as 79 per cent. in Dagenham and Edmonton to 44 per cent. in Blackburn. Further study is required of the mechanics of local government elections, and it might well start with the differentials between towns.

Health

The infant mortality rate is widely thought to have been reduced more or less to a minimum. There is, however, much scope for improvement in towns like Rochdale, Merthyr Tydfil and West Hartlepool. (Map 2, on facing page, gives an idea of the geographical distribution of infant mortality.) Bronchitis mortality, too, shows a remarkable range of variation, from almost three times the national average in Salford to about a quarter in Esher.

TABLE 18

INFANT MORTALITY, 1950-52 AND 1955-57; EXPECTATION OF LIFE, 1950-52

Infant mortality rate				Expectation of life at year One 1950-52	
Average 1950-52		Average 1955-57			
Lowest		*Lowest*		*Highest*	
Merton	15	Wimbledon	12	Chigwell	75·7
Eastbourne ⎫		Mitcham	14	Ruislip	73·1
Finchley ⎪		Merton ⎫		Epsom	73·0
Wimbledon ⎬ 17		Beckenham ⎬ 15		Coulsdon	72·5
Southgate ⎪		Solihull ⎭		Romford	72·3
Bexley ⎪		↑		↑	
Hayes ⎭					
↑					
Q1 —⊦—	23	Q1 —⊦—	20	Q3 —⊦—	70·9
Mi —⊦—	28	Mi —⊦—	23	Mi —⊦—	70·1
Q3 —⊦—	33	Q3 —⊦—	28	Q1 —⊦—	69·1
Lancaster ⎫		↓			
Merthyr ⎬ 43		Middlesbrough ⎫		Wigan ⎫	67·8
Bootle ⎭		Warrington ⎬ 33		Liverpool ⎭	
Gateshead	44	Stockton ⎭		Rhondda	67·7
Rhondda	45	Merthyr	35	Salford	67·6
Rochdale	47	W. Hartlepool	43	Carlisle	66·2
Highest		*Highest*		*Lowest*	

Note: The expectation of life figures were obtained after the analysis of Chapters III to VI had been completed. The details of calculation are shown in Appendix D.

The range of variation in expectation of life (at year one) is relatively smaller than that for infant mortality, but the differentials are still greater than might have been expected. It is a sobering thought that an inhabitant of Carlisle should on average have nine years fewer to live than a man from Chigwell.

D

TABLE 19
SPECIFIC MORTALITY AND T.B. NOTIFICATIONS, 1957

Mortality: ratio of local standardised to national rate (= 100)						T.B. notification rate	
from lung cancer		*from other cancer*		*from bronchitis*			
Lowest		*Lowest*		*Lowest*		*Lowest*	
Coulsdon	47	Colchester	75	Esher	23	Dewsbury	19
Exeter	48	Epsom	76	Epsom	35	Yarmouth	20
Swindon	49	Coulsdon	79	Worthing ⎫		Enfield	27
Gloucester	53	Wimbledon ⎫	81	Eastbourne ⎬	37	Cheltenham	31
Cambridge	59	Southall ⎭		Hove	39	Mitcham	36
Q1 –⊢	98	Q1 –⊢	98	Q1 –⊢	81	Q1 –⊢	63
Mi –⊢	116	Mi –⊢	106	Mi –⊢	106	Mi –⊢	88
Q3 –⊢	139	Q3 –⊢	114	Q3 –⊢	145	Q3 –⊢	121
Hayes	181	Barrow	134	W. Bromwich	205	Watford	169
Huyton	184	Oldham ⎫	135	Manchester	212	Tynemouth ⎫	171
Salford	190	Dagenham ⎭		Oldham	221	Gateshead ⎭	
Bootle	228	South Shields	136	Rhondda	231	South Shields	180
Barking	243	Barking	145	Salford	277	Southall	197
Highest		*Highest*		*Highest*		*Highest*	

Not too much should be made of the health indices, other than that for infant mortality, because the totals on which the indices were based, particularly for the smaller towns, are small and subject to chance fluctuations from one year to the next. But, even if only approximations, the indices are likely to be a fair guide to the range of variation, and this is shown to be substantial in every case.

Education

The only comment worth making on the education series given in Table 20 is that they follow closely the social class distributions of the population, and consequently show considerable variability.

The towns at the extremes

The above tables may well give the impression that the extreme positions are repeatedly filled by the same towns. In fact, the great majority of the towns, some 125 out of the 157 are among the extremes in one table or another. A good number of them, just under 50, however, appear only once or twice, and there are indeed a few towns which appear over and over again. Coulsdon & Purley, for example, is among the extremes 22 times (out of a possible 60), Dagenham 18 times, Huyton with Roby 17 times, Worthing 16 times, Rhondda and Hove 15 times, Epsom & Ewell, Eastbourne and Southgate 13 times, Hayes & Harlington and Bournemouth 12 times, Beckenham and Bootle 11 times. These figures relate to the five extremes at each end. One can also note the towns falling below the lower quartile and above the upper quartile. There are 60 variables, and 78 positions on each fall outside the quartiles. On average, one

TABLE 20

EDUCATION, 1951

Per cent. of occupied pop. aged 20-24 whose T.E.A. was less than 15		Per cent. of pop. aged 15-24 attending full time at an educ. estab.	
Lowest		*Highest*	
Beckenham	33·6	Coulsdon	25·0
Coulsdon	34·4	Beckenham	21·1
Southgate	36·0	Southgate	19·3
Cheltenham	41·0	Esher	18·7
Ruislip	44·4	Epsom	17·6
Q1	58·8	Q3	11·8
Mi	67·8	Mi	8·1
Q3	75·2	Q1	6·4
		West Ham ⎫ Salford ⎬ Stoke ⎭	4·6
Dudley	83·5		
Warrington	83·6	W. Bromwich	4·4
Dagenham	84·4	Barking	4·3
Nuneaton	86·1	Dudley	4·0
Stoke	86·2	Dagenham	3·8
Highest		*Lowest*	

would expect each town to be outside the quartiles about $\dfrac{60 \times 78}{157} = 30$ times. With this in mind we may note the towns which appear most and least often in these positions:

Most		*Least*	
Coulsdon & Purley	53	Bristol	12
Southgate	48	Darlington	12
Wembley	47	Watford	13
Epsom & Ewell	46	Northampton	14
Worthing	46	Leicester	15
Hove	45	York	15
Dagenham	45	Cardiff	15
Eastbourne	45	Reading	16
Bournemouth	44	Worcester	16
Bootle	44		

This list of towns occupying the extreme positions suggests the question whether much of the observed variations in the above tables may be due to the suburbs which, being in a sense 'parts of towns', might be expected to be especially 'atypical'. To shed some light on this, we can compare, for each variable, the range between the extreme values both for the 157 towns and for the non-suburbs. The definition of a suburb is arbitrary, and is here taken to include all areas of the Greater London Census conurbation (with the exception of London A.C.), together with Solihull, Huyton with Roby, Stretford, Crosby and Wallasey. This leaves a total of 108 non-suburban areas.

Table 21 shows the results. For eighteen of the variables there is no alteration in the range, while for many others the reduction is small.[1] Only for population changes between 1931 and 1951 and for the job ratio, the latter of which might in fact be used to measure the extent to which an area is suburban, has the exclusion of the suburbs notably affected the range of variation between the towns.

[1] Since the range tends to vary with the number of towns, some reduction might be expected simply because the number of towns has been reduced from 157 to 108.

TABLE 21

COMPARISON OF RANGE OF VARIATION FOR ALL TOWNS AND FOR NON-SUBURBAN TOWNS ONLY

Variable	Range (distance between extreme values)	
	All 157 towns	108 non-surbuban towns only
POPULATION SIZE AND STRUCTURE		
Population ('000)	3298	3298
% of population aged 0-14	15·3	11·9
% of population aged 15-64	12·5	10·5
% of population aged 65 or over	19·7	17·5
Females per 1000 males	568	568
Females per 1000 males, age 25-44	389	389
% of females aged 20-24 ever married	27·8	21·7
POPULATION CHANGE		
1931-51—total (%)	1015·1	188·2
1931-51—births and deaths (%)	183·6	48·7
1931-51—balance of change (%)	851·6	156·6
1951-58 (%)	38·3	38·3
Birth rate ratio, 1950-52	69	68
Birth rate ratio, 1955-57	68	64
% illegitimate births, 1950-52	6·0	5·6
% illegitimate births, 1955-57	6·8	6·4
HOUSEHOLDS AND HOUSING		
% persons in private h/hlds	14·6	14·5
% one-person h/hlds	16·6	15·8
% six-or more person h/hlds	13·4	11·8
% 1-3-room dwellings	46·5	46·5
Persons per room	0·37	0·37
% overcrowded h/hlds (composite)	19·2	18·4
% h/hlds at over 1½ persons per room	15·3	14·6
% h/hlds in shared dwellings	62·0	46·1
% h/hlds with piped water	23	23
% h/hlds with W.C.	33	33
% h/hlds with 5 amenities	76	71
% h/hlds with all 5, or only bath missing	36	35
New-housing rate, 1945-58—total	121	100
New-housing rate, 1945-58—L.A.s	86	78
% L.A. of total houses 1945-58	73·9	73·9

TABLE 21 (*Cont.*)

Variable	Range (*distance between extreme values*)	
	All 157 towns	*108 non-suburban towns only*
ECONOMIC CHARACTER		
Occupied as % of total population	25·5	25·5
% of women in labour force	20·3	20·3
% in manufacture etc.	68·1	68·1
% in all service industries	61·0	61·0
% in retail	20·2	14·1
% in finance, etc.	6·7	6·7
% in professional services	33·0	17·1
Job ratio	154	104
Commuting ratio	161	80
Per capita retail sales, 1950 (£)	206	181
SOCIAL CLASS		
% in social classes I + II	37·7	27·5
% in social classes IV + V	33·5	27·7
Social class index	197	134
Social Survey J-index, 1954	19·90	16·39
VOTING		
General elections—		
1951 poll	15·0	15·0
1955 poll	18·4	17·8
1951 % voting left	62·9	60·7
1955 % voting left	60·9	58·0
Local elections, 1956-58—		
Voting in contested elections	37	37
% uncontested seats	92	92
Votes as % of total electorate	48	48
HEALTH		
Infant mortality rate, 1950-52	32	30
Infant mortality rate, 1955-57	31	27
Expectation of life at year One, 1950-52	9·5	6·1
T.B. notification rate, 1957	178	161
Mortality rate, 1957—lung cancer	196	180
Mortality rate—other cancer	70	61
Mortality rate, 1957—bronchitis	254	240
EDUCATION		
% with terminal edn. age under 15	52·6	45·2
% aged 15-24 in full-time education	21·2	12·2

III

Differences Between Regions and Other Major Groupings of Towns

IT is obviously of interest to enquire in what ways towns in the various regions of England and Wales most differ from one another, whether there are major differences according to size of town, and so forth. This chapter aims to answer such questions. We have divided the 157 towns in our study, in turn, according to the following criteria:

        (1) by region
        (2) by size of town
        (3) by change in population, 1931-51
        (4) by social class.

This choice was decided by the general interest of the topics, rather than because of their particular analytic importance. As the subsequent three chapters (IV to VI) show, the most important factors of urban differentiation emerging from our analysis are respectively associated with social class, 'age' of the town and housing density. Of these, social class and one aspect of the 'age' of a town, namely growth or decline between 1931 and 1951, are here used as bases of classification. To these are added a regional classification, which is not included in the analysis (since region is not readily quantifiable), and division according to size of town. The latter was found in the component analysis to have surprisingly little importance in differentiating between towns, but we include it here because of its obvious interest.

For each group of towns (e.g. towns in the northern region), we compare the median values for each of the 57 characteristics with the corresponding medians of towns in the other sub-groups (e.g. regions) as well as with the overall medians of the 157 towns in England and Wales. The object of the exercise is description, and we make no attempt in this chapter to *explain* differences by reference to other 'underlying' factors. For example, five of the six towns with populations over 500,000 are in the Midlands and North, and characteristics shown as being typical of this size group may equally well be associated with regional distinctions. To follow up each difference by forming sub-groups or sub-sub-groups would not only be tedious but also methodologically imperfect, since we would generally be guessing at the underlying factors. Later chapters will, with the aid of multivariate analysis, come closer to disentangling these factors. In the present, we confine ourselves to treating one breakdown at a time.

Variations between regional groups

For the analysis in this section the towns are grouped as follows:

Region	*Contents of region*	*Number of towns*
North	Cheshire, Cumberland, Durham, Lancashire, Northumberland, Yorkshire	49
Midland & Wales	Derbyshire, Leicestershire, Lincolnshire, Northamptonshire, Nottinghamshire, Peterborough, Staffordshire, Warwickshire, Worcestershire, Glamorganshire, Monmouthshire	28
London & South-East	Essex (part), Kent, London, Middlesex, Surrey, Sussex	52
South & South-West	Bedfordshire, Berkshire, Buckinghamshire, Cambridgeshire, Devon, Dorset, Essex (part), Gloucestershire, Hampshire, Hertfordshire, Norfolk, Oxfordshire, Somerset, Suffolk, Wiltshire	28
		157

Towns in the North and the Midland & Wales regions differ markedly from those of the southern regions. For 36 out of the 57 variables the two northern regions have values either above or below those of the two southern ones; in some cases the differences are substantial. The data are summarised in Table 22.

With respect to *population size and structure*, the southern regions, and particularly London, have an older population than the northern, higher sex ratios, and fewer women aged 20-24 who are or have been married. *Population increase* was highest in London and the South-East, largely due to a relatively high degree of inward migration.

The *household and housing* structure shows significant differences. The North is particularly marked by the high proportion of small dwellings, while overcrowding is also considerably higher in the northern than in the southern regions. New housing is particularly low in London and the North, while the share of council houses in total new building is especially high in the North.

TABLE 22
Towns divided into regional groups

	England and Wales	Region			
		North	Midland and Wales	London and South-East	South and South-West
Number of towns:	(157)	(49)	(28)	(52)	(28)
Population Size and Structure		*Medians*			
Population ('000)	84	88	92	74	84
% of population aged 0-14	21·8	22·2	23·5	20·6	21·8
% of population aged 15-64	67·3	67·2	67·1	68·2	66·4
% of population aged 65 or over	10·4	10·2	9·9	10·8	11·7
Females per 1000 males	1108	1104	1054	1130	1114
Females per 1000 males, age 25-44	1042	1034	1000	1091	1047
% of females aged 20-24 ever married	48·1	49·7	51·2	44·5	48·3
Population Change					
1931-51—total (%)	11·0	1·8	9·5	34·7	18·6
1931-51—births and deaths (%)	9·0	7·3	11·7	11·3	8·3
1931-51—balance of change (%)	2·5	-5·7	-1·2	26·2	12·2
1951-58 (%)	-0·2	-0·7	1·9	-1·4	6·0
Birth rate ratio, 1950-52	96	106	103	82	95
Birth rate ratio, 1955-57	94	102	99	82	97
% illegitimate births, 1950-52	4·9	5·3	4·4	3·9	5·6
% illegitimate births, 1955-57	4·7	5·1	4·5	3·9	5·4
Households and Housing					
% persons in private h/hlds	97·5	97·7	97·5	97·7	95·9
% one-person h/hlds	9·9	10·8	8·5	9·4	10·4
% six- or more person h/hlds	7·2	8·1	9·1	6·0	7·5
% 1-3-room dwellings	10·6	14·9	8·1	9·3	11·5
Persons per room	0·74	0·77	0·75	0·73	0·71
% overcrowded h/hlds (composite)	5·9	6·8	6·5	5·5	5·5
% h/hlds at over 1½ persons per room	4·3	5·6	4·7	3·9	3·8
% h/hlds in shared dwellings	12·2	7·4	11·5	18·5	14·9
% h/hlds with piped water	94	95	92	94	93
% h/hlds with W.C.	97	96	95	98	97
% h/hlds with 5 amenities	65	59	59	82	70
% h/hlds with all 5, or only bath missing	91	91	88	94	91
New-housing rate 1945-58—total	48	44	62	32	69
New-housing rate 1945-58—L.A.s	32	32	46	20	46
% L.A. of total houses 1945-58	72·8	82·5	75·5	58·7	69·2
Economic Character					
Occupied as % of total population	59·7	61·4	62·8	61·1	57·5
% of women in labour force	32·6	33·4	30·3	33·3	31·2
% in manufacture etc.	41·6	48·5	54·1	30·8	32·2
% in all service industries	37·4	35·0	33·4	49·2	46·8
% in retail	10·4	9·7	10·0	10·7	11·3
% in finance, etc.	1·4	1·4	1·4	1·8	1·9
% in professional services	6·8	6·1	5·9	9·2	8·2
Job ratio	99	103	108	73	106
Commuting ratio	51	37	36	88	34
Per capita retail sales, 1950 (£)	125	125	135	114	160

TABLE 22 (*Cont.*)

TOWNS DIVIDED INTO REGIONAL GROUPS

	England and Wales	Region			
		North	Midland and Wales	London and South-East	South and South-West
Number of towns:	(157)	(49)	(28)	(52)	(28)
SOCIAL CLASS		*Medians*			
% in social classes I + II	15·8	14·2	13·5	23·8	17·8
% in social classes IV + V	26·0	30·9	30·5	19·2	24·4
Social class index	99	84	83	136	105
Social Survey J-index, 1954	5·5	3·00	2·31	9·80	6·52
VOTING					
General election:					
1951 poll	83·7	84·7	83·6	82·6	84·2
1955 poll	78·0	78·5	78·2	76·9	78·9
1951 % voting left	49·6	50·6	57·1	41·6	47·3
1955 % voting left	48·8	50·6	54·8	41·0	44·3
% voting in contested local elections, 1956-58	42·8	44·9	40·0	41·3	45·5
HEALTH					
Infant mortality rate, 1950-52	28	35	32	21	26
Infant mortality rate, 1955-57	23	28	28	20	21
T.B. notification rate, 1957	88	86	89	89	85
Mortality rate 1957—lung cancer	116	120	116	121	95
Mortality rate 1957—other cancer	106	113	110	106	96
Mortality rate 1957—bronchitis	106	146	122	93	81
EDUCATION					
% with terminal edn. age under 15	67·8	72·9	75·3	57·9	65·7
% aged 15-24 in full-time education	8·1	7·1	7·0	11·7	8·7

Southern towns have substantially smaller portions of the population employed in manufacturing and higher proportions in all the service trades. They consequently have higher proportions in the upper *social classes* and substantially higher proportions of jurors, as well as lower proportions voting left.

Among the *health* indices, infant mortality rates are considerably higher in the northern regions, as are bronchitis mortality rates and mortality from cancer other than lung and bronchial cancer. The latter, as well as tuberculosis notifications during 1957, do not vary systematically, though lung and bronchial cancer mortality is relatively low in the South and South-West.

The *education* figures follow the social class data; the extent of education, as measured by these indices, is substantially higher in the southern than in the northern towns.

Variations between towns of different size

For this analysis, the towns are grouped as follows:

Population (1951)	Number of towns
500,000 or over	6
250,000 –	8
100,000 –	53
65,000 –	51
50,000 –	39
	157

The numbers in the top two categories are, of course, too small to provide trustworthy averages, but the figures have been included for completeness' sake. The data are shown in Table 23.

As regards *population structure*, both age composition and sex ratio are remarkably independent of size of town. Indeed the only difference in this section worth noting is the high marriage rate in the towns with 250,000-500,000 population.

Population change naturally varies rather more with size of town. The smaller the town, the greater its relative growth between 1931 and 1951, the differential being most marked for growth due to factors other than births and deaths. Between 1951 and 1958 the tendency was in the same direction. Birth rate ratios are highest in the larger towns, and so, though only marginally, are illegitimacy rates.

In the *households and housing* group, there is a notable uniformity in the figures for household size. The proportion of dwellings with 1-3 rooms is much higher in the six large towns than elsewhere, perhaps because four of them are in the North. Overcrowding falls systematically with town size, sharing of dwellings is considerably more common in the middle-size category. There is little to say regarding household arrangements; in so far as a trend is discernible, it shows the smaller towns to be slightly better provided. It is also in these that house building has been greatest, with the lowest proportions being due to local authorities.

In terms of *economic character*, we find a greater labour force participation in the larger towns, and also a higher share of women in the labour force. The differences in industrial structure are naturally much more marked; the larger towns tend to be more heavily engaged in manufacturing and the like, while in the smallest towns covered by the study, there is a notably greater preponderance of people engaged in retail trade and in professional services. Job and commuting ratios vary in an expected manner, the smaller and more commonly suburban towns having the lower job ratios and the higher commuting ratios. Retail sales per head vary less than might have been expected between the five classes of town.

The same may be said of *social class*. The smaller towns have only slightly 'higher' social class characteristics. The J-index shows much more of an upward social class gradient with falling town size.

A noteworthy feature of the *voting* statistics is that, in both the 1951 and 1955 general elections and in the 1957 local elections, turnout was lower in the largest towns than elsewhere. Labour support, as is also well known, is greatest in these large towns.

The first of the *health* series, the 1950-52 infant mortality rate, varies little between the town-size groups, apart from the high figure for the towns with 250,000-500,000 population; this might be regarded as a freakish figure were it not for its continued appearance at the top five years later. T.B. notifications are astonishingly different for the town size groups, 133 for the largest towns, 82 for the smallest. Lung cancer mortality shows a similar though less extreme trend, and so does the bronchitis death rate.

The two *education* indices show the smaller towns to be somewhat better placed than the rest, but the differences are not remarkable.

Variations between towns grouped according to population change

We next summarise, in Table 24, the characteristics of the towns grouped according to their rate of population change between 1931 and 1951. The following categories are distinguished:

Per cent. population change 1931-51		Number of towns
plus	60·0 or over	23
	30·0 –	20
	15·0 –	28
	5·0 –	25
minus 5·0 – plus 5·0		38
up to minus 5·0		23
		157

In the *population structure* section, neither age composition nor sex ratio shows noteworthy differences. The marriage rate is somewhat lower in the towns that grew most. When we look at *population change* between 1951 and 1958 we find a continuation of the trends of the previous two decades. The towns that grew most in the earlier period continued to do so in the latter. Those that grew most between 1931 and 1951 had the lowest birth rate ratios in 1950-52, and also five years later. Illegitimacy was also lowest in the greatest growth towns.

Turning to *households and housing*, we find a far greater proportion of one-person households in the lower-growth towns, also more small dwellings, and on the whole more overcrowding. The sharing proportions are too erratic to bear easy summary. Household amenities are far more common in the towns that expanded most. In the building figures the most

TABLE 23

TOWNS DIVIDED INTO SIZE GROUPS

Number of towns:	England and Wales (157)	Towns with populations in 1951 of				
		500,000 or over (6)	250,000-under 500,000 (8)	100,000-under 250,000 (53)	65,000-under 100,000 (51)	50,000-under 65,000 (39)
		Medians				
POPULATION SIZE AND STRUCTURE						
Population ('000)						
% of population aged 0-14	21·8	22·5	23·0	22·0	21·7	21·6
% of population aged 15-64	67·3	67·5	67·2	67·3	67·3	67·2
% of population aged 65 or over	10·4	9·9	9·9	10·3	10·7	11·3
Females per 1000 males	1108	1126	1101	1108	1092	1117
Females per 1000 males, age 25-44	1042	1032	1024	1049	1042	1063
% of females aged 20-24 ever married	48·1	48·0	52·6	47·9	48·3	48·0
POPULATION CHANGE						
1931-51—total (%)	11·0	-3·5	5·8	6·1	16·1	17·0
1931-51—births and deaths (%)	9·0	6·6	9·2	8·6	11·1	7·9
1931-51—balance of change (%)	2·5	-11·3	-1·1	-2·0	9·4	11·9
1951-58 (%)	-0·2	-0·4	-1·3	-0·1	1·7	2·2
Birth rate ratio, 1950-52	96	102	106	96	95	96
Birth rate ratio, 1955-57	94	100	102	94	94	94
% illegitimate births, 1950-52	4·9	6·2	5·6	5·1	4·6	4·6
% illegitimate births, 1955-57	4·7	6·5	5·6	4·9	4·5	4·5
HOUSEHOLDS AND HOUSING						
% persons in private h/hlds	2·5	2·8	2·8	2·5	2·2	3·0
% one-person h/hlds	9·9	11·3	11·1	10·2	8·6	9·4
% six- or more person h/hlds	7·2	7·7	7·9	7·2	7·6	7·1
% 1-3-room dwellings	10·6	16·1	9·2	10·3	10·8	10·6
Persons per room	0·74	0·76	0·77	0·74	0·73	0·72
% overcrowded h/hlds (composite)	5·9	8·1	7·1	6·4	6·0	5·4
% h/hlds at over 1½ persons per room	4·3	6·3	5·5	4·6	4·2	3·9
% h/hlds in shared dwellings	12·2	12·0	12·2	19·1	12·0	10·1
% h/hlds with piped water	94	94	93	93	94	94
% h/hlds with W.C.	97	91	96	97	97	97
% h/hlds with 5 amenities	65	58	58	64	71	70
% h/hlds with all 5, or only bath missing	91	85	87	91	91	92
New-housing rate 1945-58—total	48	41	53	44	52	57
New-housing rate 1945-58—L.A.s	32	32	43	27	34	30
% L.A. of total houses 1945-58	72·8	80·0	80·9	72·8	73·1	69·0

ECONOMIC CHARACTER						
Occupied as % of total population	59·7	65·1	65·0	61·4	59·2	58·7
% of women in labour force	32·6	36·1	33·7	32·6	32·6	32·0
% in manufacture etc.	41·6	48·4	53·4	42·1	42·8	34·2
% in all service industries	37·4	37·4	35·6	36·1	37·3	44·1
% in retail	10·3	9·1	9·2	10·3	10·9	10·7
% in finance, etc.	1·4	2·6	1·7	1·4	1·4	1·4
% in professional services	6·8	6·9	6·0	6·7	6·5	8·5
Job ratio	99	113	112	93	97	96
Commuting ratio	51	29	27	46	60	69
Per capita retail sales, 1950 (£)	125	141	142	123	133	129
SOCIAL CLASS						
% in social classes I+II	15·8	14·2	14·1	15·3	16·3	17·9
% in social classes IV+V	26·0	29·3	28·9	26·0	25·9	23·2
Social class index	99	89	92	99	101	112
Social Survey J-index, 1954	5·5	3·5	3·5	5·6	4·9	6·6
VOTING						
General elections:						
1951 poll	83·7	79·9	83·6	83·8	84·2	83·4
1955 poll	78·0	71·7	76·8	77·0	79·3	78·6
1951 % voting left	49·6	52·7	54·0	50·3	49·2	45·8
1955 % voting left	48·8	50·8	52·8	50·2	48·3	44·5
% voting in contested local elections, 1956-58	42·8	34·9	37·3	40·4	44·9	44·6
HEALTH						
Infant mortality rate, 1950-52	28	29	33	28	26	26
Infant mortality rate, 1955-57	23	25	28	22	24	22
T.B. notification rate, 1957	88	133	122	89	85	82
Mortality rate 1957—lung cancer	116	142	117	119	112	105
Mortality rate 1957—other cancer	106	112	106	108	109	103
Mortality rate 1957—bronchitis	106	157	142	109	93	101
EDUCATION						
% with terminal edn. age under 15	8·1	7·0	7·3	8·1	8·6	8·8
% aged 15-24 in full-time education	67·8	73·8	72·6	68·7	66·7	64·7

TABLE 24

TOWNS GROUPED ACCORDING TO POPULATION CHANGE, 1931-51

	England and Wales	% Change 1931-51					
		Increase of 60% or more	Increase of 30%—under 60%	Increase of 15%—under 30%	Increase of 5%—under 15%	Increase or decrease of under 5%	Decrease of 5% or more
Number of towns:	(157)	(23)	(20)	(28)	(25)	(38)	(23)
		Medians					
POPULATION SIZE AND STRUCTURE							
Population ('000)	84	68	82	68	104	98	120
% of population aged 0-14	21·8	22·5	20·7	21·5	22·2	22·2	22·2
% of population aged 15-64	67·3	68·7	68·0	67·0	66·7	67·3	67·3
% of population aged 65 or over	10·4	8·8	10·2	11·6	10·3	10·5	10·7
Females per 1000 males	1108	1098	1140	1116	1090	1096	1122
Females per 1000 males, age group 25-44	1042	1096	1087	1052	1020	1027	1034
% of females aged 20-24 ever married	48·1	44·3	44·0	47·2	49·9	50·1	49·1
POPULATION CHANGE							
1931-51—total (%)	—	—	—	—	—	—	—
1931-51—births and deaths (%)	—	—	—	—	—	—	—
1951-58 (%)	-0·2	5·6	1·4	3·0	0·2	-0·9	-4·0
Birth rate ratio, 1950-52	96	85	82	97	101	103	99
Birth rate ratio, 1955-57	94	87	83	94	98	99	94
% illegitimate births, 1950-52	4·9	3·6	4·1	5·6	5·3	5·3	4·9
% illegitimate births, 1955-57	4·7	3·4	4·0	5·4	4·9	4·9	5·2
HOUSEHOLDS AND HOUSING							
Persons in private h/hlds	2·5	2·0	3·0	3·7	2·8	2·5	2·2
% one-person h/hlds	9·9	6·4	8·4	10·0	10·1	11·2	11·8
% six- or more person h/hlds	7·2	6·4	7·1	7·6	7·5	7·8	7·0
% 1-3-room dwellings	10·6	10·0	9·0	10·3	10·6	15·6	12·7
Persons per room	0·74	0·74	0·72	0·71	0·73	0·77	0·75
% overcrowded h/hlds (composite)	5·9	5·0	5·2	5·5	5·9	7·3	7·0
% h/hlds at over 1½ persons per room	4·3	3·7	3·6	3·9	3·9	5·5	5·1
% h/hlds in shared dwellings	12·2	10·7	16·3	13·7	11·9	9·3	16·3
% h/hlds with piped water	94	96	94	93	93	93	91
% h/hlds with W.C.	97	98	98	97	97	95	95
% h/hlds with 5 amenities	65	88	79	66	61	60	46
% h/hlds with all 5, or only bath missing	91	95	93	91	91	87	87
New-housing rate 1945-58—total	48	52	43	62	57	48	31
New-housing rate 1945-58—L.A.s	32	23	25	44	41	35	27
% L.A. of total houses 1945-58	72·8	48·9	55·5	72·7	74·7	80·5	85·7

ECONOMIC CHARACTER						
Occupied as % of total population	59·7	60·4	59·0	58·0	58·7	61·7	64·7
% of women in labour force	32·6	31·8	32·3	32·7	32·3	32·6	34·9
% in manufacture etc.	41·6	29·3	37·7	37·1	47·1	47·3	51·8
% in all service industries	37·4	47·8	42·7	45·4	35·7	35·5	28·5
% in retail	10·3	9·7	9·4	11·7	10·2	9·8	9·6
% in finance, etc.	1·4	1·2	1·6	1·8	1·7	1·5	1·2
% in professional services	6·8	9·3	7·8	8·6	7·2	6·1	5·6
Job ratio	99	62	81	105	104	105	99
Commuting ratio	51	86	85	41	39	37	56
Per capita retail sales, 1950 (£)	125	100	114	184	143	134	122
SOCIAL CLASS							
% in social classes I + II	15·8	23·9	22·4	17·5	14·7	14·9	13·5
% in social classes IV + V	26·0	18·3	20·9	24·4	27·0	29·5	30·9
Social class index	99	138	130	108	95	88	83
Social Survey J-index, 1954	5·5	11·7	9·9	5·3	4·4	3·9	3·3
VOTING							
General elections:							
1951 poll	83·7	84·3	83·4	84·7	83·7	83·8	83·3
1955 poll	78·0	79·7	76·5	80·0	78·3	77·3	75·7
1951 % voting left	49·6	44·1	39·4	45·6	52·4	53·1	55·1
1955 % voting left	48·8	41·9	38·2	44·0	50·8	52·4	53·4
% voting in contested local elections, 1956-58	42·8	43·0	39·0	42·3	42·3	44·8	37·1
HEALTH							
Infant mortality rate, 1950-52	28	21	22	27	30	32	39
Infant mortality rate, 1955-57	23	19	21	22	25	28	26
T.B. notification rate, 1957	88	89	87	84	82	98	88
Mortality rate 1957—lung cancer	116	126	117	102	112	113	139
Mortality rate 1957—other cancer	106	107	103	105	103	109	115
Mortality rate 1957—bronchitis	106	90	91	86	106	135	148
EDUCATION							
% with terminal edn. age under 15	8·1	11·7	11·8	8·8	7·9	7·4	7·0
% aged 15-24 in full-time education	67·8	61·5	59·1	64·7	70·2	69·9	72·4

interesting feature is the marked association between growth of town and the proportion of house building due to local authorities; the lower the former, the higher the latter.

Economic character. Here we find a greater proportion in the labour force in the less expanding towns and also slightly more women in it. More interesting is the industrial structure, showing a clear inverse association between growth of town and the proportion engaged in manufacturing and the like. The job ratio is highest for the towns that grew most between 1931 and 1951; the opposite holds for the commuting ratio. Retail sales appear to be highest in the middle groups of towns, those that grew moderately, falling off in both directions of great growth and great decline.

The various *social class* indices show a marked association with population change, the fastest-growing towns between 1931 and 1951 being those with the 'highest' social class characteristics. The *voting* figures, as usual, point in the same direction.

Infant mortality rises steeply as we move from the towns that grew most to those that grew least or declined. The other *health* indicators are relatively insensitive to this criterion of classification. What tendency there is, shows the towns that declined or grew little to have the highest lung cancer and bronchitis mortality and T.B. notifications; it seems to be the towns with moderate population rises which are most healthy as judged by these indices.

Neither of the *education* series tells a clear story; on the whole, the greater the inter-censal growth, the 'better off' are the towns educationally.

Variations between towns grouped according to social class

The final factor of classification relates to social class, as measured in census occupational categories. The 157 towns are divided into the following categories, according to the percentage of the occupied population in the two 'top' social classes I and II:

Per cent. in social classes I and II	Number of towns
25·0 or over	29
20·0 –	19
15·0 –	42
10·0 –	58
under 10·0	9
	157

The data are set out in Table 25, on pages 54-55.

Let us see first how the *population structure* varies between towns of different social class. The higher the social class, the fewer young and more old people there are, with a consequently higher sex ratio; the marriage rate falls steadily in the opposite direction.

As to *population change*, there is a marked association with migration between 1931 and 1951, the towns towards the upper social class extreme gaining far the most. Natural change varies fairly little between the town classes, and so does population change after 1951. The birth rate ratios are puzzling: for 1950-52 they show a steady rise with falling social class proportions; five years later the same holds except for the towns with less than 10 per cent. in classes I and II, where the trend is reversed. The illegitimacy rates show a curiously 'normal' distribution.

Many of the *household and housing* figures show a marked association with social class. The percentage in non-private household dwellings falls steadily as one goes down the social class scale, one-person households become slightly less common, and large households very much more so. Overcrowding rises markedly as one descends the social class scale, whilst sharing tends to fall. The possession of household amenities, as measured by the most sensitive indicator, shows a remarkably steep association with social class. The building figures are also informative: total numbers of houses built vary little between the social class groups, but the proportion of houses due to local authorities rises from 46 per cent. for the top social class to 87 per cent. for the lowest.

Economic character. The lower the social class of the town, the higher the participation in the labour force; the female share in it varies little. The proportions engaged in various industries naturally vary closely with occupation-based social class categories, and require no comment. The job and commuting ratios are also strongly associated with social class, the former inversely, the latter directly. Retail sales are puzzling, in that the figure is highest by far for the middle of the social class range (10-15 per cent. in classes I and II), falling off in either direction.

The only one of the *social class* figures worth a separate comment is the J-index. This is based on quite different criteria from that used in the census classification, but shows a clear and systematic relation to it. Direction of *voting*, if not turnout, also varies closely with social class.

Infant mortality is the *health* indicator most commonly related to social class, and the figures clearly show that this is justified. The extent of the gradient is remarkable. Bronchitis mortality rises even more steeply as one descends the social scale. T.B. notifications also jump markedly in the same direction, except for the bottom social class category, where they are at their lowest.

The *education* proportions clearly demonstrate the very marked relationship between education and social class.

E

TABLE 25

TOWNS GROUPED ACCORDING TO SOCIAL CLASS

	England and Wales	% in social classes I + II				
		25% or over	20% and under 25%	15% and under 20%	10% and under 15%	under 10%
Number of towns:	(157)	29	19	42	58	9
		Medians				
POPULATION SIZE AND STRUCTURE						
Population ('000)	84	68	84	100	92	112
% of population aged 0-14	21·8	19·8	21·3	21·6	23·2	24·2
% of population aged 15-64	67·3	67·2	67·4	67·3	67·3	67·2
% of population aged 65 or over	10·4	12·4	11·6	11·3	9·9	8·7
Females per 1000 males	1108	1208	1152	1113	1075	1040
Females per 1000 males, age 25-44	1042	1149	1099	1037	1014	987
% females aged 20-24 ever married	48·1	40·1	46·4	49·4	50·1	52·0
POPULATION CHANGE						
1931-51—total (%)	11·0	34·8	38·7	11·9	1·9	-0·6
1931-51—births and deaths (%)	9·0	9·0	8·6	8·2	10·0	11·5
1931-51—balance of change (%)	2·5	29·7	29·3	4·3	-6·4	-12·1
1951-58 (%)	-0·2	-0·2	1·6	0·5	-1·2	-0·4
Birth rate ratio, 1950-52	96	79	90	97	105	105
Birth rate ratio, 1955-57	94	82	88	97	101	94
% illegitimate births, 1950-52	4·9	4·0	5·0	5·6	4·8	3·9
% illegitimate births, 1955-57	4·7	4·1	4·8	5·5	4·5	3·4
HOUSEHOLDS AND HOUSING						
% persons in private h/hlds	2·5	2·9	2·9	2·9	2·3	1·7
% one-person h/hlds	9·9	9·9	10·1	10·3	9·6	8·0
% six- or more person h/hlds	7·2	5·7	6·4	7·0	8·4	10·5
% 1-3-room dwellings	10·6	10·6	12·9	9·4	11·7	10·5
Persons per room	0·74	0·67	0·74	0·73	0·77	0·84
% overcrowded h/hlds (composite)	5·9	4·6	5·4	5·8	7·0	9·7
% h/hlds over 1½ persons per room	4·3	3·3	3·7	4·1	5·3	7·3
% h/hlds in shared dwellings	12·2	17·2	15·9	11·9	10·0	11·3
% h/hlds with piped water	94	95	94	94	93	94
% h/hlds with W.C.	97	97	98	96	96	97
% h/hlds with 5 amenities	65	85	82	66	59	49
% h/hlds with all 5, or only bath missing	91	93	93	91	89	89
New-housing rate 1945-58—total	48	41	48	55	51	48
New-housing rate 1945-58—L.A.s	32	18	22	41	38	37
% L.A. of total houses 1945-58	72·8	46·1	61·6	72·8	82·6	87·2

TABLE 25 (*Cont.*)

TOWNS GROUPED ACCORDING TO SOCIAL CLASS

	England and Wales	% in social classes I + II				
		25% or over	20% and under 25%	15% and under 20%	10% and under 15%	under 10%
Number of towns:	(157)	29	19	42	58	9
		Medians				
ECONOMIC CHARACTER						
Occupied as % of total population	59·7	56·5	59·4	61·7	61·9	65·5
% of women in labour force	32·6	33·3	33·3	32·7	31·4	31·1
% in manufacture etc.	41·6	24·4	28·2	46·1	49·3	59·0
% in all service industries	37·4	55·2	52·2	36·4	33·6	26·8
% in retail	10·3	13·5	12·1	10·1	9·8	8·3
% in finance, etc.	1·4	2·2	1·6	1·6	1·3	1·0
% in professional services	6·8	10·6	10·0	6·7	5·9	4·6
Job ratio	99	68	78	108	101	98
Commuting ratio	51	81	76	35	49	51
Per capita retail sales, 1950 (£)	125	133	122	158	123	113
SOCIAL CLASS						
% in social classes I + II	15·8	—	—	—	—	—
% in social classes IV + V	26·0	16·4	22·0	26·2	31·8	39·8
Social class index	99	181	128	102	82	58
Social Survey J-index, 1954	5·5	11·1	9·9	5·3	3·0	1·1
VOTING						
General elections:						
1951 poll	83·7	81·9	84·7	84·7	84·2	81·2
1955 poll	78·0	76·6	80·9	79·7	77·3	73·9
1951 % voting left	49·6	33·6	42·9	50·4	55·9	67·3
1955 % voting left	48·8	31·0	40·7	49·0	53·6	64·7
% voting in contested local elections, 1956-58	42·8	40·5	46·2	46·4	39·7	37·8
HEALTH						
Infant mortality rate, 1950-52	28	21	23	26	33	36
Infant mortality rate, 1955-57	23	20	20	22	27	29
T.B. notification rate, 1957	88	81	76	91	100	68
Mortality rate 1957—lung cancer	116	104	114	113	119	140
Mortality rate 1957—other cancer	106	104	104	102	113	120
Mortality rate 1957—bronchitis	106	73	94	100	138	176
EDUCATION						
% with terminal edn. age under 15	67·8	50·0	60·7	67·2	73·7	82·1
% aged 15-24 in full-time education	8·1	15·2	11·4	8·5	6·5	5·6

Part Three

IV

Simple Relationships
between Urban Characteristics

ONE way of unravelling the relationships between the 57 variables is to take certain of them in turn as the basis for major breakdowns, and to relate the others to these classificatory variables. This was done for a few variables in Chapter III. In the present chapter we consider the correlation matrix, in which the relationships between all pairs of variables are shown in terms of product-moment correlation coefficients. Some of the relationships are straightforward, others are fairly subtle. For example, towns with high proportions of jurors on the electoral register tend on average to have relatively low infant mortality. The two are not causally connected; the association arises because both factors are related to the 'economic well-being' of the community.

To make any sense of the relationships between pairs of variables it is often in fact necessary to consider the influence of a third, a fourth, and further variables. Essentially this is what the multivariate analysis in Chapter V sets out to do. The correlation coefficients given in the present chapter are the raw material for this analysis, and are also illuminating in their own right, as descriptive data.

The matrix (Table 26) may provide answers to various kinds of question. Are the associations between variables generally high or low? For example, are the four series relating to household amenities, such as possession of a water closet and fixed bath, associated with each other, and in what ways? Can we eliminate one or other of them without much loss, or does each series tell a distinct story? Which series show the highest correlations and which the lowest? How much do the series change over time, that is, what is the relationship, for those variables for which we have data at two points of time, between the earlier and the later years? Some of these questions can be satisfactorily answered only by multivariate techniques, but even for these a consideration of the simple correlation matrix is a useful preliminary.

The interpretation of the product-moment correlation coefficient (r) is well understood. A positive value means that the two series concerned tend to move together, one increasing as the other does so. A negative value means association of the inverse type. The closer the correlation between the two series, the closer will r be to ± 1, the extremes of complete correlation; a zero value means no correlation. In the present case the signs of the coefficients are of limited meaning, since they depend on the often arbitrary way in which the basic data are ordered. Thus, if the variable relating to full-time education were measured in terms of the percentage of the 15-24 age-group *not* receiving education, instead of the other way round, all its correlation coefficients would be reversed in sign.

Three qualifications relating to the coefficients should be stressed. First, it must be understood that they refer to the towns as units, and not to the individuals comprising them.[1]

Secondly, the correlation coefficients are based on the towns treated as equal units. In the computation of any one coefficient, the pair of observations for, say, London gets no greater weight than that for the smallest town.

Thirdly, and most important, we must remember that the product-moment coefficient is a measure of linear association. Casual examination of the data suggests that a fair number of the relationships involved are non-linear, in which cases r will understate the actual degree of relationship. A solution is to transform the data into their logarithmic equivalents, which increases the symmetry of distributions and the linearity of relationships. This has been done, and all the computations have been made on transformed as well as untransformed data. We have also pursued one further approach to the measure of simple relationships, which is not troubled by assumptions of the above kind, namely that of rank correlation. Spearman rank correlation coefficients were calculated between all the variables and compared both with the correlations on the untransformed data and with those derived from log transformations.

Neither the matrix of the log-transformed values nor that of the rank

---

[1] This is best explained by an example. The matrix shows a correlation of -0.481 between the percentage of the population in the labour force and the percentage of occupied and retired males in social classes I and II. This is based on 157 pairs of observations (percentages in this case). It is, so to speak, an accident of the study that we are dealing with towns rather than, say, wards or polling districts. A correlation based on the percentages in the thousands of wards would have been different, and certainly lower, than that observed here. If, to take the example to its extreme, the correlation had been based on all the individuals making up the town populations, it would have been different again, probably substantially lower. In short, individual and group (often called ecological) correlations are different things, and the coefficients used in this study relate solely to the particular groupings employed.

For a discussion of the relationship between group and individual correlations see Yule, G. U. and Kendall, M. G., *An Introduction to the Theory of Statistics*, Charles Griffin, London, 1950; Robinson, W. S., 'Ecological Correlations and the Behaviour of Individuals', *American Sociological Review*, XV, 3 (1950); Goodman, L. A., 'Ecological Regressions and Behavior of Individuals', *American Sociological Review*, XVIII, 6 (1953), and 'Some Alternatives to Ecological Correlation', *The American Journal of Sociology*, LXIV, 6 (1959); Duncan, O. D. and Davis, B., 'An Alternative to Ecological Correlation', *American Sociological Review*, XVIII, 6 (1953); Merton, R. K. and Lazarsfeld, P. F., *Continuities in Social Research*, The Free Press, Illinois, 1950.

order values is, except in a few cases, very different from the matrix in Table 26. On average, the log-transformed coefficients are about the same as the untransformed coefficients; the rank order coefficients are slightly higher:

Average value of coefficients

Original untransformed data	0·263
Log-transformed data	0·262
Rank orders	0·281

Log transformations would act most strongly in cases where the distribution of the original variables is markedly skewed. It would reduce the coefficients in cases where the outlying values are correlated with each other, and increase them where they are uncorrelated. The rank order correlations tend to have the same effect, to an even greater degree, by reducing still further the relative importance of the outlying values. As the figures below show, in all cases where transformations make any substantial difference, the correlations tend to be increased. We show below the average values of coefficients associated with variables most strongly affected by transformation:

Variables most strongly affected by transformation	Observations in ORIGINAL form	Observations transformed into LOGS	RANK ORDER values
	Average value of coefficients		
Change in population 1931-51			
total	0·201	0·285	0·318
due to births and deaths	0·217	0·251	0·255
due to balance of causes	0·207	0·290	0·369
Population size	0·118	0·164	0·174
% in finance, etc.	0·261	0·280	0·296
New-housing rate 1945-58—total	0·174	0·184	0·210
% households in shared dwellings	0·174	0·182	0·205
% in professional services	0·275	0·272	0·336

Let us return to the original matrix in Table 26. Perhaps the most striking fact at first glance is how small most of the coefficients are. There is of course no objective dividing line between a 'large' and a 'small' correlation coefficient. If we were dealing with sample data, we could first test the statistical significance of the coefficients. With a sample of 150, correlations of ±0·210 or less would, on a one per cent. confidence level, be set aside as statistically not significant. This figure may be borne in mind, if one should wish to regard the data as a sample from a wider population of towns.

Here we are looking at the correlation coefficients as descriptive statistics, and can only make an arbitrary division between small and large correlations. We will call anything equal to or outside the limits of ±0·500, that is below −0·500 or above +0·500, a 'substantial' correlation, and anything outside ±0·750 a 'high' correlation. These limits have no logical justification, and merely provide a convenient way of describing the mass of data in the matrix.

In Table 26 correlations equal to or outside the limits of ± 0.500 are marked with an asterisk, and one sees at once that their number is small (254 out of a total of 1,653). The markings also convey how much the variables differ in the extent of their correlations with others. Some, like social class, density of housing and the proportion of people aged over 65, are substantially correlated with numerous other variables; others, like size of population, have no correlations outside the limits ± 0.500.

However, too much should not be made of such comparisons, since the number of substantial inter-correlations shown by different variables depends on the more or less accidental circumstance that the coverage of variables is more extensive in some fields than in others: just because many social class variables are included, any one of them is likely to have a fair number of high correlates.

It is instructive to look at the correlation matrix subject by subject. To make this easier, we show in Table 27 the highest intercorrelation for each variable and, as a rough measure of the amount of inter-correlation, the average of its 56 correlations with other variables.

The social class group shows the highest correlations with other variables. Its importance is borne out by the fact that out of the 254 'substantial' correlations in the table, no fewer than 138 involve one of the eight social class indicators (social classes I+II and IV+V; social class index; J-index; the two education variables; and the two variables showing the proportion of the population voting left at the General Elections of 1951 and 1955 respectively.) Another indication is that the percentage in social classes I+II is substantially correlated with 23 out of the 56 remaining variables. Social class, as reflected in these variables, is clearly a dominant factor in the differentiation of British towns.

Next, it is of interest to look at some of the variables which show little correlation with others. One of these is population size. The low correlations in this case were thought to be partly due to the non-linear relationships caused by the inclusion of very large towns. London, with a population of 3,347,982 in 1951, for example, exceeds the average size for the 157 towns by over three million, or eleven times the standard deviation. When the seven largest towns are excluded, however, the average size of the coefficients between population size and the other 56 variables remains at 0.118, and the logarithmic values give an average of only 0.164.

The lack of relationship between the size of a town and other characteristics was very clearly brought out in Table 23 of Chapter III. Here we may note that the only fair sized correlation ($+0.437$) is with the proportion of persons working in the area employed in finance, banking and insurance, and this is due to the peculiar concentration of financial institutions in one or two major centres like London and Birmingham, and virtually dis-

TABLE 27

CORRELATIONS OF EACH VARIABLE WITH (a) ALL REMAINING VARIABLES
AND (b) HIGHEST ASSOCIATED VARIABLE

Variable	(a) Average size of coefficients (ignoring signs)	(b) Most highly associated with:	
POPULATION SIZE AND STRUCTURE			
Population ('000)	0·118	% in finance, etc.	0·437
% of population aged 0-14	0·358	% of six- or more person h/hlds	0·797
% of population aged 15-64	0·191	Occupied as % of total population	0·557
% of population aged 65 or over	0·349	Females per 1000 males	0·834
Females per 1000 males	0·370	Females per 1000 males, age group 25-44	0·889
Females per 1000 males, age 25-44	0·390	Females per 1000 males	0·889
% of females aged 20-24 ever married	0·327	% aged 15-24 in full-time education	−0·758
POPULATION CHANGE			
1931-51—total (%)	0·201	Population change 1931-51, balance of change	0·996
1931-51—births and deaths (%)	0·217	Population change 1931-51, total change	0·917
1931-51—balance of change (%)	0·207	Population change 1931-51, total change	0·996
1951-58 (%)	0·185	Total new housing rate 1945-58	0·742
Birth rate ratio, 1950-52	0·370	Birth rate ratio, 1955-57	0·850
Birth rate ratio, 1955-57	0·290	Birth rate ratio, 1950-52	0·850
% illegitimate births, 1950-52	0·204	% illegitimate births, 1955-57	0·840
% illegitimate births, 1955-57	0·182	% illegitimate births, 1950-52	0·840
HOUSEHOLDS AND HOUSING			
% persons in private h/hlds	0·235	% in all service industries	−0·604
% one-person h/hlds	0·275	% of population aged 65 or over	0·720
% six- or more person h/hlds	0·329	% of population aged 0-14	0·797
% 1-3-room dwellings	0·167	% h/hlds with W.C.	−0·605
Persons per room	0·368	% h/hlds at over 1½ persons per room	0·892
% overcrowded h/hlds (composite)	0·321	% h/hlds at over 1½ persons per room	0·976
% h/hlds at over 1½ persons per room	0·327	% overcrowded h/hlds (composite)	0·976
% h/hlds in shared dwellings	0·174	Total new-housing rate 1945-58	−0·395
% h/hlds with piped water	0·187	% h/hlds with all 5 amenities or only bath missing	0·588
% h/hlds with W.C.	0·190	% h/hlds with all 5 amenities or only bath missing	0·838
% h/hlds with 5 amenities	0·335	% local authority housing 1945-58	−0·723
% h/hlds with all 5, or only bath missing	0·246	% h/hlds with W.C.	0·838
New-housing rate 1945-58—total	0·174	New housing rate 1945-58—L.A.s	0·774
New-housing rate 1945-58—L.A.s	0·278	New housing rate 1945-58—total	0·774
% L.A. of total houses 1945-58	0·372	% in social classes I + II	−0·799

TABLE 27 (*Cont.*)

Variable	(a)	(b)	
ECONOMIC CHARACTER			
Occupied as % of total population	0·297	% in manufacture, etc.	0·658
% of women in labour force	0·206	Females per 1000 males	0·570
% in manufacture etc.	0·334	% in all service industries	−0·941
% in all service industries	0·358	% in manufacture etc.	−0·941
% in retail	0·271	% in manufacture etc.	−0·720
% in finance etc.	0·261	% in finance etc.	0·544
% in professional services	0·275	% in all service industries	0·682
Job ratio	0·260	% illegitimate births 1955-57	0·539
Commuting ratio	0·219	% h/hlds with 5 amenities	0·467
Per capita retail sales, 1950 (£)	0·192	% illegitimate births 1950-52	0·566
SOCIAL CLASS			
% in social classes I + II	0·423	Social class index	0·965
% in social classes IV + V	0·402	Social class index	−0·896
Social class index	0·425	% in social classes I + II	0·965
Social Survey J-index, 1954	0·334	% in social classes I + II	0·704
VOTING			
% poll, 1951 general election	0·165	% poll, 1955 general election	0·879
% poll, 1955 general election	0·132	% poll, 1951 general election	0·879
% voting left, 1951 general election	0·398	% voting left, 1955 general election	0·972
% voting left, 1955 general election	0·395	% voting left, 1951 general election	0·972
% poll in local elections, 1956-58	0·145	% poll, 1955 general election	0·515
HEALTH			
Infant mortality rate, 1950-52	0·308	Infant mortality rate, 1955-57	0·794
Infant mortality rate, 1955-57	0·291	Infant mortality rate, 1950-52	0·794
T.B. notification rate, 1957	0·102	% overcrowded households	0·362
Mortality rate 1957—lung cancer	0·212	Occupied as % of total population	0·551
Mortality rate 1957—other cancer	0·202	% persons in private h/hlds	0·458
Mortality rate 1957—bronchitis	0·180	% voting left, 1955 general election	0·369
EDUCATION			
% with terminal edn. age under 15	0·387	% aged 15-24 in full-time education	−0·891
% aged 15-24 in full-time education	0·392	% in social classes I + II	0·946

appears (to +0·037) when the seven largest towns are omitted from the calculations. After this freakish case the next highest correlation with population size is no more than −0·302, with the proportion voting at the 1955 General Election.[1]

Other variables which have only minor correlations are the proportion of people voting in the local elections of 1956-58; the 1951 and 1955 size of poll in the general elections; and the rate of tuberculosis notifications during 1957.

Apart from noting the extremes, it is not easy to summarise the matrix, nor is it possible to consider each coefficient separately. We shall confine our remaining comments to one or two special aspects.

[1] The weakness of size as a differentiating factor was also noted by Duncan and Reiss for American towns (Duncan, O. D. and Reiss, A. J., *Social Characteristics of Urban and Rural Communities, 1950*, Wiley, New York, 1956).

In the first place, we might consider whether any variables are so highly inter-correlated that one of them might, on this ground alone, be dropped from the analysis.[1] The precise point at which to draw the line is difficult to decide, and must vary from case to case depending on the nature of the exercise.

The highest coefficient in the matrix is +0·996, between total population change 1931-51 and that part of it which is due to causes other than births and deaths. Even this high value conceals discrepancies (partly no doubt due to the skewness of both series). One town, for example, is 73rd in rank order in the first series, and 117th in the other, a difference of 45 places. If we require 100 per cent. predictability (in the sense of 'predicting' the relative value of a town for one variable in terms of another), none of the series is a sufficient substitute for any other. For many purposes, however, the kind of predictability given by a coefficient of, say, 0·900 or over would be sufficient. Only a small number of coefficients reach this level:

1. 1931-51 population change—total / Change due to births and deaths
2. 1931-51 population change—total / Change due to balance of causes
3. Households at density of over 1½ / Composite overcrowding index
   persons per room
4. % working in manufacturing, etc. / % working in all service industries
   industry
5. Social class index / % in social classes I + II
6. Social class index / % aged 15-24 in full-time education
7. % in social classes I + II / % aged 15-24 in full-time education
8. % voting left in 1951 general / % voting left in 1955 general
   election   election

Of these eight pairs, six are *technically* interdependent. For example, total population change 1931-51 is the sum of changes due to births and deaths, and to other causes. Similarly, the percentage of a population working in manufacturing, and the percentage working in service industries, are derived from the same total, and to some extent complementary. Only two of the pairs, numbers 7 and 8, are independent in a technical sense.

However, technical interdependence does not affect the question of using one series as a substitute for the other, and we can assume that little damage would be done to any further study of this kind if some of the variables in the above list were omitted.

Another matter of interest is the relationship between series on the

[1] High correlations should not in fact be the sole criterion for exclusion. One should also take into account the correlations of each of the two associated variables with all the remaining variables. Only if they have very similar correlation patterns can they be said to be interchangeable.

same topic taken at two points of time. The correlation coefficients of the five pairs of series in question are as follows:

Birth rate ratios 1950-52 and 1955-57	+0·850
% illegitimate births 1950-52 and 1955-57	+0·840
Infant mortality rates 1950-52 and 1955-57	+0·794
% poll in 1951 and in 1955 general elections	+0·879
% voting for left-wing candidates in 1951 and in 1955 general election	+0·972

All five series are reasonably consistent over time.

This is as far as we shall take our remarks on the simple relationships between variables. The predominant impression from the matrix is how low most of the correlations are, and this is itself a sign of the diversity of the towns. But the connections between the variables are in reality too complex to be brought out by simple correlations. In the next chapter we shall employ multivariate techniques to investigate them more satisfactorily.

V

Complex Relationships: Common Factors in Urban Differentiation

The multivariate approach

It is plain from the foregoing chapters that many of the 57 variables included in the analysis are interrelated. They cannot be regarded as so many independent measures of inter-town variations, but often repeat roughly the same story. This suggests the question, whether all or most of the variation between towns, as shown by the 57 variables, can be expressed in a much smaller number of major factors; and, if so, how many such factors are adequate for the purpose, how much of the total variation they account for, and what meaning can be given to them. To answer these questions we need the aid of multivariate techniques.

Kendall has defined multivariate analysis as 'the branch of statistical analysis which is concerned with the relationships of sets of dependent variates', and has differentiated two kinds of situation, according to whether one is concerned with *dependence* or *interdependence*. In the former 'one or more of the variates is selected for us by the conditions of the problem and we require to investigate the way in which it depends on the other variates—the so-called but badly-named "independent" variates'. In the study of interdependence 'we are concerned with the relationship of a set of variates among themselves, no one being selected as special in the sense of a dependent variate'.[1]

In social research the first of these situations predominates. More often than not, one is seeking to investigate the dependence of a certain variable —say, admission to Borstal institutions, or suicide rates, or a mortality indicator—on a number of other variables. Such problems are often tackled by means of multiple regression analysis, and there are numerous illustrations of its application in the literature. This approach seemed inappropriate here, since it was not our aim to investigate to what extent any one variable among the 57 depended on the rest. We could admittedly have taken several of the variables in turn as 'dependent' and found that combination of three or four of the remainder which best explained the

[1] Kendall, M. G., *A Course in Multivariate Analysis*, Charles Griffin, London, 1957, p. 6.

inter-town differences on, first, one variable, then another, and so on. But this seemed pointless, and would also have involved serious technical difficulties.

It seemed more appropriate to treat this study as a case of interdependence and to approach it by the technique of *component analysis*. The essence of this is to investigate how much of the total variability (between towns) exhibited in the 57 primary variables can be accounted for, and expressed, in a smaller number of new independent variates. These new variates, which are functions of the primary variables, are the so-called principal components, hereafter referred to simply as *components*. The technique ensures that the first component accounts for the greatest possible proportion of the total variance of all 57 variables; that the second component is uncorrelated with the first, and accounts for the greatest possible part of the variance; and so on in descending order. As a way of determining the *number* of components necessary to give an adequate summary of the mass of data the technique is useful and appropriate. Its major problems arise in the interpretation of the components. These are mathematical artefacts, and not individual series taken from among the 57; and as such they need not have an easily interpretable meaning.

The component analysis

The details of component analysis—for which a computing programme was available for the Mercury Digital Computer of the University of London Computing Unit—are described in Kendall[1] and we will not attempt more than a brief summary here.

The starting-point of our analysis is the correlation matrix[2] (shown in Table 26). From this matrix are ultimately derived a series of equations expressing the new variates (ξ_j) in terms of the primary variables (x'_i).[3] Concretely, the first new variate (ξ_1) looks as follows:

$$\xi_1 = -0{\cdot}023x'_1 - 0{\cdot}163x'_2 + \ldots + 0{\cdot}215x'_{57}$$

the weights $-0{\cdot}023$, $-0{\cdot}163$ etc. being derived from the analysis. These weights are sometimes known as factor coefficients. The complete set of coefficients for this first variate is given in the first column of Table 28. The higher the weight attached to a particular variable, the greater the
• importance of the variable for that particular component. We can next evaluate ξ_1 for each town from the 57 values $x'_1 \ldots x'_{57}$; this is in the nature of a straightforward index number, the weights used being those just described. We then have a new set of 157 values, one for each town.

---

[1] *op. cit.* Ch. 2.
[2] A component analysis can start from a so-called dispersion matrix composed of variances and covariances of pairs of variables; a correlation matrix is equivalent to a dispersion matrix for the variables in standardised form.
[3] For purposes of calculating ξ_j the variables are expressed in standardised form.

TABLE 28

COMPONENT ANALYSIS—FACTOR COEFFICIENTS FOR FIRST FOUR PRINCIPAL COMPONENTS

Primary variable	Component			
	I	II	III	IV
POPULATION SIZE AND STRUCTURE				
Population ('000)	−0·023	0·091	−0·082	0·125
% of population aged 0-14	−0·163	−0·171	0·152	0·114
% of population aged 15-64	−0·017	−0·127	−0·248	−0·176
% of population aged 65 or over	0·154	0·229	0·031	0·013
Females per 1000 males	0·177	0·160	−0·051	0·125
Females per 1000 males, age 25-44	0·202	0·043	−0·019	0·153
% of females aged 20-24 ever married	−0·166	0·072	0·099	−0·179
POPULATION CHANGE				
1931-51—total (%)	0·038	−0·243	0·099	0·132
1931-51—births and deaths (%)	−0·031	−0·282	0·082	0·122
1931-51—balance of change (%)	0·051	−0·230	0·100	0·131
1951-58 (%)	0·022	−0·117	0·279	−0·012
Birth rate ratio, 1950-52	−0·185	0·029	0·193	0·092
Birth rate ratio, 1955-57	−0·135	0·013	0·247	0·082
% illegitimate births, 1950-52	0·007	0·267	0·069	−0·021
% illegitimate births, 1955-57	0·008	0·251	−0·029	−0·048
HOUSEHOLDS AND HOUSING				
% persons in private h/hlds	−0·096	−0·137	−0·167	−0·005
% one-person h/hlds	0·070	0·298	−0·087	0·086
% six- or more person h/hlds	−0·159	−0·099	0·139	0·184
% 1-3-room dwellings	−0·061	0·107	−0·083	0·202
Persons per room	−0·179	−0·089	−0·079	0·217
% overcrowded h/hlds (composite)	−0·155	0·011	−0·078	0·294
% h/hlds at over 1½ persons per room	−0·161	0·000	−0·065	0·298
% h/hlds in shared dwellings	0·050	0·040	−0·197	0·116
% h/hlds with piped water	0·069	−0·119	−0·004	−0·199
% h/hlds with W.C.	0·077	−0·133	0·046	−0·092
% h/hlds with 5 amenities	0·152	−0·205	0·013	0·046
% h/hlds with all 5, or only bath missing	0·106	−0·163	0·028	−0·132
New-housing rate 1945-58—total	−0·024	−0·039	0·328	−0·055
New-housing rate 1945-58—L.A.s	−0·123	0·040	0·269	−0·060
% L.A. of total houses, 1945-58	−0·187	0·112	−0·063	−0·038
ECONOMIC CHARACTER				
Occupied as % of total population	−0·133	−0·091	−0·231	−0·090
% of women in labour force	0·062	0·110	−0·258	0·015
% in manufacture, etc.	−0·165	−0·012	−0·165	−0·190
% in all service industries	0·179	0·026	0·161	0·162
% in retail	0·134	0·077	0·131	0·147
% in finance, etc.	0·112	0·169	0·036	0·122
% in professional services	0·144	−0·020	0·092	0·104
Job ratio	−0·107	0·191	0·018	−0·157
Commuting ratio	0·047	−0·203	−0·222	0·036
Per capita retail sales, 1950 (£)	0·040	0·235	0·077	−0·092
SOCIAL CLASS				
% in social classes I + II	0·225	−0·043	−0·011	0·040
% in social classes IV + V	−0·210	0·063	0·063	0·077
Social class index	0·218	−0·072	−0·037	0·006
Social Survey J-index, 1954	0·170	−0·101	0·034	0·038
VOTING				
% poll, 1951 general election	−0·051	−0·091	0·040	−0·281
% poll, 1955 general election	−0·007	−0·084	0·093	−0·287
% voting left, 1951 general election	−0·208	−0·025	−0·063	−0·040
% voting left, 1955 general election	−0·207	−0·017	−0·045	−0·025
% poll in local elections, 1956-58	0·033	0·083	0·146	−0·176

TABLE 28 (*Cont.*)

Primary variables	Component			
	I	II	III	IV
HEALTH				
Infant mortality rate, 1950-52	−0·157	0·089	0·094	0·085
Infant mortality rate, 1955-57	−0·149	0·077	0·127	0·063
T.B. notification rate, 1957	−0·045	−0·014	0·019	0·142
Mortality rate 1957—lung cancer	−0·078	−0·122	−0·185	0·100
Mortality rate 1957—other cancer	−0·092	−0·025	−0·126	0·098
Mortality rate 1957—bronchitis	−0·095	0·014	−0·091	−0·008
EDUCATION				
% with terminal edn. age under 15	−0·204	0·034	0·013	−0·024
% aged 15-24 in full-time education	0·215	−0·038	−0·003	0·036

Bedford, for example, has the value 0·193, Luton −0·104, and so on. These values, which we call component scores, appear in Table 31 (pp. 84-88).

So much for the first variate. We proceed by eliminating the effect of the first variate from the matrix, and then repeating the analysis to obtain a second set of weights from the residual matrix. The equation here is

$$\xi_2 = 0 \cdot 091 x'_1 - 0 \cdot 171 x'_2 + \ldots - 0 \cdot 038 x'_{57}$$

The complete set of weights is shown in the second column of Table 28, and similarly for later components. The second set of component scores is derived in the same manner as before. The process is repeated another four times, thus yielding a total of six components. In theory it could be continued until the matrix is exhausted (i.e. until all coefficients were zero), but there is in fact no point in extracting components which account for only a tiny part of the variance.

The result of main interest is the proportion of the total inter-town variance accounted for by each of the components. The first component accounts for 30 per cent., the second for 13 per cent., the third for 10 per cent., the fourth for 7 per cent., and the fifth and sixth for 4 per cent. each, making a total of 69 per cent. We shall, in the remainder of this analysis, concentrate on the first four components which between them accounted for 60 per cent. of the total variance. Put another way, the variation between the towns, as contained in the 57 variables, can be regarded as attributable to four major factors, accounting for three fifths of the total, and a number of minor factors which account for the remainder.

General assessment of the components

The figures given in the preceding paragraph are considerably lower than those found in some other published examples of component analysis. Stone,[1] in a well-known analysis of 17 economic series, extracted three components accounting between them for 97 per cent. of the total variance.

[1] Stone, J. R. N., 'The Interdependence of Blocks of Transactions', *Journal of the Royal Statistical Society, Supp.*, 9, 1, 1947.

F

Pearce and Holland, in an agricultural enquiry,[1] summarised four variables relating to tree measurements by two components accounting for over 90 per cent. of the total variation. Many similar findings could be quoted.

Such results set alongside our own might be regarded as discouraging. But then our analysis was done on an unusually large, and heterogeneous set of variables. This was intentional. We brought together as wide a representation of urban data as we could find, and one might, if anything, be surprised that *as much* as 60 per cent. of the total variation in the 57 series can be expressed by four components.

However, as the percentages are relatively low, we need to be doubly careful in interpreting the components. To begin with, a special analysis enables us at least to test the consistency of the components. We divide the 157 towns into a 'Northern' and a 'Southern' section, the dividing line being roughly a diagonal drawn across England from the Wash to the Bristol Channel, and then carry out a separate component analysis for each section. The results are summarised below:

Component	North	South
	Per cent. of total variance accounted for	
I	24·0	27·5
II	14·3	19·0
III	8·7	14·6
IV	6·7	5·1
Total I-IV	53·7	66·2

The figures are reassuring. The pattern of components is broadly similar for the two halves of the country, and a study of the factor coefficients confirmed that the *nature* of the components in the northern and southern towns is very similar. The figures suggest that the variables closely associated with the first three components are more relevant in differentiating between towns in the south than in the north.

There are other technical points which may affect the reality or size of the principal components. We commented in Chapter IV on the non-linearity of some of the relationships between variables and on the unsuitability of the product-moment coefficient for measuring correlation in these cases. Since the component analysis is based on the correlation coefficients, its results could well be distorted by such non-linearities. We therefore repeated it, both on the logarithms of the primary observations and on the rank order values shown in Appendix B. The correlation matrices resulting from these calculations were discussed in Chapter IV above. We show here the resulting principal components side by side with the original analysis:

[1] Pearce, S. C. and Holland, D. A., 'Some Applications of Multivariate Methods in Botany', *Applied Statistics*, IX, 1, 1960.

Component	Observations in ORIGINAL form	Observations transformed into LOGS	Observations as RANK ORDER values
	Per cent. of total variance accounted for		
I	30·1	30·7	31·9
II	13·2	13·6	13·5
III	9·8	9·6	11·2
IV	7·3	6·3	6·5
Total I-IV	60·4	60·2	63·1

It is reassuring that the analysis on the transformed observations has produced a pattern of components very similar to those found for the original data. The rank order analysis produces only slightly larger values of the components.

Other technical difficulties are less easily disposed of, and we hope to look further into (a) the importance of attenuation effects in the correlation coefficients; (b) consequences of the fact that the original observations are based on different total numbers, both in the sense that the towns differ greatly in size and in that the variables relate to different populations and sub-populations; and (c) the problem of testing the statistical significance of the results.

Interpretation of the components

Meanwhile, let us consider what meaning can be given to the components. The strength of the relationship between a variable and a component is measured by the correlation coefficient between them, and these coefficients are given in Table 29 (on pp. 74-75). For more convenient reading of the results, we have extracted for each of the first four components the variables showing the highest correlations.

COMPONENT I

Primary variables showing the ten highest correlations with component I[1]

% in social classes I + II	0·931
Social class index	0·903
% aged 15-24 in full-time education	0·891
% in social classes IV + V	− 0·871
% voting left, 1951 general election	− 0·860
% voting left, 1955 general election	− 0·859
% with terminal education age under 15	− 0·845
Sex ratio, 25-44	0·836
% of new houses built by local authorities	− 0·773
Birth rate ratio, 1950-52	− 0·765

[1] Note that the signs have the same significance as in the correlation matrix. They indicate the *direction* in which the variable is related to the component. The component score was computed in such a way that the highest score indicates high social class. Its relationship with the percentage in social classes IV + V is therefore negative in the sense that the higher the score, the lower the percentage in social classes IV + V.

It is evident, and a glance at the correlation matrix opposite page 58 will confirm, that the leading coefficients here belong to variables highly correlated with the social class indices. The first component can with little doubt be regarded as reflecting social class differentiation, and it accounts for almost one third of the total variance.

COMPONENT II

Primary variables showing the ten highest correlations with Component II

% of one-person households	0·817
Population change, 1931-51, due to births and deaths	−0·773
% illegitimate births, 1950-52	0·732
% illegitimate births, 1955-57	0·688
Population change, 1931-51—total change	−0·667
Per capita retail sales	0·643
Population change, 1931-51, due to causes other than births and deaths	−0·630
% population aged 65 or over	0·628
% households with all 5 household amenities	−0·563
Commuting ratio	−0·557

The high coefficients associated with the second component are notably related to population growth during the period 1931 to 1951. During this time the highest increase was recorded in suburban areas, such as Huyton with Roby (near Liverpool) which increased over tenfold from about 5,000 to over 55,000 and the London suburbs of Ruislip-Northwood and Chigwell. Older towns like London A.C. and Rhondda or the old centres of the wool trade like Bradford and Dewsbury, lost population as people left the inner areas for the new estates outside the city boundaries, or left the town altogether.

Other factors associated with this movement of population are the proportion of single-person households and of the elderly, both of which tend to rise in the old areas as the young families move to new homes; better housing amenities in the new areas, where houses are built complete with internal water supply, water closets and bathrooms; and low per capita retail sales due to the lack of balance between housing and shopping facilities in the new housing estates. The areas of recent development are also characterised by high commuting ratios, since a large proportion of the resident occupied population go to work in other areas.

COMPONENT III

Primary variables showing the ten highest correlations with Component III

New-housing rate, 1945-58—total building	0·776
Population change, 1951-58	0·661
New-housing rate, 1945-58—local authority building	0·636
% of women in labour force	−0·610
% of population aged 15-64	−0·587
Birth rate ratio, 1955-57	0·584

COMPONENT III (*cont.*)

Occupied as % of total population	−0·546
Commuting ratio	−0·525
Households in shared dwellings	−0·467
Birth rate ratio, 1950-52	0·456

The third component is most closely associated with two groups of variables: (*a*) developments after 1951, and (*b*) the working population in 1951. The first group includes the building of new houses between 1945 and 1958 (72 per cent. of the total in this period in England and Wales were built between the beginning of 1951 and the end of June 1958), population change between 1951 and 1958, and the birth rate in the years 1955 to 1957.

The second component, as we saw, is related to developments between the years 1931 and 1951. Some of the areas which had expanded in this period were largely built up by 1951, and received little additional population. In other areas, such as Romford, Chigwell and Solihull, expansion continued; new houses were built and the population followed. At the other extreme we find a group of towns whose population for the first time showed a decline in this period after 1951. Chesterfield, Barking and Ilford are examples.

The other set of variables closely associated with the third component includes the proportion of the population aged 15-64, the proportion of the population aged 15 or over in gainful employment, the proportion of women in the labour force, and the commuting ratio. All these variables relate to 1951.

COMPONENT IV

Primary variables showing the ten highest correlations with Component IV

Households at over 1½ persons per room	0·608
Overcrowded households (composite index)	0·599
% poll, 1955 general election	−0·586
% poll, 1951 general election	−0·573
Persons per room	0·442
% 1-3-room dwellings	0·413
% households with piped water	−0·405
% working in manufacturing etc. industry	−0·389
% six- or more person households	0·375
% females aged 20-24 ever married	−0·366

The fourth component is strongly associated with housing conditions and particularly with overcrowding. This is especially noteworthy in view of the fact that the components are independent of one another; overcrowding clearly plays a role of its own, independent either of social class, or of the age of the area, as expressed in the first three components. Other variables important for the fourth component are the two indices of participation in the General Elections of 1951 and 1955, absence of an internal piped water supply, and the proportion of women aged 20-24 ever married.

TABLE 29

Correlations of variables with each of the first four principal component scores

Primary variable	Correlation coefficients between variable and component score			
	I	II	III	IV
Population Size and Structure				
Population ('000)	−0·096	0·250	−0·194	0·255
% of population aged 0-14	−0·674	−0·470	0·360	0·234
% of population aged 15-64	−0·069	−0·349	−0·587	−0·360
% of population aged 65 or over	0·637	0·628	0·074	0·027
Females per 1000 males	0·735	0·437	−0·121	0·255
Females per 1000 males, age 25-44	0·836	0·119	−0·044	0·312
% of females aged 20-24 ever married	−0·687	0·199	0·234	−0·366
Population Change				
1931-51—total (%)	0·156	−0·667	0·234	0·268
1931-51—births and deaths (%)	−0·128	−0·773	0·193	0·248
1931-51—balance of change (%)	0·213	−0·630	0·237	0·267
1951-58 (%)	0·092	−0·321	0·661	−0·024
Birth rate ratio, 1950-52	−0·765	0·079	0·456	0·188
Birth rate ratio, 1955-57	−0·558	0·035	0·584	0·166
% illegitimate births, 1950-52	0·026	0·732	0·162	−0·042
% illegitimate births, 1955-57	0·033	0·688	−0·068	−0·098
Households and Housing				
% persons in private h/hlds	−0·398	−0·374	−0·397	−0·010
% one-person h/hlds	0·289	0·817	−0·207	0·176
% six- or more person h/hlds	−0·659	−0·272	0·328	0·375
% 1-3-room dwellings	−0·253	0·293	−0·195	0·413
Persons per room	−0·739	−0·244	−0·187	0·442
% overcrowded h/hlds (composite)	−0·644	0·030	−0·185	0·599
% h/hlds at over 1½ persons per room	−0·665	0·001	−0·154	0·608
% h/hlds in shared dwellings	0·205	0·110	−0·467	0·236
% h/hlds with piped water	0·286	−0·327	−0·009	−0·405
% h/hlds with W.C.	0·321	−0·365	0·109	−0·188
% h/hlds with 5 amenities	0·631	−0·563	0·030	0·094
% h/hlds with all 5, or only bath missing	0·440	−0·446	0·067	−0·270
New-housing rate, 1945-58—total	−0·101	−0·108	0·776	−0·112
New-housing rate, 1945-58—L.A.s	−0·509	0·110	0·636	−0·123
% L.A. of total houses, 1945-58	−0·773	0·306	−0·150	−0·078
Economic Character				
Occupied as % of total population	−0·553	−0·249	−0·546	−0·184
% of women in labour force	0·256	0·302	−0·610	0·031
% in manufacture, etc.	−0·682	−0·034	−0·391	−0·389
% in all service industries	0·741	0·070	0·382	0·331
% in retail	0·556	0·210	0·309	0·300
% in finance, etc.	0·462	0·462	0·086	0·249
% in professional services	0·596	−0·055	0·218	0·212
Job ratio	−0·442	0·524	0·042	−0·320
Commuting ratio	0·193	−0·557	−0·525	0·073
Per capita retail sales, 1950 (£)	0·164	0·643	0·183	−0·188
Social Class				
% in social classes I + II	0·931	−0·118	−0·026	0·082
% in social classes IV + V	−0·871	0·172	0·149	0·157
Social class index	0·903	−0·197	−0·088	0·011
Social Survey J-index, 1954	0·705	−0·278	0·080	0·077
Voting				
% poll, 1951 general election	−0·209	−0·250	0·094	−0·573
% poll, 1955 general election	−0·029	−0·231	0·219	−0·586
% voting left, 1951 general election	−0·860	−0·069	−0·148	−0·081
% voting left, 1955 general election	−0·859	−0·045	−0·107	−0·051
% poll in local elections, 1956-58	0·138	0·227	0·345	−0·360

TABLE 29 (*Cont.*)

Primary variable	Correlation coefficients between variable and component score			
	I	II	III	IV
HEALTH				
Infant mortality rate, 1950-52	−0·648	0·244	0·223	0·174
Infant mortality rate, 1955-57	−0·616	0·212	0·300	0·128
T.B. notification rate, 1957	−0·188	−0·039	0·045	0·289
Mortality rate, 1957—lung cancer	−0·324	−0·335	−0·438	0·204
Mortality rate, 1957—other cancer	−0·382	−0·068	−0·299	0·200
Mortality rate, 1957—bronchitis	−0·392	0·038	−0·216	−0·016
EDUCATION				
% with terminal edn. age under 15	−0·845	0·092	0·031	−0·049
% aged 15-24 in full-time education	0·891	−0·105	−0·007	0·074

General discussion of the components

The components have the vital characteristic, already referred to, of being independent of each other. The importance of this is brought out if we think back to the correlation matrix. The correlation between two variables had limited meaning since it could often be due, in a causal sense, to the intervention of a third. Thus the positive correlation of 0·649 between the J-index and the proportion of persons aged 15-24 in full-time education was probably due to a relationship of each with a third factor, namely social class. In the case of the components no such possibility arises. Their independence means that a classification in terms of, say, the second component is strictly independent of a classification in terms of the first or third or fourth component.

This should be borne in mind in commenting on the meaning of the components. These, as we saw, are weighted averages of the primary variables, the latter contributing in very different degrees to the different components. This constitutes a basis on which some meaning can be assigned to them. In the case of the first component, the weights are greater, and therefore the association stronger, for those primary variables which are directly or indirectly associated with social class. This formalises the results of Chapter IV, where the social class indices and their correlates were seen to play a dominant role. We can now assign a value to the degree of dominance, for the first component has been shown to account for 30 per cent. of total variability.

Of equal interest, and less easily observable in the matrix, is the nature of the other components, though they naturally account for decreasing portions of the total variance. The second component, which is independent of the others, is related to characteristics associated with the 'age' of an area.

The third component has been found to be associated with development during the years 1951 to 1958. The changes reflected in the second component had by then largely come to a halt, and the importance of the third is that it stresses the rapid changes which occur in urban conditions, and the need, consequently, for constant reassessment of the data over time.

Finally, the fourth component underlines the importance of housing conditions as a differentiating factor independent of social class and of stage of development. In other words, when we have classified areas according to the occupational status of their populations, and according to whether they are old or newly developed towns, each group can be further sub-divided into towns with a high degree of overcrowding (Sunderland, Gateshead and South Shields, for example) and those with relatively little overcrowding (Merthyr Tydfil and the Rhondda).[1]

These attempts at interpretation should not lead one to regard component analysis as a magical process whereby the structure of British towns can be transformed from a state of statistical chaos to a system of well ordered functional groups. It may produce an ordering which makes sense, but its generality is restricted by the choice of the primary series. If we had analysed a different set of 57 variables, the components extracted would have been different. Up to a point 'what comes out' depends on 'what goes in'. All we can say is that the selection of variables was dictated by the data available, and was not made with an eye on the component analysis. We aimed to get as representative and far-ranging a set of variables as could be compiled. But this does not alter the fact that the results apply only to this particular set of data.

How far the process of selection has influenced the findings is difficult to say. Social class would probably emerge as a dominant factor in any set of variables covering the major aspects of urban structure. The second component, also, has high correlations spread over a wide variety of variables, ranging from demographic characteristics to housing and retail sales. The third component would have disappeared in its present form had we failed to include the series relating to events since 1951, but this makes it no less valuable.

None of these considerations is of great importance to the analysis. It is sufficient to realise that the problem of the 'input-output' relationship exists and to acknowledge the limited generality of the results.

The 'representation' of different variables by the principal components

The first purpose of the component analysis is to try to represent the body of data contained in the fifty-seven series by a smaller number of major variables. We have extracted six components, four of which could be given some recognisable meaning. To what extent can these new variables be said to 'represent' the fifty-seven? Arithmetically the answer has already been given. The six components 'represent' the fifty-seven primary variables to the extent that the former account for roughly two thirds of the total variance contained in the latter. But it is clear from Table 29 that some of the variables are better represented than others. This can be more clearly seen in Table 30, which shows the percentage of the

See group 7 in the classification of Chapter VI.

variance of each primary variable accounted for by the four components separately and combined.[1] These figures are simply the squares of the correlation coefficients. For example, the correlation coefficient between population size and component I is −0·096, the square of which is 0·0092. This indicates that roughly 1 per cent. of the total variation in population size is accounted for by component I; the other percentages for this variable are 6·25 (component II), 3·76 (component III) and 6·50 (component IV), showing that components I-IV between them account for 17·4 per cent. of its total variance.

A few features of Table 30 are worth noting. In the *population size and structure group*, there is one variable—population size itself—for which less than a fifth of the total variance is accounted for by the first four components. At the other extreme, there are the proportions in the outside age groups and the sex ratios, which are almost wholly accounted for by these four components. In the case of the old—the proportion aged 65 or over—the first two components account for 80 per cent. of the total variation.

Among the *population change* variables, only the birth rate ratio series are to any appreciable extent accounted for by component I. In the 1931-51 change figures, it is component II that accounts for the bulk of the variability, while in the 1951-58 series it is component III.

The *housing* variables are very diverse. In some cases, the four components explain a great share of the inter-town variance: the percentage of one-person households (82 per cent.), persons per room (84 per cent.), percentage of households living at more than $1\frac{1}{2}$ persons per room (84 per cent.) are outstanding examples. In other cases, a third or less of the variance is due to these components. The importance of component II as regards one-person households, and of component III as regards house building, is clearly brought out.

In the *economic* group none of the variables are notably dependent on these four components, although there are two cases where the total contribution exceeds 70 per cent. These are the proportions in manufacturing and in service industries, both largely accounted for by component I.

The *social class* group is striking for the very high dependence of the variables on component I. As expected, this applies particularly to the indices based on occupations. The *voting* direction figures are also highly dependent on component I.

In the *health* group the infant mortality rates are explained in considerable measure by component I. Curiously, the other variables are evidently related more to factors not covered by these components. Finally, there are the *education* series, variation in both of which is in considerable measure accounted for by the first component.

[1] A list of the variables which are best and least-well accounted for by the four components was given in Table 3, page 16.

TABLE 30

PERCENTAGE OF VARIANCE OF EACH OF 57 PRIMARY VARIABLES ACCOUNTED FOR BY THE
PRINCIPAL COMPONENTS

Primary variable	Per cent. of variance accounted for by: Component				
	I	II	III	IV	I-IV
POPULATION SIZE AND STRUCTURE					
Population ('000)	0·92	6·25	3·76	6·50	17·44
% of population aged 0-14	45·43	22·09	12·96	5·48	85·95
% of population aged 15-64	0·48	12·18	34·46	12·96	60·07
% of population aged 65 or over	40·58	39·44	0·55	0·07	80·64
Females per 1000 males	54·02	19·10	1·46	6·50	81·09
Females per 1000 males, age 25-44	69·89	1·42	0·19	9·73	81·23
% of females aged 20-24 ever married	47·20	3·96	5·48	13·40	70·03
POPULATION CHANGE					
1931-51—total (%)	2·43	44·49	5·48	7·18	59·58
1931-51—births and deaths (%)	1·64	59·75	3·72	6·15	71·27
1931-51—balance of change (%)	4·54	39·69	5·62	7·13	56·97
1951-58 (%)	0·85	10·30	43·69	0·06	54·90
Birth rate ratio; 1950-52	58·52	0·62	20·79	3·53	83·47
Birth rate ratio; 1955-57	31·14	0·12	34·11	2·76	68·12
% illegitimate births, 1950-52	0·07	53·58	2·62	0·18	56·45
% illegitimate births, 1955-57	0·11	47·33	0·46	0·96	48·87
HOUSEHOLDS AND HOUSING					
% persons in private h/hlds	15·84	13·99	15·76	0·01	45·60
% one-person h/hlds	8·35	66·75	4·28	3·10	82·48
% six- or more person h/hlds	43·43	7·40	10·76	14·06	75·65
% 1-3-room dwellings	6·40	8·58	3·80	17·06	35·85
Persons per room	54·61	5·95	3·50	19·54	83·60
% overcrowded h/hlds (composite)	41·47	0·09	3·42	35·88	80·87
% h/hlds at over 1½ persons per room	44·22	0·00	2·37	36·97	83·56
% h/hlds in shared dwellings	4·20	1·21	21·81	5·57	32·79
% h/hlds with piped water	8·18	10·69	0·01	16·40	35·28
% h/hlds with W.C.	10·30	13·32	1·19	3·53	28·35
% h/hlds with 5 amenities	39·82	31·70	0·09	0·88	72·49
% h/hlds with all 5, or only bath missing	19·36	19·89	0·45	7·29	46·99
New-housing rate 1945-58—total	1·02	1·17	60·22	1·25	63·66
New-housing rate 1945-58—L.A.'s	25·91	1·21	40·45	1·51	69·08
% L.A. of total houses, 1945-58	59·75	9·36	2·25	0·61	71·97
ECONOMIC CHARACTER					
Occupied as % of total population	30·58	6·20	29·81	3·39	69·98
% of women in labour force	6·55	9·12	37·21	0·10	52·98
% in manufacture, etc.	46·51	0·12	15·29	15·13	77·05
% in all service industries	54·91	0·49	14·59	10·96	80·95
% in retail	30·91	4·41	9·55	9·00	53·87
% in finance, etc.	21·34	21·34	0·74	6·20	49·63
% in professional services	35·52	0·30	4·75	4·49	45·07
Job ratio	19·54	27·46	0·18	10·24	57·41
Commuting ratio	3·72	31·02	27·56	0·53	62·85
Per capita retail sales, 1950 (£)	2·69	41·34	3·35	3·53	50·92
SOCIAL CLASS					
% in social classes I+II	86·68	1·39	0·07	0·67	88·81
% in social classes IV+V	75·86	2·96	2·22	2·46	83·51
Social class index	81·54	3·88	0·77	0·01	86·21
Social Survey J-Index, 1954	49·70	7·73	0·64	0·59	58·66

TABLE 30 (*Cont.*)

Primary variable	Component				I-IV
	I	II	III	IV	
VOTING					
% poll, 1951 General Election	4·37	6·25	0·88	32·83	44·33
% poll, 1955 General Election	0·08	5·34	4·80	34·34	44·56
% voting Left, 1951 General Election	73·96	0·48	2·19	0·66	77·28
% voting Left, 1955 General Election	73·79	0·20	1·14	0·26	75·40
% poll in local elections, 1956-58	1·90	5·15	11·90	12·96	31·92
HEALTH					
Infant mortality rate, 1950-52	41·99	5·95	4·97	3·03	55·94
Infant mortality rate, 1955-57	37·95	4·49	9·00	1·64	53·08
T.B. notification rate, 1957	3·53	0·15	0·20	8·35	12·24
Mortality rate 1957—lung cancer	10·50	11·22	19·18	4·16	45·07
Mortality rate 1957—other cancer	14·59	0·46	8·94	4·00	27·99
Mortality rate 1957—bronchitis	15·37	0·14	4·67	0·03	20·20
EDUCATION					
% with terminal edn. age under 15	71·40	0·85	0·10	0·24	72·59
% aged 15-24 in full-time education	79·39	1·10	0·00	0·55	81·04

This analysis has yielded some interesting results. Social class has been shown to be a very discriminating factor in urban differentiation, while two others, development between 1931 and 1951 and between 1951 and 1958, are, as expected, associated with variables such as birth rates, age structure of the population, new housing and so forth. This emphasises the importance of stage of development as a factor in urban differentiation.

The next step is to use the results of the above analysis in deriving a classification of towns, in other words to group towns according to the four principal components. It needs to be stressed that, since the components reflect some urban features more closely than others, the classification based on them also has limited generality.

A Classification of Towns

A CLASSIFICATION of towns can take many forms. A method common in American writing[1] is to group towns according to economic function, as expressed in the distribution of the labour force among various kinds of industry. We did not pursue this approach beyond classifying towns according to simple occupational and industrial indices. Any of the 57 variables can of course be used for arranging the towns into 'types', and, in Chapter III, we classified them in respect of four major variables which seemed important as discriminators of town types.

Clearly these classifications overlap. Towns which appear in the 'uppermost' group in one classification tend again to be found in the 'uppermost' group in another. Such relationships have been examined, first, by means of correlation coefficients and secondly by component analysis. As a result, we now have four principal components, which can be reasonably interpreted in terms of the primary variables, and therefore four component scores for each town. Bedford for example has scores of 0·193, −0·116, 0·231, −0·173, Luton −0·104, 0·160, 0·076, −0·284, etc. The towns can be classified according to these four sets of values which now take the place of the fifty-seven primary variables.

This classification is done mainly by visual means. The process can be explained by reference to Figure 2 (facing) which shows the towns plotted according to the first two components. Component I is measured along the vertical axis, component II along the horizontal axis. A rough classification can be arrived at by gathering adjacent towns on the diagram into groups. Some of the towns fall into natural clusters by reason of their distance from other groups of towns. An example are the seaside resorts in the top left-hand side of the diagram. Lower down in the diagram the towns are spread more evenly, and grouping involves an arbitrary decision on the total number of groups desired and the lines used to separate one group of towns from the other.

The real problem arises when we try to visualise the towns, not in two-dimensional space as in the diagram, but classified in four dimensions, according to the four components. We find ourselves virtually in the posi-

[1] Kneedler, G. M., 'Functional Types of Cities', *Public Management*, XXVII, 1945; Harris, C. D., 'A Functional Classification of Cities in the United States', *Geographical Review*, XXXIII, 1, 1943; Nelson, H. J., 'A Service Classification of American Cities', *Economic Geography*, XXI, 3, 1955; Duncan and Reiss, *op. cit.*

tion of the astronomer who looks up at the stars, trying to ascertain not only the distance between them on a plane but also in depth, while the whole universe curves away into a fourth dimension, at right angles to the other three.

Fortunately, the independence of the components makes it relatively simple to calculate the distance between any two points in space, and to cluster the towns in such a way that the distance between a town and the centre of the group to which it is assigned is less than the distance from it to the centre of other groups. As an example, let us consider the classification of Blackpool. This lies between two groups of, respectively, seaside resorts and other non-industrial towns which include Bath, Cambridge and Southend. In order to allocate Blackpool to one or other of these groups, we need to find the centres of the two groups and to measure the distance of Blackpool from each. The town is then assigned to the nearest group.

This principle, adapted to four dimensions, is used in the classification below. The actual process is however more complicated than in the above example, in which an initial visual grouping was possible and the only remaining problem was to assign marginal towns like Blackpool. In the four-dimensional case, there is no question of 'seeing' the basic clusters. However, one circumstance eases the task. Since the first two components account for 43 per cent. of the total variance, as against the 17 per cent. accounted for by the next two, the classification will be dominated by the first two components. Geometrically, if the first component is plotted in a vertical direction and the second component in a horizontal direction, the vertical distances between towns is considerably larger than the horizontal distance. Both, on the same reasoning, exceed the distance from the plane to the third dimension, and this in turn is larger than the distance to the fourth dimension. We can, in other words, imagine the towns as clusters of points hovering at no great distance from a plane of considerable expanse.

The first stage, therefore, is to plot the towns as in Figure 2, and to obtain from this diagram 'hypothetical' groups formed in the way described above, by grouping together adjacent towns. The hypothetical groups are shown by the circles in Figure 2. Subsequently this hypothetical grouping can be tested by calculating the distance, in four-dimensional space, from each town to the group mean.

An example will make this clear. Group 3, in its hypothetical form, consists of 23 towns, each with four component scores which are the four co-ordinates determining the position of the town in space. Summing the twenty-three scores for component I, and dividing by 23, produces the group mean for component I. Group means for the other three components are obtained in a similar way. The four means are the co-ordinates of the central point of the group.

The next step is to calculate the distance from each town in the group to this central point. An example of the calculation is given in the footnote below.[1] Two towns may be close to each other on the plane shown in Figure 2 but, when another dimension is introduced, one of them may lie close to the plane, while the other is a considerable distance from it. Brentford & Chiswick, the example used to illustrate the computation, is in fact moved to a different group as a result of the distance calculations. Group 3, to which Brentford & Chiswick (an industrial suburb of London) had been assigned, includes a number of former market towns like Peterborough, Ipswich, Bristol and others. Once account is taken of the third and fourth components, most towns in the group remain broadly in a cluster, while Brentford & Chiswick, and one or two others like Acton and Leyton (both of which have a third component score very much lower than the other members) separate off from the remainder. We can visualise Brentford & Chiswick, Leyton and Acton as hovering in space far below the other towns in the group.

After computing the distance between each town and the mean of the group to which it had been provisionally assigned, we can look at the towns which, like Brentford & Chiswick, were furthest away from the means. Two major modifications of the hypothetical classification are then open to us:

1. We could assign the town to another group; Cheltenham, for example, had originally been assigned to group 1, but was found, when its distances from the means both of groups 1 and 2 were computed, to be considerably nearer to group 2.

2. We could take a number of towns which, like Brentford & Chiswick, differ substantially from their means, and form them into a new cluster. This was done with group 13 (see Table 31 below), since it was found that a large number of towns which had previously been distributed amongst various groups all deviated considerably and in the same direction with respect to component III. Brentford & Chiswick, Acton and Tottenham, for example, though similar to towns in group 3 with respect to components I and II, are found to differ considerably when account is taken of component III.

[1] Component	Mean scores for group 3	Co-ordinates of Brentford & Chiswick	Col. (1) – col.(2)	Col. (3) squared
	(1)	(2)	(3)	(4)
I	−0·004	0·021	−0·025	0·000625
II	−0·150	−0·150	0·000	0·000000
III	0·160	−0·493	0·653	0·426409
IV	−0·121	−0·004	0·125	0·015625
			Sum of squares =	0·442659

The square root of 0·442659 = 0·665 is the distance of Brentford & Chiswick from the centre of group 3.

The treatment adopted was to some extent determined by the number of groups we wanted for the final classification. We decided arbitrarily to aim at groups of at least ten towns. This means that small groups, though both homogeneous and different from others, were in fact combined with another group. Examples are Gateshead, South Shields and Sunderland, which deviate considerably from the group to which they were assigned by virtue of their poor housing conditions.

There are some exceptions to the aim of having at least ten towns per group. Both London A.C., at one extreme, and Huyton with Roby, at the other, are too different from other towns to be included in any group. Hayes & Harlington, Barking and Dagenham similarly are formed into a group of their own because of the considerable distance between each and any other group.

Table 31 shows the towns allocated to groups, together with their component scores. We also indicate the direction in which the towns deviate to a substantial degree from the means. For example, a single asterisk on component I for Hove means that the town is at least 200 units above the group mean. The direction of the deviation is, of course, conventional, depending on the direction of the component score. In the first component, a single asterisk means that the town has a higher, and a double asterisk a lower, social class level than the average town in this group. In the second component, the older towns have a single asterisk, those of more recent development a double; similarly with component III, where relatively rapid increase in population and the factor associated with it, is marked with a single asterisk. In component IV, a single asterisk marks the towns with higher housing density and related factors.

The smaller the number of asterisks in a group, the more homogeneous that group tends to be. It is clear from Table 31 that some of the groups are in fact much more homogeneous than others. Only one group, 14, with three towns, has no substantial deviants; group 2 has one. On the other hand, in group 7, nine out of the eleven towns are deviants. No amount of reshuffling of towns between the groups seemed likely to produce a better classification. We could, however, further subdivide the groups in order to arrive at a greater degree of homogeneity within them. We might, for example, divide group 7 into four sections, containing:

(i) Gateshead, South Shields, Sunderland
(ii) Merthyr Tydfil, Rhondda, Warrington
(iii) Salford, West Ham
(iv) West Hartlepool, Barnsley, West Bromwich.

The general procedure would be to separate from the main groups those towns which are marked in Table 31 with asterisks.

TABLE 31

FINAL CLASSIFICATION OF TOWNS, WITH COMPONENT SCORES
(OMITTING DECIMALS)

Note: Asterisks indicate substantial deviations (200 or more) from group means, one asterisk showing a positive, and two asterisks a negative, deviation.

A. *Mainly resorts, administrative and commercial towns*

Group 1 (mainly *seaside* resorts)

	Component scores			
	I	II	III	IV
Group mean	680	−472	95	165
Worthing	955*	−437	309*	152
Hove	872	−570	−80	323
Hastings	590	−541	181	168
Eastbourne	758	−431	134	−27
Bournemouth	724	−581	130	285
Torquay	651	−484	124	198
Southport	674	−385	−84	106
Harrogate	705	−449	135	140
Brighton	349**	−489	113	228
Blackpool	524	−348	−10	74

Group 2 (mainly *spas, professional and administrative* centres)

Group mean	275	−175	211	−72
Bath	376	−213	71	−32
Cheltenham	205	−374	344	81
Poole	268	−15	270	−80
Oxford	219	−187	40	−89
Cambridge	367	−185	198	−109
Exeter	244	−213	217	−69
Maidstone	207	−144	235	−96
Bedford	193	−116	231	−173
Colchester	193	−134	377	−254
Southend-on-Sea	479*	−134	122	102

Group 3 (mainly *commercial* centres with some industry)

Group mean	−8	−141	180	−133
Southampton	−86	−69	317	5
Portsmouth	28	−158	222	−98
Plymouth	−80	−129	244	−28
Bristol	40	−70	42	−53
Gloucester	−36	−99	227	−117
Great Yarmouth	20	−262	280	−245
Norwich	49	−257	169	−205
Ipswich	24	−78	289	−252
Lincoln	−73	−181	261	−243
Peterborough	−3	−165	267	−210
Reading	42	−155	142	−66
Northampton	64	−122	−30**	−276
Lancaster	−52	−203	99	−162
Worcester	−9	−169	136	−66
York	44	−72	89	−234
Cardiff	−102	−71	126	125*

TABLE 31 (*cont.*)

B. *Mainly industrial towns*

   Group 4 (including most of the traditional *railway* centres)

	I	II	III	IV
		Component scores		
Group mean	− 218	− 111	99	− 167
Crewe	− 261	47	28	− 319
Darlington	− 148	− 47	66	− 70
Swindon	− 168	− 43	336*	− 221
Doncaster	− 163	− 6	198	− 234
Derby	− 279	− 134	− 4	− 274
Carlisle	− 191	− 107	173	− 7
Chesterfield	− 214	42	140	− 156
Barrow in Furness	− 244	45	94	− 147
Mansfield	− 243	− 32	180	− 216
Coventry	− 304	114*	144	− 220
Sheffield	− 254	− 15	− 138**	− 77
Wakefield	− 227	− 131	116	− 102
Stockport	− 103	− 79	− 103**	− 143
Newcastle under Lyme	− 258	188*	160	− 152

   Group 5 (including many of the large *ports* as well as two Black Country towns)

	I	II	III	IV
Group mean	− 339	− 91	67	172
Birkenhead	− 322	11	74	128
Liverpool	− 379	− 180	91	450*
Grimsby	− 366	− 178	324*	44
Hull	− 426	− 143	123	152
Tynemouth	− 329	− 55	154	317
Newport	− 327	− 28	87	120
Swansea	− 257	− 21	66	79
Newcastle upon Tyne	− 367	− 151	− 95	426*
Wolverhampton	− 307	− 38	− 27	− 70**
Birmingham	− 313	− 129	− 132	77

   Group 6 (mainly *textile* centres of Yorkshire and Lancashire)

	I	II	III	IV
Group mean	− 222	− 230	− 136	− 105
Huddersfield	− 126	− 229	− 167	− 60
Halifax	− 201	− 386	− 191	89
Leeds	− 229	− 335	− 155	152*
Dewsbury	− 460**	− 304	− 7	138*
Bradford	− 259	− 337	− 119	81
Keighley	− 164	− 170	− 171	− 213
Bolton	− 142	− 105	− 194	− 217
Burnley	− 264	− 204	− 164	− 349**
Blackburn	− 92	− 186	− 186	− 343**
Bury	− 98	− 184	− 101	− 258
Manchester	− 213	− 200	− 120	81
Oldham	− 347	− 240	− 244	− 89
Preston	− 276	− 141	− 96	− 131
Rochdale	− 305	− 308	− 234	− 207
Leicester	− 98	− 173	− 40	− 214
Nottingham	− 280	− 177	19	− 139

G

TABLE 31 (*Cont.*)

Group 7 (including the industrial towns of the *north-east seaboard* and *mining* towns of Wales)

| | Component scores | | | |
	I	II	III	IV
Group mean	−586	−91	−14	218
Gateshead	−751	−44	−159	553*
South Shields	−598	−244	97	570*
Sunderland	−617	−141	192*	582*
West Hartlepool	−562	−50	318*	216
Barnsley	−620	−140	209*	104
West Ham	−564	−63	−368**	201
West Bromwich	−611	80	−20	144
Salford	−460	−82	−322**	32
Warrington	−616	−138	−82	29
Merthyr Tydfil	−466	−89	65	−16**
Rhondda	−579	−95	−81	−20**

Group 8 (including the more recent *metal manufacturing* towns)

Group mean	−485	132	89	−20
Stockton-on-Tees	−465	112	334*	53
Scunthorpe	−431	249	440*	−231**
Middlesbrough	−507	−8	352*	152
Thurrock	−382	242	272	−113
Nuneaton	−419	137	190	−233**
Rotherham	−427	118	164	−177
Bootle	−735**	292	−128	301*
Dudley	−557	107	−24	139
Walsall	−488	21	67	148
Stoke-on-Trent	−592	46	−91	−72
St. Helens	−574	180	32	69
Wigan	−448	73	−46	−28
Smethwick	−385	−34	−319**	−231**
Oldbury	−382	319	−251**	−61

C. *Suburbs and suburban type towns*

Group 9 (mainly '*exclusive*' residential suburbs)

Group mean	786	206	−54	60
Coulsdon & Purley	1030*	344	173*	62
Epsom & Ewell	906	203	108	40
Esher	636	255	117	37
Bromley	624	56	45	83
Sutton & Cheam	713	227	−125	103
Wanstead & Woodford	729	215	−71	24
Beckenham	806	332	−187	−20
Finchley	694	66	−248	113
Southgate	934	157	−298**	102

TABLE 31 (*cont.*)

Group 10 (mainly *older mixed residential* suburbs)

	I	II	III	IV
Group mean	411	82	−177	57
Wood Green	255	−33	−389**	76
Hornsey	473	−80	−366	200
Ealing	260	159	−296	−18
Hendon	457	143	−301	83
Wimbledon	619*	−121**	−238	136
Ilford	429	258	−226	−50
Heston & Isleworth	303	224	−247	−116
Twickenham	476	113	−158	34
Croydon	351	−19	−80	−31
Surbiton	538	288*	−96	60
Crosby	457	24	92*	234
Wallasey	311	32	190*	124

The header row for Component scores spans columns I, II, III. (Component scores label appears above columns I–III.)

Group 11 (mainly *newer mixed residential* suburbs)

Group mean	341	495	5	17
Chigwell	210	604	260*	136
Orpington	475	424	344*	62
Solihull	426	552	304*	−47
Hornchurch	193	585	218*	−72
Chislehurst & Sidcup	128**	511	52	89
Ruislip-Northwood	510	603	141	66
Bexley	383	460	28	31
Harrow	469	396	−212**	25
Carshalton	272	446	−196**	223*
Wembley	400	422	−418**	−155
Merton & Morden	280	437	−467**	−173

Group 12 (including *light industry* suburbs, *national defence* centres and towns within the sphere of influence of large conurbations)

Group mean	37	210	86	−142
Gosport	62	219	443*	−112
Gillingham	77	84	310*	−167
Romford	128	277	296*	90*
Luton	−104	160	76	−284
Uxbridge	94	330	141	−96
Watford	94	18	−21	−146
Slough	−112	220	5	−169
Enfield	55	243	−176**	−183
Mitcham	34	330	−302**	−209

TABLE 31 (*cont.*)

Group 13 (mainly *older working-class*, and *industrial* suburbs)

	Component scores			
	I	II	III	IV
Group mean	−57	25	−419	−31
Willesden	−106	−67	−570	241*
Tottenham	−226	−93	−538	120
East Ham	−108	65	−299	31
Leyton	72	−36	−401	−27
Brentford & Chiswick	21	−150	−493	−4
Southall	−30	181	−246	−87
Edmonton	−36	234*	−402	−66
Walthamstow	−54	69	−412	−67
Acton	−62	−70	−534	−169
Stretford (Lancs.)	−42	114	−294	−285**

Group 14 (mainly *newer industrial* suburbs)

	I	II	III	IV
Group mean	−441	498	−343	39
Hayes & Harlington	−282	595	−263	−61
Barking	−409	422	−376	32
Dagenham	−632	476	−391	146

D. *Towns not allocated to any group*

	I	II	III	IV
London A.C.	−59	−599	−498	537
Huyton with Roby	−301	1289	573	850

Group 1, another example, could be divided into three sub-groups as follows:

    (i) Hove, Worthing
   (ii) Hastings, Eastbourne, Bournemouth,
       Torquay, Southport, Harrogate
  (iii) Brighton, Blackpool.

If, on the other hand, larger groups were required, a possible combination would be:

	Groups	Number of towns
(A) ⎱	1	10
(B) ⎰	2, 3, London A.C.	27
(C) ⎱	4, 5, 6	40
(D) ⎰	7, 8	25
(E) ⎱	9, 10, 11	32
(F) ⎰	12, 13, 14, Huyton with Roby	23

An even wider grouping is suggested by the brackets which combine groups A with B, C with D, E with F, containing respectively 37, 65 and 55 towns.

The groups are arbitrary not only as regards their number, but also with respect to the boundaries dividing one from another. There seems at first glance no reason why the horizontal lines which separate group 2 from 3; 3 from 4; 4 from 5; and 5 from 7, could not each be shifted up or down a little, without detracting from the homogeneity of a group. The limits of this process, however, lie in the co-ordinates of the other two components, not shown in Figure 2, which may determine the closeness of marginal towns to one or other of the adjacent groups. Nor does it matter greatly where the dividing lines are drawn, as long as we can clearly distinguish between the more extreme types of towns.

The degree of homogeneity of the groups is shown in Figure 3 (p. 90), which also gives the distance between the centre points of the groups. The more homogeneous a group, the smaller the 'within-group' distance, i.e. the average distance of each town to the group centre, given inside the circle. The diagram again shows that some of the groups are very much more homogeneous than others. The extreme cases are, on the one hand, the sixteen towns of group 3, with an average distance from the centre of the group of only 0·151 units; and, at the other extreme, group 7 with eleven towns, which, on average, are 0·304 units distant from the mean. The 'within-group' distances should be compared with the 'between-group' distances, i.e. between one group and others adjacent to it. Group 1, for example, has a relatively high 'within-group' distance (0·210), but this compares with the distance (0·569) of group 1 from the group nearest it, group 2.

The general aim of the classification is to minimise 'within-group' distances and to maximise those between groups, subject to having, wherever possible, ten or more towns in a group. We might have waived the latter condition and aimed instead at equal homogeneity for each group. This would lead us, for example, to combine groups 4 and 5; to sub-divide group 7; and similarly group 8. This is a point meriting further consideration.

In spite of the arbitrariness of the above procedure, it is striking how nearly the classification it has produced accords with the past development and present industrial structure of the towns in each group. A general degree of agreement there must be, since the historical development and present industry are reflected in some of the primary variables. The distribution of industry, for example, gives rise to the occupational and social classification which is the essence of the first component. Similarly the later development of the suburbs, as compared with the industrial towns, tends to place the suburbs in a different position on the diagram from that of the industrial towns.

Nevertheless it is gratifying that the final classification corresponds so well to one's common-sense knowledge of British towns. It is clearly more satisfactory to have a group of towns which can reasonably be labelled 'textile centres' and which have common elements in social class and stage of historical development, than a group which has these characteristics,

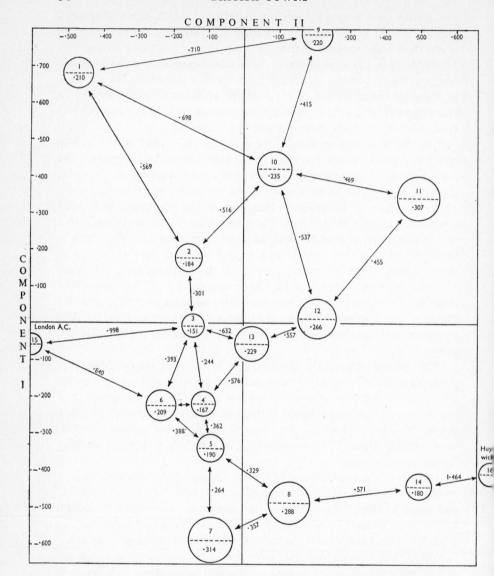

FIG. 3. COMPARISON OF 'BETWEEN' AND 'WITHIN' GROUP DISTANCES

Distances between means of adjacent groups are shown besides arrows connecting circles; average distances between individual towns and their group means are shown inside the circles which are also proportionate in size to 'within' group distances. The top figure in each circle is the group number.

Note: 1. The distances have been calculated in four-dimensional space, but are shown only on a plane. The space between the circles does not, therefore, necessarily correspond to the calculated distance.

       2. Circles 15 and 16 each consist of one town only. No 'within' group distance can therefore be shown.

but contains such diverse contents, to take an extreme and fortunately fictitious example, as London, Ipswich, Epsom and Bury. The isolation of London County also confirms that the classification has some roots in reality, for Rasmussen's description of London as 'The Unique City'[1] is surely well justified.

How well the components differentiate the towns can be seen if we now take a closer look at Figure 2.

Non-industrial towns

In the first place, the suburbs are well separated from the non-suburban towns, while the seaside resorts stand out well from both these groups. Within each of the two major groups, self-contained towns and suburbs, we find a sub-division which corresponds well with the industrial characteristics of the towns. In the north-west quadrant of the diagram lie the seaside resorts, most of them on the south coast of England, with their major preoccupations of retailing and catering and their confluence of elderly and retired middle-class people.

As we progress downwards through the diagram, the towns become increasingly industrialised. First there is a group of mixed spas and professional towns, headed by the university cities of Oxford and Cambridge, and including spas like Cheltenham and Bath, and centres of administration like Exeter.

Still further down in the diagram lies another group of towns (group 3) which, though not dominated by industry, harbours important industries. The cathedral town of Worcester, on the edge of the black country, is a good example. Like most other towns in this group, it has a long history, and is still a vital commercial centre. In addition it has a fair amount of industry, such as the manufacture of gloves and of Worcester porcelain, besides some general engineering.

Industrial towns

Further towards the south-west quadrant are the textile towns, divided into the old wool towns, like Halifax, Bradford, Dewsbury and Leeds, and the Lancashire cotton towns of Oldham, Burnley, Bolton, Manchester, etc. The wool centres in particular are amongst the oldest of the industrial towns; they are completely built up and have been losing population for a number of years.

To the right of the textile towns, and distinguished from them, both on components II and III, lies a group including the towns which were either made by the coming of the railways or else were revivified by them—such as Swindon, Crewe, Darlington, Doncaster and Derby.

Further down lies a group which includes many of the ports, such as Liverpool, Grimsby, Hull, Newport, Tynemouth and Birkenhead, as well as two of the Midlands towns, Birmingham and Wolverhampton.

[1] Rasmussen, Steen Eiler, *London: The Unique City*, Jonathan Cape, London, 1937.

Further down still, we come to a group which includes four of the towns of the north-eastern seaboard, the three mining areas of Merthyr Tydfil, Rhondda and Barnsley, besides an assorted number of other areas. This group, characterised generally by areas of low social class, is less homogeneous than those discussed so far. The towns differ particularly with respect to the fourth component, which indicates overcrowded housing conditions.

The last group of industrial towns includes the metal producing and processing towns of Smethwick, Rotherham, Middlesbrough, Walsall, Scunthorpe and Oldbury, as well as the remaining Staffordshire towns Stoke-on-Trent and Newcastle under Lyme.

Suburban towns

The suburbs, as the number of asterisks in groups 9 to 14 indicates, are considerably less homogeneous than are the non-suburban towns. The factors which distinguish between them are, roughly speaking, social class and stage of development.

Group 9, including Coulsdon & Purley, which we singled out for comment in Chapter II, lies furthest towards the top of the diagram. This is the group of middle to upper-middle class residential suburbs spread around London.

Lower down lie two groups of largely middle-class residential areas, one (Group 11) of more recent vintage than the other (Group 10). A characteristic town in the older group is Twickenham with large stretches of detached houses, giving way near the middle of the towns to streets of inter-war working-class terrace houses. There is little manufacturing industry in Twickenham, but some government departments have offices and laboratories there.

Group 11 is similar in many respects, but differs in the period in which its growth occurred. In areas such as Chigwell, Orpington and Solihull, the expansion has continued since 1951, whereas others, such as Wembley, were fully built up by that time.

None of the towns in the next group (Group 12) are purely, or even mainly, residential. Watford is well known for its printing industry, Mitcham is a centre of light engineering, Uxbridge a Royal Air Force base. This group also includes a number of towns near the fringes of Greater London such as Luton and Slough, as well as two towns which are not suburbs, namely Gillingham and Gosport. Gillingham is part of the historical trilogy (with Chatham and Rochester) characterised by its extensive naval dockyards; Gosport similarly is a naval base.

Group 13 is very different in character from the others. It contains the old, densely built up, and in some cases highly industrialised, northern and eastern suburbs of London, as well as Stretford near Manchester. Brentford & Chiswick, for example, is the seat of heavy engineering industry.

Like many of the inner Metropolitan boroughs which it resembles, it has been losing population for some time.

The last group contains only the three areas of Hayes & Harlington, Dagenham and Barking, all of them fairly heavily industrialised but of more recent vintage than towns in the previous group.

Concluding remarks

Perhaps the most relevant criticism of a general classification involving the analysis of fifty-seven variables is that, though it may be of *some* relevance to many aspects of urban structure, it does not reproduce with exactness any single aspect of urban differentiation.

But our multi-purpose classification is meant to be an average classification, and it has the advantages and disadvantages of any average. The main weakness of the classification obtained lies in the fact that the four components from which it is derived account for only 60 per cent. of the total variation. It accounts, however, for a greater part of some variables than of others, and we indicated in the previous chapter the fields which are most adequately reflected. Finally, it must again be stressed that the classification is in no sense uniquely determined. Thus, the decision to aim at groups containing about 10 towns was arbitrary, and many different restrictions could be justified. What is general is the *nature* of the process by which the classification was derived, and we hope that future researchers will use, and refine, this process under different circumstances.

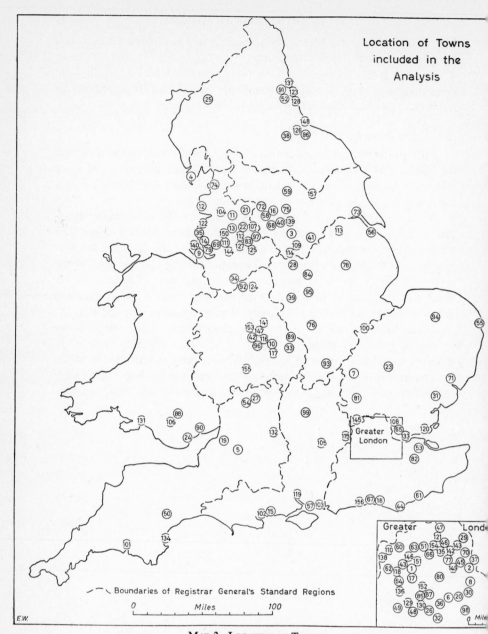

MAP 3. LOCATION OF TOWNS

The 157 towns in England and Wales with populations of
50,000 or more in 1951, as numbered on the map:

Acton	1	Beckenham	6	Blackburn	11
Barking	2	Bedford	7	Blackpool	12
Barnsley	3	Bexley	8	Bolton	13
Barrow-in-Furness	4	Birkenhead	9	Bootle	14
Bath	5	Birmingham	10	Bournemouth	15

APPENDIX A

The Variables and their Sources

THE choice of variables was dictated largely by the data available for local government authority areas. In defining individual variables—e.g. choosing how to represent age distribution—arbitrary decisions were unavoidable, but we aimed to use indicators which would best discriminate between towns and which were relevant to social and economic policy. In certain cases, standardised rates were used. Most of the data relate to 1951, but a few series for more recent years were also included. The three series not used in the main analysis are marked S 1, S 2 and S 3 below.

Population size and structure
1. *Enumerated population, Census, 1951*

     Source: There are a number of sources for the 1951 Census population. The simplest, giving the population for all local authority areas is: General Register Office, Census 1951, England and Wales, *General Tables*, London: H.M.S.O., 1956.

2. *Per cent. of the population aged 0-14, 1951*
3. *Per cent. of the population aged 15-64, 1951*
4. *Per cent. of the population aged 65 or over, 1951*

     Source: General Register Office, Census 1951, England and Wales, *County Reports*, London: H.M.S.O., various years.

The age structure has been described by three segments in common use: population under working age; the working population[1]; the aged.

5. *Females per 1,000 males, 1951*
6. *Females per 1,000 males, age group 25-44, 1951*

     Source: General Register Office, Census 1951, England and Wales; *County Reports*, London: H.M.S.O., various years.

Previous studies have shown how markedly the sex ratios differ for different age groups. The lure of the city lights attracts young unmarried women to the central areas of large towns. Many of them then marry, and (particularly the better off) move to the suburbs. At a later age, or if the marriage is ended prematurely, some of them will move once more, perhaps to the coastal resorts and country towns. Since men tend to die earlier than women, the more old people an area contains, the greater will be the surplus of women.

[1] An alternate definition of the working population is men aged 15-64, women aged 15-59.

This type of migration tends to be highly selective both in terms of social class and for different parts of a town. In London, for example, it is the upper-class residential areas of Hampstead and South Kensington which attract many of the young women who come to London. In the older areas of inner London, on the other hand, what influx there is in the way of young women tends to be offset by the greater proportion of old people who stay behind as the young married couples move to the suburbs. An analysis which treats only entire local authority areas will not adequately reflect such selective migration.

We included the overall ratio of women to men, and the ratio for a particular age group, 25-44, which is fairly large and yet isolates the sex ratio from the effect of differential mortality in old age.

7. *Per cent. of women aged 20-24 ever married (married, divorced or widowed), 1951*

Source: General Register Office, Census 1951, England and Wales, *County Reports*, London: H.M.S.O., various years.

Since the marriage rate rises with increasing age, the overall marriage rate is less informative than that for a specific age group. We selected an age group which was known to show very considerable variation between areas.

Population change and birth rates

8. *Change in population 1931-51—total change as per cent. of 1931 population*

9. *Change in population 1931-51—change due to births and deaths as per cent. of 1931 population*

10. *Change in population 1931-51—change due to balance of causes as per cent. of 1931 population*

11. *Change of population 1951-58—total change as per cent. of 1951 population*

Source: Items 8-10. General Register Office, Census 1951, England and Wales, *General Tables*, London: H.M.S.O., 1956.

Item 11. 1951 population: *op. cit.*

1958 population: General Register Office, *Annual Estimates of the Population of England and Wales and of Local Authority Areas 1958*, London: H.M.S.O., 1958.

Figures for populations of towns have been given in each Census since 1801; annual estimates have been prepared by the General Register Office since 1911. It should therefore be relatively simple to study population changes for any period since the beginning of the nineteenth century. The difficulty is that both the definition for Census purposes and the administrative boundaries of towns have changed considerably over time. Although the Census reports generally indicate the changes that have taken place between one Census and another, care must be taken in analysing the growth of towns over a substantial period.[1]

Population change can be due to natural increase, migration and to extension of boundaries. For descriptive purposes the distinctions may not matter, but if we wish to relate population change to, say, housing structure or the industrial character of the town, the distinction between growth by immigration into an empty tract on the periphery of the town, and growth due to the incorporation of built-up areas, is vital.

In order to minimise these complications, only the more recent period 1931-58, divided into two segments 1931-51 and 1951-58, has been taken into account. Figures for the period 1931-51 exclude changes due to alterations in boundaries. Changes in boundaries in the 1951-58 period were confined to 22 towns. Towns with changes of one per cent. or more arising out of boundary changes (irrespective of normal population growth or decline) are Southampton (14·2 per cent.), Dudley (5·8), Worcester (3·7) St. Helens (2·9), Ipswich (2·5), Preston (2·1), Brighton (1·9), Crosby (1·8), Oldham (1·5), Gloucester (1·5), Nottingham (1·3) and Gateshead (1·0).

The data on changes between 1931-51 are particularly illuminating because they can be divided up into changes due to natural causes (births and deaths) and a balance, largely made up of migration.

12. *Birth rate: ratio of local standardised to national rate, average 1950-52*
13. *Birth rate: ratio of local standardised to national rate, average 1955-57*
    Source: General Register Office, *The Registrar-General's Statistical Review of England and Wales*, Parts I or II for the years 1950, 1951, 1952, 1955, 1956 and 1957, London: H.M.S.O., various years.

The General Register Office publish for each local authority area annual figures giving *inter alia* the number of births, legitimate and illegitimate; the crude birth rate (live births per 1,000 population); a comparability factor which takes account of sex and age differences between areas; and the birth rate ratio, which is the crude rate multiplied by the comparability factor and divided by the rate for England and Wales. In order to avoid fluctuations arising from chance events in any one year, the ratios were averaged over three years.

14. *Per cent. of illegitimate to total live births, average 1950-52*
15. *Per cent. of illegitimate to total live births, average 1955-57*
    Source: General Register Office, *The Registrar-General's Statistical Review of England and Wales*, Parts I or II, for the years 1950, 1951, 1952, 1955, 1956 and 1957, London: H.M.S.O., various years.

[1] For a discussion of area definitions used in past Censuses see Interdepartmental Committee on Social and Economic Research, *Guides to Official Sources, No. 2, Census Reports of Great Britain, 1801-1931*, London: H.M.S.O., 1951.

Households and housing

16. *Per cent. of persons living in dwellings occupied by non-private households*, 1951
    Source: General Register Office, Census 1951, England and Wales, *County Reports*, H.M.S.O., London, various years.

Non-private households are largely made up of military establishments (which in England and Wales as a whole accounted for almost a quarter of all persons in such households), mental and mental deficiency hospitals, hotels and large boarding-houses, educational establishments, and so forth. The proportion of persons in non-private households helps to explain peculiarities in the demographic and industrial structure of a small number of areas.

17. *Per cent. of private households with one person*, 1951
18. *Per cent. of private households with six or more persons*, 1951
    Source: General Register Office, Census 1951, England and Wales, *Housing Report*, London: H.M.S.O., 1956.
19. *Per cent. of dwellings, occupied or vacant, with* 1-3 *rooms*, 1951
    Source: General Register Office, Census 1951, England and Wales, *Housing Report*, London: H.M.S.O., 1956.

Items 17-19 were selected from a large number of possible indices of household and dwelling size, as being conveniently available and giving a suitable summary of the situation.

20. *Average number of persons per room*, 1951
21. *Per cent. of private households in overcrowded condition*, composite index (criterion of overcrowding: 1-3 person households—density at over one person per room; 4 or more person households —density at over one and a half persons per room), 1951
22. *Per cent. of private households with over* $1\frac{1}{2}$ *persons per room*, 1951
    Source: General Register Office, Census 1951, England and Wales, *County Reports*, London: H.M.S.O., 1956.

Of the three indices of housing density one is an average while the other two estimate the degree of overcrowding. A number of overcrowding indices are in common use and are described in the 1951 Census Housing Report (*op. cit.*). Our first index is a composite, based on the following assumptions:

   (i) Each single person, living alone, has at least one room
  (ii) Households of 2-7 persons must have at least one living-room, and at least one bedroom for every two persons
 (iii) Same as (ii) for households of 8 or more persons, except that these must have at least *two* living-rooms (not used for sleeping).

On these assumptions, overcrowded households would be defined as follows: 1-3-person households—more than one person per room; 4 or more person households—more than one and a half persons per room.

(Note however that the 9-person household with six rooms is an exception, since it would require 7 rooms to meet the above standards.)

Side by side with the complex index of overcrowding, we used a simpler index: the proportion of households with more than $1\frac{1}{2}$ persons per room. This differs from the composite index only in one respect—the 3-person households require 3 rooms to avoid overcrowding in the first index, and only 2 rooms in the second.

Neither standard is rigorous, particularly when we remember that 'rooms' include a kitchen which is used for living or eating. A three-room flat with a sizeable kitchen, used for a family of six adults or children, would not be considered overcrowding on our definition, but it is scarcely comfort.

23. *Per cent. of private households living in shared dwellings*, 1951
    Source: General Register Office, Census 1951, England and Wales,
    County Reports, London: H.M.S.O., various years.

Two or more households are defined as sharing a dwelling if they do not have separate access to the street or to a common landing. This commonly occurs in multi-storey houses in which each storey is occupied by a separate household, and where the dwelling is not divided off from the rest of the house by a separate front door.

24. *Per cent. of private households in undivided dwellings with exclusive use of piped water*, 1951
25. *Per cent. of private households in undivided dwellings with exclusive use of the W.C.*, 1951
26. *Per cent. of private households in undivided dwellings with exclusive use of all five household amenities (piped water, W.C., kitchen sink, cooking stove and fixed bath)*, 1951
27. *Per cent. of private households in undivided dwellings with exclusive use either of all five amenities, or with only the bath shared or missing*, 1951
    Source: General Register Office, Census 1951, England and Wales,
    Housing Report, London: H.M.S.O., 1956.

The possession of household amenities has been tabulated in the 1951 Census for each of five amenities: piped water, W.C., kitchen sink, cooking stove and fixed bath, taken separately and for various combinations. Further classifications are possible, for example, according to whether the amenity is missing, shared or for the exclusive use of the household; and according to whether the household is in a shared or single unit dwelling. The number of households in which an amenity is completely missing is, for most of the arrangements, too small to warrant its use as an index. This suggests using a combination of 'none or sharing' of the amenity, or its complement 'exclusive use of'. Similarly, we found that the bulk of the sharing was in households where the *dwelling* was shared. Since sharing of dwelling was already included separately, we standardised for this factor

H

by considering the sharing or absence of the amenity only in unshared dwellings.

This left the question of which amenities to include in the analysis. A case might be made for including all five, since correlations between them were not high. In the end it was decided to study the extremes; absence of exclusive use of piped water and of the W.C. on the one hand, the use of all five amenities on the other. This latter index is almost identical with the exclusive use of a fixed bath, since almost all households which have a bath also have the other amenities. We therefore added a third index: shared or no bath *and* exclusive use of all other four amenities.

One difficulty arises in the interpretation of the data for the piped water supply. The General Register Office consider that some householders mis-understood the intent of the question, and thought they were sharing piped water if there was 'common participation in the whole plumbing system supplying taps exclusively used by other households'.[1]

28. *Total number of new houses completed between* 1.4.1945 *and* 30.6.1958 *per* 1,000 *population in* 1951

29. *New houses completed between* 1.4.1945 *and* 30.6.1958 *by local authorities per* 1,000 *population in* 1951

30. *New houses built by local authorities between* 1.4.1945 *and* 30.6.1958 *as per cent. of total new houses built in this period*

Source: Ministry of Housing and Local Government, *Housing Return for England and Wales*, 30th June, 1958, Appendix, London: H.M.S.O., 1958. For 1951 population figures: Census 1951 (*op. cit.*).

Figures of new housing are published quarterly for each local authority area, in the form of cumulative totals beginning in 1945. To obtain a picture of achievement relative to size of the area, the figures may be related either to the total stock of housing, or to the population living in the area. Both procedures raise problems. The stock of housing in 1945 is unknown, whereas the 1951 figure obtainable from the Census already includes a number of new houses. Alternatively, we may consider only housing built since 1951 and relate this to the stock of housing in 1951. Such a comparison may, however, work out to the detriment of the authorities which made an early start and had already built a substantial number of houses by 1951.

The difficulties of relating new housing to population figures are similar. Since population tends to follow new housing, areas with con-siderable in-migration between 1945 and 1951 following in the wake of new housing would be at a disadvantage in an inter-town comparison compared with areas with little new housing and an outflow of population up to 1951. The magnitude of population changes, however, appears to be

[1] General Register Office, Census 1951, England and Wales, *General Report*, London: H.M.S.O., 1958, p. 56.

small compared with differences between local authorities in providing new housing.

Economic character

31. *Occupied population as per cent. of total resident population aged* 15 *or over,* 1951

32. *Women as per cent. of the total occupied population,* 1951
    Source: General Register Office, Census 1951, England and Wales, *Occupation Tables,* H.M.S.O., London, 1956.

33. *Per cent. of population working in the area, in manufacture, agriculture and mining* (Standard Industrial Classification Groups I-XVI), 1951

34. *Per cent. of population working in the area, in all service industries* (S.I.C. Groups XX-XXIV), 1951

35. *Per cent. of population working in the area, in retail trades* (S.I.C. Nos. 243, 245 and 246), 1951

36. *Per cent. of population working in the area, in insurance, banking and finance* (S.I.C. Group XXI), 1951

37. *Per cent. of population working in the area, in professional services* (S.I.C. Group XXIII), 1951
    Source: General Register Office, Census 1951, *Industry Tables,* London: H.M.S.O., 1957.

The data in items 33 to 37 differ from other series in so far as they apply not to the resident population but to the population working in the area. Where there is a considerable daily flow of commuters into and out of the area, the resident population may be quite different from the population working there. In Acton (Middlesex), for example, where no fewer than 177 people come into the town, or leave it each working day, per 100 resident occupied population, the working population is a largely different body of persons from the resident population. In most areas the difference is much smaller.

Unfortunately, the Census practice of tabulating the night resident population in terms of occupations, and the 'day' population in terms of industry, makes it impossible to compile equivalent series for the resident population and hence to compare the industrial composition of the 'day' and 'night' populations.

38. *Job ratio* (*population working in the area per* 100 *resident occupied population*), 1951

39. *Commuting ratio* (*number of persons either living in the area but working outside it or working in the area but living outside it, per* 100 *occupied resident population*), 1951
    Source: General Register Office, Census 1951, England and Wales, *Report on Usual Residence and Workplace,* H.M.S.O., London, 1956.

These two ratios measure the relationship between the resident occupied population and the population working in the area. The job ratio was
designed by Ruth Glass for an analysis of journeys to work in the Greater
London region.[1] It divides the population working in the area by the
occupied population living there. The higher the job ratio, therefore, the
greater the inflow of population. The City of London, for example, with a
resident occupied population in 1951 of 3,591 and a net daily *inflow* of
334,912 has a job ratio of 9,430. At the other extreme is an area like
Huyton with Roby, a suburb of Liverpool, with a resident occupied population of 24,330 and a net daily *outflow* of 17,576. The job ratio for Huyton
is 28.

One disadvantage of the job ratio is that it considers only the *net* flow.
An area with a job ratio of 100 may have a large inflow of workers balan-
cing a large outflow (for example, in a fashionable London suburb, shop
assistants and domestic workers taking the place of the City workers); a
job ratio of 100 may, on the other hand, also mean total self-sufficiency
without either inflow or outflow.

We therefore computed the commuting ratio, which is simply the sum
of workers leaving an area, together with the number entering it, divided
by the occupied resident population.[2]

In considering the relationship between resident and working (or
'night' and 'day') population, the two indices should be read side by side.

   40. *Per capita retail sales*, 1950
        Source: *Board of Trade, Census of Distribution and Other Services
             1950*, Volume I, London: H.M.S.O., 1953.

The per capita retail sales indicate the amount of shopping in an area,
which is a function both of the financial strength of the community and of
local shopping facilities. In many newly established areas, for example,
lack of proper shops will lead residents to do their shopping elsewhere,
particularly for consumer durables, even though spending power may be
substantial.

Social class
   41. *Per cent. of occupied and retired males in social classes I or II*, 1951
   42. *Per cent. of occupied and retired males in social classes IV or V*, 1951
   43. *Social class index*, 1951
        Source: General Register Office, Census 1951, England and Wales,
             County Reports, London: H.M.S.O., various years.

The Registrar-General groups occupations into five social classes for
purposes of Census tabulations and analyses of vital statistics. The term
'social class' in this context is not ideal since it conjures up visions of a

---

[1] Ruth Glass, 'London on the Move', *The Times*, 18th and 19th June, 1956.
[2] An alternative denominator would be the total resident occupied population
plus the total population working in the area.

more sophisticated classification than is involved in this elementary grouping of occupations. The occupations are classified as follows:

		Per cent. of occupied and retired males, England and Wales, 1951
Class I	Professional, etc. occupations	3·3
Class II	Intermediate occupations	14·5
Class III	Skilled occupations	53·0
Class IV	Partly skilled occupations	16·1
Class V	Unskilled occupations	13·1
		100·0

Details of the allocation of occupations to these groups are given in the One Per Cent. Sample Tables of the 1951 Census.[1]

For purposes of analysis, the five social classes can be variously combined. We chose combinations of the classes at either end of the scale, since group III shows little variation between areas.

The social class index is an average of the two groups. It is calculated as follows:

Two ratios are formed:

$$(a) \quad \frac{\text{per cent. in social classes I}+\text{II in town } k}{\text{average per cent. in social classes I}+\text{II in all 157 towns}}$$

$$(b) \quad \frac{\text{average per cent. in social classes IV}+\text{V in all 157 towns}}{\text{per cent. in social classes IV}+\text{V in town } k}$$

The index equals $\frac{(a)+(b)}{2} \times 100$

44. *The Social Survey J-index: per cent. of voters on Electoral Register who are jurors, 1954*

Source: Central Office of Information, The Social Survey, *Some Useful Data when Sampling the Population of England and Wales*, London: H.M.S.O., 1956.

The J-index is well-known to sample survey experts as a stratification factor. It was included in the present analysis in order to show its relationship to other social class indices. It is fairly clear that the J-index is more useful for the purpose for which it was created than for a comparison of large towns in different regions of the country.

Voting

45. *Per cent. of electorate polling in the 1951 general election*
46. *Per cent. of electorate polling in the 1955 general election*
47. *Per cent. of votes cast for Labour or other left-wing candidates in the 1951 general election*

[1] General Register Office and General Registry Office, Scotland, Census 1951, Great Britain, *One Per Cent. Sample Tables*, Part I, London: H.M.S.O., 1952.

48. *Per cent. of votes cast for Labour and other left-wing candidates in the 1955 general election*
      Source: *The Times Guide to the House of Commons 1951, and 1955,* London: The Times, 1951 and 1955.

These data apply to Parliamentary Constituencies, which generally coincide with, or are little different from, local authority areas, particularly in the case of County Boroughs. In other cases, especially among the London suburbs, agreement is less good. The relationship between Parliamentary Constituencies and local authority areas in 1951 is described in the 1951 Census County Reports (*op. cit.*).

49. *Per cent. of electorate voting in contested areas at local government elections, 1956-58*
      Source: General Register Office, *The Registrar-General's Statistical Review of England and Wales* for the years 1956, 1957 and 1958, Part II, Civil Tables, London: H.M.S.O., various years.

This, the only series on local government elections included in the analysis, was found to contain only some of the information relevant to local elections. Generally speaking, the smaller the number of seats contested, the greater the voting participation of the electorate in the seats that remain. A summary picture, combining the two aspects of local elections, seats contested, and voting, is given by the number of votes cast as a proportion of the total electorate in the area. The following supplementary series were then compiled:

S1. *Per cent. of seats uncontested in local government elections, 1956-58*
S2. *Votes cast as per cent. of total electorate, local government elections, 1956-58*
      Source: General Register Office, *The Registrar-General's Statistical Review of England and Wales* for the years 1956, 1957 and 1958, Part II, Civil Tables, London: H.M.S.O., various years.

Health

50. *Infant mortality rate (deaths under one year of age per 1,000 related live births), average 1950-52*
51. *Infant mortality rate (deaths under one year of age per 1,000 related live births), average 1955-57*
      Source: General Register Office, *The Registrar-General's Statistical Review of England and Wales* for the years 1950, 1951, 1952, 1955, 1956 and 1957, Parts I or II, London: H.M.S.O., various years.

S3. *Estimation of expectation of life at year One, 1950-52*
      Source: The estimates are based on data derived from *The Registrar-General's Statistical Reviews* (*op. cit.*) for the

years 1950-52. The method employed is described in Appendix D.

52. *Notifications of respiratory tuberculosis among men aged* 15-44, *per* 100,000 *related population*, 1957

53. *Deaths from selected causes* (ratio of local to national rate adjusted for sex and age differences); *cancer of the lung* (malignant neoplasm—lung and bronchus), 1957

54. *Deaths from selected causes* (ratio of local to national rate adjusted for sex and age differences): *other forms of cancer* (malignant neoplasm—other sites), 1957

55. *Deaths from selected causes* (ratio of local to national rate adjusted for sex and age differences); *bronchitis*, 1957

Source: All data were made available by courtesy of the General Register Office. Deaths from malignant neoplasm of lung and bronchus are also published in: General Register Office, *The Registrar-General's Quarterly Return for England and Wales*, Quarter ended 31st March 1958, London: H.M.S.O., 1958.

The following data on the state of public health are published annually by the Registrar-General for each local authority in England and Wales (and therefore for each of the 157 towns):

Morbidity: Number of notifications of infectious diseases for 19 separate diseases—*Registrar-General's Statistical Review* (*op. cit.*), Part II, Medical Tables. Notifications for a smaller number of diseases are also published weekly—General Register Office, *The Registrar-General's Weekly Return for England and Wales*, London: H.M.S.O.

Mortality: Total number of deaths; crude and standardised death rates; deaths of children under one year and under four weeks of age; and stillbirths, are published in the annual *Statistical Review* (*op. cit.*). In addition, deaths from certain causes are published each year for towns with populations in 1951 of 25,000 or over in *The Registrar-General's Quarterly Return for England and Wales* (*op. cit.*), distinguishing the following causes of death: malignant neoplasm of lung and bronchus; whooping cough; diphtheria; tuberculosis; influenza; acute poliomyelitis; pneumonia; coronary and arteriosclerotic heart disease.

In addition, there is a wealth of material available for county boroughs, but not for other towns; for example, in the Registrar-General's Decennial Supplement[1] on area mortality, admissions to mental hospitals,[2] etc.

We selected two indices corresponding to mortality occurring respec-

[1] General Register Office, Registrar-General's Decennial Supplement, England and Wales 1951, *Occupational Mortality*, Parts I and II, London: H.M.S.O., 1954 and 1958.
[2] General Register Office, *The Registrar-General's Statistical Review of England and Wales* for the three years 1954-56. *Supplement on Mental Health*, London: H.M.S.O., 1960.

tively under and over one year of age. The infant mortality rates, already available in published form, were extracted for the years 1950-52 and 1955-57 respectively; while Mr N. H. Carrier devised a new technique for computing the expectation of life at year One for local authority areas in England and Wales, which is a summary index of that part of mortality not already accounted for by the infant mortality rate. This is explained in Appendix D.

In addition, we were interested in three specific diseases with possible social implications: bronchitis; malignant cancer of the lung; and other forms of malignant cancer. Data are published for cancer of the lung, but not for the other two. They were, however, made available to us by the General Register Office, for one specific year. As the number of cases involved is small for many of the towns, it would have been preferable to have combined several years. Comparable figures were in fact collected for the three years 1956-58 for deaths from cancer of the lung. The product-moment correlation between the 1957 figures and the data for the three years combined is very nearly unity (0·993) which indicates that there was in most towns little year-to-year fluctuation. Nevertheless, there may be fluctuation for individual towns, and not too much should be made of the values given in Appendix B for any particular town.

As the mortality data for specific causes of death are likely to be influenced by differences in the sex and age distribution of towns, some form of standardisation was desirable. This took the form of multiplying the raw data by the Registrar-General's Comparability Factor, as published in the *Statistical Review* (*op. cit.*) for 1957. The procedure is not quite satisfactory since the comparability factor is not intended for application to specific causes of death, but it is an adequate approximation.

Only one series is given for morbidity, namely the number of notifications of respiratory tuberculosis in 1957. Tuberculosis no longer accounts for as large a share of premature deaths as it did some years ago. Even so, the data seemed worth including. It was again necessary to make allowance for age and sex differentials; we obtained from the General Register Office figures of notifications for a group with a relatively high incidence of notifications, namely, men aged 15-44. The figures were available for one year only, and because of the small numbers involved, are subject to the same restrictions as the mortality data.

Education

56. *Per cent. of the occupied population aged* 20-24 *whose terminal age was under* 15, 1951

57. *Per cent. of the population aged* 15-24 *attending full-time at an educational establishment*, 1951

   Source: General Register Office, Census 1951, England and Wales, *County Reports*, London: H.M.S.O., various years.

All education statistics, with the exception of those contained in the Census, are published for County Boroughs and for Counties, since these are the local education authorities. We were therefore restricted to the Census figures relating to the age at which full-time education was terminated and to the proportion of the population still attending full-time educational institutions. The age groups were chosen as those most indicative of the recent educational experience of a large section of the population.

I

APPENDIX B

The Complete Data—
Arranged by Town and Subject Matter

Notes

1. The towns are listed by county and within each county in the order of County Boroughs, followed by Municipal Boroughs and Urban Districts. Counties are in alphabetical order, with one exception: Hampshire, whose official name until recently was Southampton, will be found under 'S'.

2. For each town, the actual values of the variables are given, together with the corresponding rank order values. Where a rank value consists of an integer and a fraction, the fraction has for the sake of simplicity been omitted.

3. The variables refer to 1951 unless otherwise stated. They are given in abbreviated form. For full titles and explanatory notes, see Appendix A.

4. A map showing the positions of the towns appears on page 94.

Index of the 157 towns in England and Wales (cont.)

| | Bedfordshire | | | | Berkshire | | Buckinghamshire | | Cambridgeshire | | Cheshire | | | | | |
| | BEDFORD | | LUTON | | READING | | SLOUGH | | CAMBRIDGE | | BIRKENHEAD | | STOCKPORT | | WALLASEY | |
	Value	Rank	Value	Rank	Value	Rank	Value	Rank	Value	Rank	Value	Rank	Value	Rank	Value	Rank
POPULATION SIZE AND STRUCTURE																
Population ('000)	53	149	110	54	114	50	66	116	82	84	143	36	142	37	101	66
% of population aged 0-14	21·1	101	22·9	53	22·1	72	23·3	44	20·2	124	24·6	23	21·6	89	22·9	53
% of population aged 15-64	66·9	94	68·0	43	66·0	121	68·7	25	67·4	70	65·3	135	67·2	82	65·0	141
% of population aged 65 or over	12·0	41	9·1	125	12·0	41	8·0	147	12·4	26	10·1	95	11·2	61	12·1	38
Females per 1000 males	1117	68	1051	124	1115	70	1066	111	1157	34	1081	99	1138	42	1184	27
Females per 1000 males, age 25-44	1013	111	994	128	1042	79	1024	101	1053	68	1000	124	1083	43	1141	24
% of females 20-24 ever married	45·9	111	52·1	31	46·8	99	48·6	71	43·8	122	44·8	116	49·7	61	44·7	117
POPULATION CHANGE																
1931-51—total (%)	24·6	50	56·6	25	17·5	62	97·8	15	16·1	67	-5·9	137	12·1	74	3·1	102
1931-51—births and deaths (%)	6·7	108	18·0	27	8·1	93	30·6	8	6·7	108	9·8	73	4·4	127	5·3	121
1931-51—balance of change (%)	17·9	46	38·6	28	9·4	63	67·2	16	9·4	63	-15·7	142	7·7	69	-2·2	99
1951-58 (%)	12·1	10	7·2	26	3·3	44	10·8	14	13·5	8	0·1	76	-0·2	79	1·6	63
Birth rate ratio, 1950-52	99	68	96	81	97	74	91	103	94	91	118	11	96	81	107	36
Birth rate ratio, 1955-57	118	9	99	58	96	74	89	108	88	110	110	16	104	37	110	16
% illegitimate births, 1950-52	6·7	18	5·1	72	6·1	29	4·9	79	5·7	41	5·4	60	5·1	72	5·0	75
% illegitimate births, 1955-57	5·8	35	5·4	52	6·3	24	4·8	75	5·4	52	4·7	80	4·7	80	4·7	80
HOUSEHOLDS AND HOUSING																
% persons in private h/hlds	96·2	119	97·9	54	96·6	111	97·9	54	95·5	123	96·4	116	98·2	44	98·3	38
% one-person h/hlds	11·0	53	6·9	133	10·2	69	6·6	138	12·5	33	10·1	73	11·1	51	10·8	55
% six- or more person h/hlds	7·0	88	7·2	80	8·7	41	8·9	36	6·2	111	11·1	11	5·8	120	7·8	65
% 1-3-room dwellings	6·9	136	5·6	148	8·4	115	10·1	89	9·5	94	9·5	94	12·0	69	6·6	141
Persons per room	0·66	140	0·74	76	0·73	85	0·78	40	0·64	150	0·78	40	0·69	120	0·67	135
% overcrowded h/hlds (composite)	3·9	133	5·6	91	6·9	55	7·4	48	3·4	143	10·7	16	3·8	136	4·7	118
% h/hlds at over 1½ persons per room	2·7	140	3·9	94	5·4	45	5·6	42	2·0	152	8·3	16	3·0	129	3·0	129
% h/hlds in shared dwellings	15·7	63	12·5	76	17·6	50	12·7	74	13·3	71	20·8	35	4·1	145	18·3	47
% h/hlds with piped water	95	52	95	52	94	76	93	95	91	119	93	95	94	76	95	52
% h/hlds with W.C.	98	39	98	39	97	72	96	94	96	94	97	72	87	144	98	39
% h/hlds with 5 amenities	65	81	70	63	55	125	79	39	64	87	65	81	59	108	82	31
% h/hlds with 5, or bath missing	94	34	94	34	93	52	91	80	90	91	92	67	82	135	95	18
New-housing rate 1945-58—total	65	42	85	10	47	83	69	31	64	46	39	102	41	97	49	77
New-housing rate 1945-58—L.A.s	45	43	44	46	34	72	48	36	49	31	27	100	28	95	34	72
% L.A. of total houses 1945-58	69·0	94	51·3	130	72·8	79	69·4	92	76·2	62	68·8	95	67·4	98	70·3	89

ECONOMIC CHARACTER																
Occupied as % of total population	58·6	99	64·8	32	59·1	93	65·7	21	57·8	107	59·4	87	63·9	41	54·9	142
% of women in labour force	31·3	98	32·2	83	32·1	84	33·6	59	34·0	53	29·7	116	36·6	27	30·6	111
% in manufacture etc.	39·8	84	67·8	146	33·5	107	67·8	6	22·7	133	38·7	89	56·9	34	18·3	139
% in all service industries	43·7	55	22·8	137	48·1	45	22·1	149	58·3	22	35·4	92	28·5	118	58·1	23
% in retail	12·7	37	7·4		13·5	27	6·0	150	12·1	46	10·3	79	9·0	105	17·2	7
% in finance, etc.	2·2	34	1·1	119	2·7	11	1·2	106	2·2	34	1·4	83	1·1	119	2·0	41
% in professional services	8·5	52	4·3	138	9·2	40	3·8	145	19·2	4	6·1	93	5·5	117	10·0	33
Job ratio	108	47	115	23	102	70	125	9	113	29	99	79	90	98	48	150
Commuting ratio	44	88	28	126	34	107	59	71	31	116	66	61	54	76	62	68
Per capita retail sales, 1950	202	3	140	65	190	11	148	56	189	12	113	111	119	102	80	144
SOCIAL CLASS																
% in social classes I + II	19·9	49	15·6	83	17·4	64	16·5	71	23·4	35	14·4	99	18·1	58	23·0	37
% in social classes IV + V	24·5	91	25·8	84	26·0	78	25·9	81	22·1	113	34·6	24	26·5	72	23·2	102
Social class index	107	54	93	82	98	67	95	73	123	37	77	123	99	64	119	44
Social Survey J-index, 1954	3·87	101	5·62	77	7·92	44	6·72	60	3·27	108	6·83	58	6·26	69	10·52	32
VOTING																
General elections—1951 poll	87·1	13	87·6	7	86·8	17	84·3	63	84·4	61	82·8	103	84·8	53	79·7	143
1955 poll	81·8	22	83·1	8	84·1	3	79·8	49	78·5	71	75·7	112	79·4	58	72·3	142
1951 % voting left	43·5	113	47·3	98	50·5	75	54·8	48	41·2	120	55·0	46	45·3	106	36·7	133
1955 % voting left	44·5	101	42·2	111	50·2	72	53·2	48	42·4	110	53·5	44	44·6	99	36·6	127
Local elections 1956-58: % voting in contested elections	43	61	44	53	49	19	41	80	43	61	38	102	48	24	47	31
% uncontested seats	45	25	4	99	11	77	39	32	16	67	22	54	2	107	8	87
Votes as % of total electorate	20	133	42	34	45	16	27	113	37	64	31	99	48	6	43	26
HEALTH																
Infant mortality rate, 1950-52	26	90	27	84	26	90	25	96	19	146	39	14	35	30	31	57
Infant mortality rate, 1955-57	18	137	22	88	21	102	23	78	24	71	31	11	28	41	25	64
Expect. of life at year One, 1950-52	71·2	27	71·3	22	71·0	34	71·3	22	71·8	9	69·3	112	69·0	122	69·4	107
T.B. notification rate, 1957	125	31	108	52	122	35	56	130	85	86	74	106	43	148	83	91
Mortality rate 1957—lung cancer	105	100	132	43	89	129	140	35	59	153	103	105	140	35	112	89
Mortality rate 1957—other cancer	84	150	103	102	90	141	87	145	103	102	118	27	130	7	108	72
Mortality rate 1957—bronchitis	86	111	89	105	89	105	94	94	68	139	161	25	187	10	94	94
EDUCATION																
% with terminal edn. age under 15	59·8	115	69·6	66	63·4	101	66·7	83	50·1	141	70·0	63	76·4	29	55·0	130
% aged 15-24 in full-time education	12·0	34	7·2	104	8·5	72	8·1	80	15·2	16	8·4	74	8·4	74	12·7	30

| | Cheshire | | Cumberland | | Derbyshire | | | | Devon | | | | | | Dorset | |
| | CREWE | | CARLISLE | | DERBY | | CHESTERFIELD | | EXETER | | PLYMOUTH | | TORQUAY | | POOLE | |
	Value	Rank	Value	Rank	Value	Rank	Value	Rank	Value	Rank	Value	Rank	Value	Rank	Value	Rank
POPULATION SIZE AND STRUCTURE																
Population ('000)	52	150	68	110	141	38	69	106	76	91	208	19	53	148	83	80
% of population aged 0-14	22·3	63	21·6	89	21·7	84	22·4	62	21·1	101	22·2	67	17·6	149	21·5	93
% of population aged 15-64	67·4	70	68·3	33	67·7	53	67·5	63	66·2	118	67·3	77	64·5	147	64·2	148
% of population aged 65 or over	10·3	85	10·1	95	10·6	75	10·1	95	12·7	21	10·5	76	17·9	6	14·3	16
Females per 1000 males	1040	138	1112	75	1061	117	1046	133	1159	33	1005	151	1325	8	1191	23
Females per 1000 males, age 25-44	987	136	1056	65	967	147	1000	124	1064	53	993	132	1239	6	1150	18
% of females 20-24 ever married	54·5	15	47·7	86	54·3	17	51·6	36	45·6	111	54·5	15	42·5	131	50·2	51
POPULATION CHANGE																
1931-51—total (%)	8·5	87	18·3	59	-0·9	117	6·9	93	11·7	76	-2·4	128	14·9	72	37·9	37
1931-51—births and deaths (%)	6·0	112	8·4	89	8·4	89	12·0	54	4·8	126	7·4	99	-5·4	151	8·6	82
1931-51—balance of change (%)	2·5	78	9·9	62	-9·3	123	-5·1	104	6·9	70	-9·8	127	20·3	45	29·3	33
1951-58 (%)	-2·0	106	2·4	50	-5·2	146	-1·6	99	1·8	60	4·0	39	-5·2	146	6·5	28
Birth rate ratio, 1950-52	99	68	112	22	97	74	93	96	93	96	109	31	81	130	95	87
Birth rate ratio, 1955-57	94	83	107	30	97	69	84	119	94	83	107	30	78	141	93	90
% illegitimate births, 1950-52	4·0	108	5·2	67	6·0	33	4·3	98	6·1	29	7·1	9	7·2	7	5·4	60
% illegitimate births, 1955-57	5·4	52	4·5	88	5·8	35	4·5	88	5·1	64	5·4	52	5·7	39	5·5	46
HOUSEHOLDS AND HOUSING																
% persons in private h/hlds	98·9	16	96·1	120	96·3	118	97·0	98	94·2	136	92·5	144	87·2	155	97·1	94
% one-person h/hlds	8·8	95	9·9	78	9·8	81	7·3	126	10·2	69	12·6	30	14·4	14	9·6	83
% six- or more person h/hlds	6·9	93	9·5	23	8·4	49	9·4	26	8·3	52	7·4	75	6·5	103	7·8	65
% 1-3-room dwellings	7·2	130	26·8	15	7·4	127	10·8	77	10·6	80	8·2	117	13·2	59	8·7	108
Persons per room	0·71	106	0·80	30	0·71	106	0·77	48	0·71	106	0·81	25	0·66	140	0·69	120
% overcrowded h/hlds (composite)	3·5	141	8·5	30	5·6	91	6·8	57	5·1	108	8·4	32	5·3	103	4·1	128
% h/hlds at over 1½ persons per room	2·9	133	6·6	29	4·3	79	5·3	50	3·7	103	5·3	50	3·9	94	2·9	133
% h/hlds in shared dwellings	4·7	143	7·5	121	10·1	95	8·7	106	15·8	61	47·6	5	18·4	46	12·0	81
% h/hlds with piped water	96	27	93	95	94	76	96	27	93	95	92	108	88	141	93	95
% h/hlds with W.C.	98	39	90	139	98	39	98	39	96	94	96	94	94	119	96	94
% h/hlds with 5 amenities	60	101	66	76	53	132	55	125	72	55	77	45	70	63	77	45
% h/hlds with 5, or bath missing	93	52	87	114	93	64	94	34	91	80	89	100	85	126	91	80
New-housing rate 1945-58—total	51	73	76	21	56	64	65	42	56	64	68	33	42	95	78	17
New-housing rate 1945-58—L.A.s	43	50	64	5	51	26	47	39	42	53	55	20	22	122	38	61
% L.A. of total houses 1945-58	83·8	39	84·8	32	90·8	11	71·2	85	74·7	72	80·9	48	53·3	128	48·5	136

114

The following table is printed rotated on the page. Each of the eight areas is given as a pair of figures (an actual value and an index value).

	1 val	1 idx	2 val	2 idx	3 val	3 idx	4 val	4 idx	5 val	5 idx	6 val	6 idx	7 val	7 idx	8 val	8 idx
ECONOMIC CHARACTER																
Occupied as % of total population	59·4	87	61·8	64	61·6	66	58·6	99	55·3	136	55·6	134	49·8	151	52·8	148
% of women in labour force	28·5	126	33·4	61	31·0	104	27·2	134	32·3	81	23·0	153	35·5	34	31·4	96
in manufacture etc.	52·5	49	34·6	103	57·4	33	53·3	48	22·2	134	29·0		13·1	152	35·9	100
% in all service industries	22·6	147	41·1	66	26·8	134	33·4	101	53·6	32	53·1	35	66·6	8	42·4	61
% in retail	8·2	126	11·4	53	7·7	132	11·0	61	12·1	46	9·4	100	16·4	10	11·0	61
% in finance, etc.	0·9	140	1·9	48	1·0	132	1·4	83	3·1	7	1·5	71	2·6	15	1·2	106
% in professional services	3·3	150	6·8	77	5·5	117	7·4	59	12·7	70	5·8	108	8·9	46	7·7	59
Job ratio	119	17	99	79	148	3	105	58	121	14	110	43	104	65	86	107
Commuting ratio	35	104	27	131	59	71	48	82	33	111	17	155	21	147	40	93
Per capita retail sales, 1950	119	102	188	13	165	33	156	44	174	26	116	107	188	13	105	120
SOCIAL CLASS																
% in social classes I + II	9·8	149	14·2	103	11·8	134	13·8	110	19·9	49	11·9	132	26·3	28	20·5	47
% in social classes IV + V	25·4	86	27·6	63	28·8	55	32·1	39	23·5	99	25·9	81	21·9	116	26·2	76
Social class index	78	118	86	97	78	118	110	50	83	106	131	31	106	56	106	56
Social Survey J-index, 1954	0·88	153	2·39	123	2·09	135	2·13	130	4·62	87	7·02	54	6·61	62	16·88	6
VOTING																
General elections—1951 poll	86·5	23	87·4	10	83·5	83	84·2	65	84·1	68	85·3	42	80·0	137	85·0	48
1955 poll	81·5	30	82·3	17	77·2	89	79·9	47	79·3	61	78·0	78	75·5	116	80·9	32
1951 % voting left	52·2	67	46·8	100	59·9	22	63·7	14	40·6	123	50·8	73	27·8	152	36·4	135
1955 % voting left	52·5	55	49·5	76	54·7	35	57·6	22	43·7	104	46·8	92	25·4	153	34·5	133
Local elections 1956-58:																
% voting in contested elections	34	130	54	3	38	102	42	71	51	10	49	19	37	108	42	71
% uncontested seats	0	132	27	45	10	81	25	48	37	34	0	132	54	17	57	13
Votes as % of total electorate	34	82	39	53	35	74	33	87	34	82	49	4	22	123	19	139
HEALTH																
Infant mortality rate, 1950-52	40	10	31	57	31	57	35	30	28	76	31	57	27	84	28	76
Infant mortality rate, 1955-57	29	27	24	71	26	57	26	57	21	102	20	116	22	88	25	64
Expect. of life at year One, 1950-52	69·3	112	66·2	157	69·7	97	70·1	78	70·6	51	69·7	97	70·4	64	71·3	22
T.B. notification rate, 1957	37	151	76	104	89	76	56	130	60	121	112	47	50	140	76	104
Mortality rate 1957—lung cancer	140	35	114	82	113	86	98	116	48	156	79	142	104	103	84	136
Mortality rate 1957—other cancer	105	86	116	33	102	106	119	23	93	135	97	121	95	130	96	125
Mortality rate 1957—bronchitis	107	74	57	145	106	78	147	36	75	129	74	131	74	131	52	149
EDUCATION																
% with terminal edn. age under 15	82·6	8	69·0	72	73·9	44	76·3	30	64·7	96	58·6	120	53·4	133	71·6	53
% aged 15-24 in full-time education	5·6	139	7·1	107	5·6	139	7·7	91	12·0	34	7·1	107	13·1	29	11·1	43

Durham   Essex

	DARLINGTON		GATESHEAD		SOUTH SHIELDS		SUNDERLAND		WEST HARTLEPOOL		STOCKTON-ON-TEES		EAST HAM		SOUTHEND-ON-SEA	
	Value	Rank	Value	Rank	Value	Rank	Value	Rank	Value	Rank	Value	Rank	Value	Rank	Value	Rank
POPULATION SIZE AND STRUCTURE																
Population ('000)	85	76	115	47	107	57	182	22	73	98	74	95	121	45	152	32
% of population aged 0-14	22·2	67	24·4	26	24·7	20	25·7	7	25·7	7	25·3	11	21·6	89	20·4	119
% of population aged 15-64	66·9	94	66·4	114	65·6	131	65·1	139	65·0	141	65·8	125	68·0	43	64·6	145
% of population aged 65 or over	10·9	68	9·2	121	9·7	104	9·2	121	9·3	116	8·9	129	10·4	80	15·0	12
Females per 1000 males	1091	91	1075	105	1109	77	1102	83	1064	115	1041	136	1064	115	1211	19
Females per 1000 males, age 25-44	1048	75	1034	87	1079	46	1058	62	1014	108	1000	124	994	128	1121	30
% of females 20-24 ever married	46·8	99	47·4	92	48·9	67	45·7	109	50·6	45	50·8	42	50·7	44	47·4	92
POPULATION CHANGE																
1931-51—total (%)	17·8	61	-7·6	141	-5·8	136	-2·4	128	4·6	100	9·5	84	-15·1	151	17·0	64
1931-51—births and deaths (%)	8·5	86	10·3	69	8·6	82	12·6	52	13·0	48	14·6	39	7·6	97	2·1	136
1931-51—balance of change (%)	9·3	65	-17·9	147	-14·4	140	-15·0	141	-8·4	118	-5·1	104	-22·7	152	14·9	50
1951-58 (%)	-2·0	106	-4·5	139	1·9	58	2·0	56	2·4	50	4·1	37	-8·2	154	4·1	37
Birth rate ratio, 1950-52	97	74	115	17	117	12	127	4	128	3	125	6	87	117	90	108
Birth rate ratio, 1955-57	96	74	108	25	110	16	124	5	129	4	122	7	78	141	87	113
% illegitimate births, 1950-52	5·8	36	3·7	123	4·7	86	3·7	123	4·9	79	3·8	116	3·5	136	5·7	41
% illegitimate births, 1955-57	5·5	46	3·5	124	3·6	119	3·7	115	4·4	92	3·7	115	3·8	110	5·3	58
HOUSEHOLDS AND HOUSING																
% persons in private h/hlds	98·0	49	98·7	20	98·3	38	98·0	49	98·2	44	98·5	29	98·5	29	97·1	94
% one-person h/hlds	8·6	100	10·2	69	13·1	20	12·1	38	9·0	92	7·8	115	9·9	78	12·8	27
% six- or more person h/hlds	8·3	52	10·9	13	7·7	67	10·7	15	11·1	11	11·3	10	6·3	108	5·9	117
% 1-3-room dwellings	19·9	22	50·1	1	44·7	2	31·8	9	27·4	14	14·9	42	9·2	102	11·1	75
Persons per room	0·79	35	0·97	1	0·87	8	0·95	3	0·82	21	0·82	21	0·78	40	0·68	128
% overcrowded h/hlds (composite)	8·1	36	20·9	1	14·7	4	17·7	2	10·5	17	9·8	22	7·0	53	4·6	119
% h/hlds at over 1½ persons per room	6·2	35	16·5	1	10·2	5	13·7	2	9·4	11	8·3	16	5·1	59	3·3	121
% h/hlds in shared dwellings	7·9	114	6·6	131	3·8	148	31·1	14	6·3	134	8·5	108	35·2	12	25·4	21
% h/hlds with piped water	95	52	85	148	81	154	75	157	87	144	91	119	91	119	91	119
% h/hlds with W.C.	98	39	92	129	71	154	92	129	98	39	98	39	96	94	96	94
% h/hlds with 5 amenities	68	71	45	147	45	147	64	87	51	134	64	87	62	92	79	39
% h/hlds with 5, or bath missing	94	34	82	135	64	154	72	149	83	130	89	100	89	100	90	91
New-housing rate 1945-58—total	44	91	40	100	72	25	82	14	67	36	78	17	26	136	55	66
New-housing rate 1945-58—L.A.s	32	80	38	61	62	8	72	3	55	20	59	11	23	115	24	110
% L.A. of total houses 1945-58	73·5	74	94·0	5	86·8	21	87·0	18	82·5	43	75·5	67	85·7	27	43·3	144

	V	I	V	I	V	I	V	I	V	I	V	I	V	I	V	I
ECONOMIC CHARACTER																
Occupied as % of total population	57·5	112	60·0	75	55·4	135	58·2	102	56·8	120	58·6	99	62·9	50	52·3	149
% of women in labour force	28·9	124	30·7	108	27·1	136	29·2	120	26·4	140	26·1	91	31·8	91	30·8	107
% in manufacture etc.	47·8	62	56·5	39	37·9	95	51·5	53	44·6	71	44·0	72	26·4	125	27·0	124
% in all service industries	32·9	104	27·9	127	37·5	78	32·6	105	35·1	93	37·9	76	37·4	79	54·8	31
% in retail	11·2	56	9·6	96	13·0	34	10·5	75	11·5	51	13·8	26	13·9	24	15·1	17
% in finance, etc.	1·4	83	1·1	119	1·4	83	1·2	106	1·4	83	1·3	96	1·3	96	2·3	27
% in professional services	5·7	112	5·3	120	7·7	59	6·7	80	5·9	102	6·0	97	4·5	136	7·2	70
Job ratio	105	58	88	102	80	116	103	68	95	88	87	104	62	135	78	120
Commuting ratio	24	141	69	58	33	111	23	144	37	99	65	62	93	20	39	95
Per capita retail sales, 1950	159	40	88	134	99	127	124	85	120	99	139	66	122	94	147	58
SOCIAL CLASS																
% in social classes I + II	15·2	88	10·6	144	11·9	132	11·5	138	13·1	118	13·5	113	11·6	136	27·4	25
% in social classes IV + V	26·5	72	34·2	26	35·8	19	34·0	28	36·7	14	36·0	17	30·8	44	19·1	127
Social class index	91	87	67	141	69	136	70	135	71	134	73	131	74	128	143	27
Social Survey J-index, 1954	3·92	99	2·33	124	1·45	146	1·95	136	2·97	113	2·14	129	4·41	91	12·60	17
VOTING																
General elections—1951 poll	87·1	13	84·7	56	80·5	135	83·0	99	86·6	20	88·0	3	82·9	100	79·8	141
1955 poll	82·3	17	75·7	112	71·6	146	76·6	99	81·8	22	83·8	5	74·0	130	74·1	129
1951 % voting left	49·2	84	60·7	19	56·0	40	51·9	70	52·6	63	55·7	42	62·7	16	36·9	132
1955 % voting left	47·4	89	60·6	16	59·6	20	50·6	67	51·6	60	54·4	37	61·6	14	31·1	142
Local elections 1956-58:																
% voting in contested elections	46	40	33	136	35	124	42	71	44	53	38	102	32	141	41	80
% uncontested seats	30	40	8	87	42	27	74	4	21	58	0	132	0	132	14	70
Votes as % of total electorate	32	92	31	99	19	139	11	154	35	74	38	59	32	92	34	82
HEALTH																
Infant mortality rate, 1950-52	29	67	44	3	39	14	39	14	39	14	42	7	22	122	23	112
Infant mortality rate, 1955-57	31	11	29	27	26	57	29	27	43	1	33	4	21	102	19	127
Expect. of life at year One, 1950-52	69·3	112	68·4	136	69·1	118	68·8	130	68·8	130	69·4	107	69·9	90	70·7	45
T.B. notification rate, 1957	95	67	171	3	180	2	125	31	98	100	126	83	117	43	77	101
Mortality rate 1957—lung cancer	125	56	154	23	119	74	116	78	105	27	106	53	145	26	127	50
Mortality rate 1957—other cancer	104	94	104	94	136	2	104	94	118	12	69	81	118	27	107	76
Mortality rate 1957—bronchitis	106	78	163	23	174	16	138	45	183			136	119	64	77	126
EDUCATION																
% with terminal edn. age under 15	72·9	47	82·4	9	69·7	65	76·6	27	68·3	76	69·8	64	68·4	75	57·7	121
% aged 15-24 in full-time education	7·3	100	5·4	146	5·6	139	5·5	144	7·0	110	7·8	88	7·5	94	12·4	32

	WEST HAM		BARKING		CHIGWELL		COLCHESTER		DAGENHAM		HORNCHURCH		ILFORD		LEYTON	
	Value	Rank	Value	Rank	Value	Rank	Value	Rank	Value	Rank	Value	Rank	Value	Rank	Value	Rank
POPULATION SIZE AND STRUCTURE																
Population ('000)	171	26	78	88	52	153	57	137	115	48	104	65	185	21	106	58
% of population aged 0-14	24·2	27	23·3	44	30·1	2	20·8	108	25·8	6	23·0	50	20·3	121	20·2	124
% of population aged 15-64	66·6	106	69·8	8	62·9	154	67·5	63	69·3	17	68·7	25	69·5	13	67·6	58
% of population aged 65 or over	9·2	121	6·9	154	7·0	153	11·7	48	4·9	157	8·3	141	10·2	90	12·2	34
Females per 1000 males	1051	124	1041	136	1066	111	1044	134	1021	149	1071	108	1129	54	1131	51
Females per 1000 males, age 25-44	975	141	1007	116	1049	73	1071	50	980	139	1053	68	1079	46	1051	70
% of females 20-24 ever married	52·0	32	47·6	88	48·7	70	47·2	94	47·0	96	47·9	84	43·4	123	46·9	97
POPULATION CHANGE																
1931-51—total (%)	-41·9	157	52·5	26	217·1	3	16·9	66	28·2	44	164·3	8	40·9	34	-17·4	152
1931-51—births and deaths (%)	6·9	106	23·6	16	21·5	20	10·0	72	27·4	11	35·5	6	13·3	43	5·0	124
1931-51—balance of change (%)	-48·8	157	28·9	34	195·6	3	6·9	70	0·8	87	128·8	8	27·6	35	-22·4	151
1951-58 (%)	-3·5	125	-4·2	136	18·0	4	10·6	15	-0·4	83	15·6	7	-3·1	118	-6·8	152
Birth rate ratio, 1950-52	105	41	93	96	103	48	94	91	95	87	91	103	79	138	80	133
Birth rate ratio, 1955-57	91	100	74	150	79	136	100	53	78	141	106	34	75	147	72	155
% illegitimate births, 1950-52	4·8	84	2·8	152	3·6	131	5·5	55	3·1	146	2·8	152	3·3	143	3·7	123
% illegitimate births, 1955-57	5·2	61	3·2	138	3·5	124	4·7	80	3·4	129	2·2	156	2·7	151	3·9	105
HOUSEHOLDS AND HOUSING																
% persons in private h/hlds	98·6	24	99·7	2	98·4	32	85·1	157	99·4	11	97·7	70	96·9	103	97·1	94
% one-person h/hlds	10·7	58	6·1	145	5·2	153	10·5	62	3·7	157	5·5	151	8·5	103	12·2	37
% six- or more person h/hlds	8·9	36	8·5	46	9·2	31	6·8	97	12·9	5	6·4	105	5·3	139	4·8	152
% 1-3-room dwellings	13·6	54	26·3	17	17·0	31	9·5	94	26·4	16	10·0	91	6·3	144	10·3	86
Persons per room	0·88	7	0·90	4	0·79	35	0·67	135	0·97	1	0·75	66	0·71	106	0·75	66
% overcrowded h/hlds (composite)	12·0	8	10·1	19	5·4	100	3·8	136	11·6	9	4·8	115	4·4	123	5·8	83
% h/hlds at over 1½ persons per room	9·5	10	7·8	19	3·7	103	2·9	133	9·9	7	3·5	114	2·9	133	4·0	90
% h/hlds in shared dwellings	47·0	6	15·8	61	6·3	134	5·6	140	11·3	88	10·7	91	24·6	23	43·2	8
% h/hlds with piped water	88	141	96	27	96	27	92	108	96	27	97	27	97	10	91	119
% h/hlds with W.C.	94	119	98	39	99	8	96	94	98	39	98	39	99	9	96	93
% h/hlds with 5 amenities	35	155	78	42	88	16	57	116	93	4	91	9	91	9	46	144
% h/hlds with 5, or bath missing	85	126	96	9	95	18	91	80	96	9	95	18	97	3	89	100
New-housing rate 1945-58—total	31	126	36	111	61	50	78	17	32	123	111	3	29	131	10	156
New-housing rate 1945-58—L.A.s	27	100	34	72	23	115	48	36	23	115	27	100	18	132	8	155
% L.A. of total houses 1945-58	86·3	24	92·6	6	37·8	148	62·3	113	72·5	81	23·8	157	60·6	117	80·7	50

ECONOMIC CHARACTER, SOCIAL CLASS, VOTING, HEALTH, EDUCATION

	1 val	1 idx	2 val	2 idx	3 val	3 idx	4 val	4 idx	5 val	5 idx	6 val	6 idx	7 val	7 idx	8 val	8 idx
ECONOMIC CHARACTER																
Occupied as % of total population	65·6	23	65·3	26	59·4	87	55·9	131	66·8	9	59·6	83	58·7	96	61·6	66
% of women in labour force	33·7	57	31·4	96	28·3	128	27·9	132	31·1	103	28·0	130	31·9	89	34·6	46
% in manufacture etc.	46·0	67	40·5	81	16·0	144	29·0	116	73·7	3	37·4	96	40·2	83	41·6	79
% in all service industries	27·0	132	25·4	140	45·3	51	56·3	26	18·5	153	42·9	58	42·9	58	39·2	74
% in retail	8·4	122	6·4	147	9·2	101	10·4	77	5·3	153	10·7	67	13·9	24	12·1	46
% in finance, etc.	0·8	145	0·6	152	1·3	96	1·4	83	0·4	156	0·8	145	2·3	27	1·1	119
% in professional services	4·4	137	4·6	133	9·8	34	11·1	19	3·6	147	9·3	38	8·9	46	10·1	31
Job ratio	112	34	79	118	49	149	117	21	91	96	44	153	57	140	61	137
Commuting ratio	100	11	100	11	88	31	29	123	106	9	86	37	85	40	92	24
Per capita retail sales, 1950	113	111	82	141	61	156	167	32	87	136	65	154	125	80	110	116
SOCIAL CLASS																
% in social classes I+II	8·7	152	10·3	148	24·2	31	16·7	68	7·7	157	22·4	41	25·4	29	13·5	113
% in social classes IV+V	41·8	3	35·4	21	21·6	120	21·7	119	36·5	16	21·2	123	17·4	137	24·0	95
Social class index	55	155	65	147	126	34	106	56	57	152	123	37	144	26	91	87
Social Survey J-index, 1954	3·96	97	6·54	64	17·04	5	5·48	80	3·70	103	11·66	21	10·04	35	6·41	67
VOTING																
General elections—1951 poll	76·9	155	81·9	122	83·4	88	84·8	53	77·7	149	86·1	32	83·7	79	82·2	113
1955 poll	66·7	157	73·5	136	79·7	52	80·5	39	68·9	153	82·0	19	76·0	108	74·3	126
1951 % voting left	77·4	3	67·4	7	35·8	138	45·8	104	76·1	4	47·3	98	41·6	117	57·8	31
1955 % voting left	73·8	4	69·2	6	47·5	87	44·5	101	73·9	3	44·1	103	39·1	117	53·4	46
Local elections 1956-58: % voting in contested elections	22	154	38	102	47	31	50	14	21	155	44	53	33	136	27	150
% uncontested seats	8	87	46	24	0	132	11	77	12	73	0	132	0	132	0	132
Votes as % of total electorate	20	133	18	143	47	10	45	16	19	139	40	46	33	87	27	113
HEALTH																
Infant mortality rate, 1950-52	26	90	21	133	21	133	21	133	28	76	25	96	19	146	23	112
Infant mortality rate, 1955-57	22	88	21	102	17	144	18	137	22	88	20	116	18	137	21	102
Expect. of life at year One, 1950-52	69·2	116	69·4	107	75·7	1	72·0	6	70·0	84	71·4	20	71·0	34	70·4	64
T.B. notification rate, 1957	67	113	43	148	99	59	82	94	46	145	65	115	112	47	58	127
Mortality rate 1957—lung cancer	174	8	243	1	159	17	72	148	157	21	102	108	125	56	109	93
Mortality rate 1957—other cancer	109	67	145	1	96	125	75	157	135	3	96	125	95	130	94	133
Mortality rate 1957—bronchitis	169	17	106	78	83	116	53	148	190	9	105	82	104	85	131	58
EDUCATION																
% with terminal edn. age under 15	77·7	22	77·3	24	62·1	104	71·5	54	84·4	3	66·1	86	55·8	125	68·7	73
% aged 15-24 in full-time education	4·6	152	4·3	155	11·4	42	5·7	135	3·8	157	9·5	56	11·8	37	5·6	139

119

	ROMFORD		THURROCK		WALTHAM-STOW		WANSTEAD & WOODFORD		BRISTOL		GLOUCESTER		CHELTENHAM		WATFORD	
	Value	Rank	Value	Rank	Value	Rank	Value	Rank	Value	Rank	Value	Rank	Value	Rank	Value	Rank
POPULATION SIZE AND STRUCTURE																
Population ('000)	88	73	82	82	121	44	62	126	443	7	67	113	63	122	73	97
% of population aged 0-14	20.9	106	25.2	14	21.2	98	20.8	108	22.2	67	22.6	59	21.8	80	20.4	119
% of population aged 15-64	63.6	151	66.7	102	68.1	39	67.2	82	66.5	110	67.0	90	64.6	145	68.3	33
% of population aged 65 or over	15.5	9	8.1	145	10.7	72	12.0	41	11.3	58	10.4	80	13.6	17	11.3	58
Females per 1000 males	1065	113	978	154	1123	61	1185	26	1113	73	1048	130	1248	11	1129	54
Females per 1000 males, age 25-44	1043	78	944	154	1058	62	1145	23	1020	105	955	151	1125	28	1050	71
% of females 20-24 ever married	55.1	12	55.7	8	49.1	65	39.8	144	47.5	90	51.8	35	48.9	67	46.4	104
POPULATION CHANGE																
1931-51—total (%)	132.6	10	32.7	42	-8.9	144	42.9	33	9.7	83	20.4	54	25.3	48	24.9	49
1931-51—births and deaths (%)	26.3	13	18.4	26	6.9	106	8.9	80	8.2	91	10.1	70	3.3	133	11.0	64
1931-51—balance of change (%)	106.3	10	14.3	52	-15.8	143	34.0	29	1.5	84	10.3	61	22.0	44	13.9	54
1951-58 (%)	29.2	1	28.6	2	-5.9	149	-0.7	85	-1.1	90	1.7	61	9.2	20	0.3	72
Birth rate ratio, 1950-52	116	14	112	22	82	126	79	138	100	62	103	48	108	33	87	117
Birth rate ratio, 1955-57	95	77	100	53	74	150	74	150	97	69	107	30	107	30	94	83
% illegitimate births, 1950-52	4.0	108	4.3	98	3.8	116	2.9	149	4.3	98	5.6	49	7.7	3	4.5	93
% illegitimate births, 1955-57	3.1	143	3.9	105	4.0	102	3.4	129	4.5	88	5.6	43	7.0	11	4.9	70
HOUSEHOLDS AND HOUSING																
% persons in private h/hlds	98.5	29	95.1	128	99.6	5	96.8	108	96.5	113	94.0	138	94.7	132	97.7	70
% one-person h/hlds	6.1	145	6.2	142	10.2	69	9.2	89	11.0	53	8.7	97	14.2	18	8.5	103
% six- or more person h/hlds	7.6	70	8.8	39	5.7	124	4.9	150	7.1	84	9.3	28	7.2	80	6.8	97
% 1-3-room dwellings	16.6	34	10.3	86	11.9	70	9.5	94	8.8	106	5.1	153	16.3	36	8.4	115
Persons per room	0.80	30	0.80	30	0.75	66	0.66	140	0.73	85	0.73	85	0.72	94	0.71	106
% overcrowded h/hlds (composite)	7.1	51	6.6	61	5.5	96	3.0	150	6.2	73	6.6	61	6.2	73	5.4	100
% h/hlds at over 1½ persons per room	4.8	64	5.1	59	3.8	98	1.9	153	3.7	103	4.6	72	4.5	76	3.8	98
% h/hlds in shared dwellings	11.7	85	12.2	78	28.3	18	17.2	52	23.7	25	20.1	39	19.7	41	14.1	67
% h/hlds with piped water	96	27	94	76	90	130	94	76	92	108	92	108	89	137	93	95
% h/hlds with W.C.	97	72	94	119	94	119	97	72	96	94	97	72	94	119	97	72
% h/hlds with 5 amenities	87	20	71	61	54	129	85	28	67	73	60	101	59	108	72	55
% h/hlds with 5, or bath missing	95	18	90	91	87	114	93	52	90	91	90	91	86	121	91	80
New-housing rate 1945-58—total	70	28	69	30	23	143	46	85	54	67	60	55	87	7	63	46
New-housing rate 1945-58—L.A.s	34	72	43	50	18	132	26	106	46	41	51	26	64	5	46	41
% L.A. of total houses 1945-58	48.8	135	62.6	111	79.5	54	56.2	123	85.2	29	85.8	26	73.3	76	72.8	79

	1	2	3	4	5	6	7	8	9	10	11	12	13	14	15	16
ECONOMIC CHARACTER																
Occupied as % of total population	60·4	73	60·2	74	63·5	43	57·2	115	57·8	107	60·9	71	122	56·6	61·1	70
% of women in labour force	29·1	122	24·9	149	34·7	44	33·3	63	31·0	104	30·1	115	43	34·8	32·7	75
% in manufacture etc.	25·1	127	42·8	77	57·2	35	19·6	137	38·4	93	27·6	123	121	28·2	45·6	68
% in all service industries	46·5	49	27·1	131	30·9	108	59·0	20	40·7	68	49·9	44	34	53·2	37·3	81
% in retail	15·4	14	6·7	144	9·6	96	14·1	21	9·6	96	12·6	39	16	15·2	10·6	72
% in finance, etc.	2·0	41	0·6	152	1·1	119	2·0	41	2·3	27	1·6	64	21	2·4	2·2	34
% in professional services	10·1	31	4·6	133	5·2	122	14·1	8	8·9	46	8·6	50	18	11·3	6·5	84
Job ratio	64	131	112	34	74	123	45	152	100	25	106	51	85	96	111	38
Commuting ratio	87	34	39	95	82	42	92	24	23	144	46	84	99	37	69	58
Per capita retail sales, 1950	161	38	83	140	107	117	113	111	124	85	185	17	7	193	187	15
SOCIAL CLASS																
% in social classes I + II	19·0	55	11·7	135	14·6	97	36·5	5	17·0	65	15·6	83	41	22·4	19·3	53
% in social classes IV + V	23·7	97	38·3	12	23·1	105	13·1	153	27·6	63	24·2	93	113	22·1	23·7	97
Social class index	107	54	66	144	96	71	199	4	94	78	97	69	42	120	108	51
Social Survey J-index, 1954	12·68	16	6·42	66	7·65	50	16·46	10	5·85	72	5·06	82	71	5·88	7·59	51
VOTING																
General elections—1951 poll	83·8	76	82·8	103	84·0	71	83·4	88	82·9	100	85·5	39	95	83·2	87·2	11
1955 poll	75·5	116	75·2	119	76·9	94	76·0	108	76·4	104	80·9	32	58	79·4	82·4	16
1951 % voting left	49·0	88	65·5	11	56·5	38	35·8	138	53·0	59	48·8	89	115	42·9	47·9	96
1955 % voting left	52·5	55	66·2	9	53·2	48	27·0	151	50·8	65	50·9	64	114	40·7	48·0	84
Local elections 1956-58:																
% voting in contested elections	33	136	25	152	31	144	33	136	37	108	49	19	71	42	47	31
% uncontested seats	0	132	20	61	0	132	4	99	35	35	30	40	36	34	6	93
Votes as % of total electorate	33	87	17	145	31	99	32	92	25	118	34	82	113	27	44	19
HEALTH																
Infant mortality rate, 1950-52	24	103	28	76	24	103	19	146	21	133	29	67	25	36	22	122
Infant mortality rate, 1955-57	21	102	24	71	21	102	23	78	19	127	21	102	27	29	18	137
Expect. of life at year One, 1950-52	72·3	5	71·6	12	70·6	51	71·5	17	70·1	78	70·5	58	34	71·0	70·8	41
T.B. notification rate, 1957	54	132	86	83	88	79	43	148	113	45	92	71	154	31	169	5
Mortality rate 1957—lung cancer	144	27	105	100	166	11	105	100	93	125	53	154	133	85	119	74
Mortality rate 1957—other cancer	97	121	93	135	129	9	84	150	89	143	85	147	86	105	113	47
Mortality rate 1957—bronchitis	98	91	109	71	116	67	101	88	81	117	134	52	152	47	89	105
EDUCATION																
% with terminal edn. age under 15	67·6	80	76·0	32	67·8	80	47·7	147	65·8	89	56·5	124	154	41·0	64·5	99
% aged 15-24 in full-time education	8·2	77	5·5	144	7·2	104	17·4	6	8·8	66	7·9	84	44	11·0	9·5	56

| | Kent | | | | | | | | | | | | | | Lancashire | |
| | BECKENHAM | | BEXLEY | | BROMLEY | | CHISLEHURST & SIDCUP | | GILLINGHAM | | MAIDSTONE | | ORPINGTON | | BARROW IN FURNESS | |
	Value	Rank	Value	Rank	Value	Rank	Value	Rank	Value	Rank	Value	Rank	Value	Rank	Value	Rank
POPULATION SIZE AND STRUCTURE																
Population ('000)	75	93	89	71	64	119	84	79	71	100	54	144	63	121	67	111
% of population aged 0-14	19·8	133	21·9	76	20·5	116	25·2	14	21·5	93	21·3	95	24·1	29	23·5	42
% of population aged 15-64	67·9	47	69·5	13	66·9	94	66·7	102	67·6	58	67·4	70	65·5	134	65·8	125
% of population aged 65 or over	12·3	30	8·6	136	12·6	22	8·1	145	10·9	68	11·3	58	10·4	80	10·7	72
Females per 1000 males	1197	21	1079	101	1208	20	1093	89	957	156	1108	79	1115	70	1029	46
Females per 1000 males, age 25-44	1148	20	1089	41	1170	14	1081	44	952	152	1041	81	1110	32	993	132
% of females 20-24 ever married	38·4	147	46·5	102	41·5	134	48·3	77	54·5	15	47·4	92	44·4	120	50·0	56
POPULATION CHANGE																
1931-51—total (%)	48·4	29	172·2	6	34·6	39	208·8	4	14·6	73	20·4	54	145·0	9	1·9	107
1931-51—births and deaths (%)	9·5	76	35·7	5	9·0	78	31·1	7	11·3	60	8·5	86	28·1	10	7·9	94
1931-51—balance of change (%)	38·9	27	136·5	5	25·6	39	177·7	4	3·3	76	11·9	58	116·9	9	-6·0	110
1951-58 (%)	0·7	67	1·7	61	2·9	48	5·6	31	10·2	16	4·6	33	16·2	6	-4·5	139
Birth rate ratio, 1950-52	78	143	78	143	87	117	96	81	101	58	96	81	92	99	107	36
Birth rate ratio, 1955-57	81	132	87	113	84	119	91	100	101	48	91	100	110	16	97	69
% illegitimate births, 1950-52	2·3	157	4·0	108	3·7	123	3·3	143	5·1	72	5·6	49	3·6	131	4·5	93
% illegitimate births, 1955-57	2·8	148	2·8	148	4·4	92	3·2	138	4·8	75	4·8	75	2·6	153	4·1	99
HOUSEHOLDS AND HOUSING																
% persons in private h/hlds	98·3	38	99·7	2	97·8	62	97·9	54	90·5	149	92·0	146	95·2	126	97·7	70
% one-person h/hlds	8·7	97	6·3	141	9·9	78	6·4	140	10·0	76	9·3	87	6·8	135	8·6	100
% six- or more person h/hlds	4·7	154	5·2	141	5·4	135	8·2	56	6·7	100	7·2	80	6·3	108	8·4	49
% 1-3-room dwellings	6·8	137	6·3	144	10·1	90	17·1	30	6·7	139	7·6	123	12·9	61	11·5	71
Persons per room	0·63	153	0·72	94	0·67	135	0·77	48	0·67	135	0·69	120	0·70	115	0·75	66
% overcrowded h/hlds (composite)	2·4	156	4·1	128	3·8	136	5·5	96	3·4	143	3·6	139	3·0	150	5·9	80
% h/hlds at over 1½ persons per room	1·4	156	2·7	140	2·8	136	4·5	76	2·3	146	2·8	136	2·2	148	4·9	62
% h/hlds in shared dwellings	16·6	57	12·0	81	17·0	56	7·0	128	10·1	95	8·2	112	5·2	142	9·2	104
% h/hlds with piped water	95	52	96	27	94	76	95	52	95	52	91	119	95	52	96	27
% h/hlds with W.C.	98	39	98	39	98	39	98	39	98	39	97	72	97	72	99	8
% h/hlds with 5 amenities	88	16	89	13	78	42	87	20	61	95	60	101	86	24	60	101
% h/hlds with 5, or bath missing	95	18	95	18	93	52	94	34	94	34	90	91	94	34	95	18
New-housing rate 1945-58—total	32	123	51	73	51	73	38	106	61	50	67	36	105	4	39	102
New-housing rate 1945-58—L.A.s	11	149	22	122	24	110	19	128	41	55	44	46	36	66	33	76
% L.A. of total houses 1945-58	33·1	152	44·0	143	47·5	137	48·9	134	66·8	99	65·8	105	34·0	150	85·0	30

ECONOMIC CHARACTER · SOCIAL CLASS · VOTING · HEALTH · EDUCATION

The table below is printed sideways on the page. Each of the eight regions is given as a pair of columns — a value column and an index column.

Variable	(1) val	(1) idx	(2) val	(2) idx	(3) val	(3) idx	(4) val	(4) idx	(5) val	(5) idx	(6) val	(6) idx	(7) val	(7) idx	(8) val	(8) idx
ECONOMIC CHARACTER																
Occupied as % of total population	55·3	136	59·6	83	56·8	120	60·8	72	57·1	117	56·4	126	56·5	124	55·7	133
% of women in labour force	31·2	101	29·0	123	33·1	69	30·9	106	22·4	155	31·6	93	29·4	119	23·9	152
% in manufacture etc.	39·4	89	17·8	140	17·8	140	33·9	105	10·3	157	31·1	111	28·4	119	56·1	41
% in all service industries	41·8	63	60·6	16	61·1	15	47·8	47	75·4	1	52·4	39	51·6	42	27·9	127
% in retail	9·9	89	22·6	2	17·3	6	9·7	93	10·4	77	11·2	56	11·0	61	9·1	103
% in finance, etc.	1·8	55	2·6	15	2·8	9	1·1	119	0·9	140	2·7	11	1·2	106	1·1	119
% in professional services	9·0	44	10·4	29	11·5	17	10·6	26	3·9	143	10·5	28	16·7	6	4·9	127
Job ratio	57	140	29	156	68	127	56	142	64	131	118	19	62	135	109	46
Commuting ratio	98	14	88	31	85	40	86	37	57	73	45	86	73	53	19	151
Per capita retail sales, 1950	84	139	97	128	169	29	78	147	76	148	192	9	87	136	103	122
SOCIAL CLASS																
% in social classes I+II	41·2	2	21·6	45	32·1	15	22·6	39	13·9	109	17·6	62	33·2	9	12·8	122
% in social classes IV+V	10·5	156	18·3	132	16·4	142	21·8	117	20·1	124	26·4	74	17·4	137	29·7	50
Social class index	237	2	130	33	167	16	121	39	103	60	97	69	165	17	79	114
Social Survey J-index, 1954	16·53	9	9·84	37	11·51	25	12·19	19	1·50	144	11·66	21	15·26	11	4·29	94
VOTING																
General elections—1951 poll	82·4	110	87·8	5	81·0	132	88·0	3	85·5	39	80·5	135	82·0	118	86·2	29
1955 poll	76·5	102	82·6	13	75·2	119	84·9	2	79·5	56	77·1	90	79·4	58	80·7	36
1951 % voting left	32·6	144	48·5	92	34·5	140	49·2	84	46·3	102	43·4	114	37·3	130	56·9	36
1955 % voting left	31·0	143	45·7	97	31·8	139	41·9	113	44·5	101	42·1	112	27·6	150	53·2	48
Local elections 1956-58: % voting in contested elections	39	94	47	31	43	61	45	47	45	47	49	19	42	71	43	61
% uncontested seats	0	132	0	132	0	132	3	104	4	99	5	95	0	132	15	69
Votes as % of total electorate	39	53	47	10	43	26	40	46	43	26	47	10	33	87	39	53
HEALTH																
Infant mortality rate, 1950-52	23	112	17	153	18	150	22	122	29	67	24	103	21	133	38	18
Infant mortality rate, 1955-57	15	154	22	88	20	116	22	88	26	57	19	127	19	127	28	41
Expect. of life at year One, 1950-52	71·6	12	70·6	51	71·6	12	71·7	10	70·8	41	70·2	74	72·0	6	69·0	122
T.B. notification rate, 1957	80	97	99	59	124	33	121	38	132	24	166	7	128		114	44
Mortality rate 1957—lung cancer	83	138	128	47	91	127	120	68	114	82	78	143	120	68	101	110
Mortality rate 1957—other cancer	109	67	115	36	97	121	112	51	110	61	83	152	95	130	134	5
Mortality rate 1957—bronchitis	77	126	128	61	93	96	90	102	90	102	91	101	80	120	77	126
EDUCATION																
% with terminal edn. age under 15	33·6	157	57·0	123	50·0	142	61·5	108	61·3	110	64·8	94	50·8	140	61·5	108
% aged 15-24 in full-time education	21·1	2	12·3	33	15·2	16	10·7	45	6·8	114	9·7	53	15·0	19	8·8	66

Lancashire

	BLACKBURN		BLACKPOOL		BOLTON		BOOTLE		BURNLEY		BURY		LIVERPOOL		MANCHESTER	
	Value	Rank	Value	Rank	Value	Rank	Value	Rank	Value	Rank	Value	Rank	Value	Rank	Value	Rank
POPULATION SIZE AND STRUCTURE																
Population ('000)	111	52	147	34	167	27	75	92	85	75	59	132	789	3	703	4
% of population aged 0-14	19·8	133	16·4	156	21·1	101	27·7	3	20·5	116	20·5	116	26·0	5	22·8	55
% of population aged 15-64	67·3	77	68·4	30	67·8	49	65·2	137	67·3	77	67·1	86	65·1	139	67·5	63
% of population aged 65 or over	12·9	19	15·2	11	11·1	64	7·1	151	12·2	34	12·4	26	8·9	129	9·7	104
Females per 1000 males	1163	32	1247	12	1136	45	1032	143	1135	47	1152	35	1134	48	1122	62
Females per 1000 males, age 25-44	1064	54	1152	17	1062	59	974	142	1050	71	1063	57	1087	42	1033	90
% of females 20-24 ever married	48·1	79	44·5	118	48·4	74	43·1	127	54·0	18	50·3	48	40·6	138	47·9	84
POPULATION CHANGE																
1931-51—total (%)	-9·4	145	38·7	36	-5·7	135	-2·4	128	-13·5	148	0·8	112	-7·9	142	-8·3	143
1931-51—births and deaths (%)	-2·0	148	-7·5	154	2·0	137	16·7	29	-1·4	147	1·6	138	13·0	48	5·5	118
1931-51—balance of change (%)	-7·4	114	46·2	23	-7·7	115	-19·1	149	-12·1	133	-0·8	94	-20·9	150	-13·8	137
1951-58 (%)	-4·5	139	-1·8	102	-3·4	123	8·8	21	-4·3	137	-1·3	93	-3·3	121	-3·7	129
Birth rate ratio, 1950-52	90	108	73	149	94	91	134	2	99	68	96	81	126	5	110	28
Birth rate ratio, 1955-57	94	83	82	127	94	83	137	2	101	48	99	58	122	7	108	25
% illegitimate births, 1950-52	4·9	79	6·5	24	4·9	79	3·9	113	6·5	24	6·0	33	5·7	41	6·8	15
% illegitimate births, 1955-57	4·9	70	8·0	3	5·2	61	3·1	143	5·4	52	5·5	46	5·2	61	7·7	8
HOUSEHOLDS AND HOUSING																
% persons in private h/hlds	97·8	62	88·9	153	98·6	24	96·4	116	97·8	62	97·6	74	97·0	88	97·3	86
% one-person h/hlds	13·2	19	12·6	30	12·4	35	7·5	122	13·0	22	12·8	27	10·7	58	11·9	40
% six- or more person h/hlds	4·8	152	5·1	144	5·6	127	16·2	2	5·0	148	5·3	139	13·2	4	8·3	52
% 1-3-room dwellings	10·3	86	7·5	125	13·5	55	6·8	137	12·9	61	17·0	31	12·7	63	10·6	80
Persons per room	0·69	120	0·65	145	0·71	106	0·86	10	0·71	106	0·70	115	0·82	21	0·74	76
% overcrowded h/hlds (composite)	3·2	147	5·3	103	4·0	131	12·2	7	3·9	133	3·5	141	12·5	5	5·9	80
% h/hlds at over 1½ persons per room	2·7	140	3·6	110	3·5	114	9·6	9	3·2	124	3·1	126	10·2	5	4·8	64
% h/hlds in shared dwellings	3·4	152	15·9	60	4·0	147	21·1	33	3·1	153	2·7	155	17·3	51	10·0	99
% h/hlds with piped water	95	52	93	95	96	27	94	76	97	10	96	27	91	119	95	52
% h/hlds with W.C.	98	39	96	94	96	94	94	39	96	94	91	135	96	94	98	39
% h/hlds with 5 amenities	45	147	85	28	54	129	65	81	42	152	56	120	57	116	61	95
% h/hlds with 5, or bath missing	92	67	92	67	91	80	93	52	94	34	87	114	87	114	92	67
New-housing rate 1945-58—total	25	139	45	88	32	123	68	33	25	139	41	97	38	106	36	111
New-housing rate 1945-58—L.A.s	22	122	20	126	27	100	67	4	23	115	29	93	32	80	30	87
% L.A. of total houses 1945-58	86·7	23	44·2	142	85·5	28	97·7	1	91·9	8	70·9	86	84·6	34	84·1	37

ECONOMIC CHARACTER																
Occupied as % of total population	66·8	9	55·0	141	66·1	18	65·5	25	67·7	5	64·4	34	62·3	59	66·3	15
% of women in labour force	41·2	1	35·7	31	38·5	9	31·4	96	40·9	2	37·8	17	34·9	41	37·7	18
% in manufacture etc.	59·9	27	21·3	136	60·6	19	33·5	107	60·2	25	60·3	22	35·0	102	45·1	69
% in all service industries	27·5	130	61·5	14	28·1	125	34·3	151	28·5	118	28·5	118	39·8	72	40·9	67
% in retail	8·6	117	15·4	14	8·6	117	5·6	151	8·8	114	8·2	126	9·9	89	9·9	89
% in finance, etc.	1·2	106	1·9	48	1·1	119	1·0	132	1·4	83	1·3	96	2·9	8	3·5	6
% in professional services	5·6	114	6·4	87	5·2	122	3·0	152	5·6	114	5·9	102	7·4	65	7·2	70
Job ratio	105	58	91	96	101	72	111	38	99	79	101	72	113	29	121	14
Commuting ratio	25	137	23	144	33	111	92	24	27	131	41	91	35	104	56	74
Per capita retail sales, 1950	127	77	178	23	123	90	68	151	124	85	124	85	123	90	179	22
SOCIAL CLASS																
% in social classes I+II	14·9	91	23·1	36	14·2	103	8·0	155	13·7	111	15·7	81	12·1	128	14·2	103
% in social classes IV+V	29·1	53	22·7	107	29·1	53	43·6	1	30·9	43	31·4	41	37·6	13	30·4	46
Social class index	85	100	120	42	84	103	52	157	80	111	84	103	68	139	82	108
Social Survey J-index, 1954	2·76	115	8·26	43	2·96	114	4·43	90	2·99	112	1·90	137	6·48	65	4·78	85
VOTING																
General elections—1951 poll	89·0	1	74·0	157	84·8	53	81·2	130	88·7	2	86·5	23	77·2	153	79·5	145
1955 poll	83·1	8	67·2	156	79·1	63	75·7	112	83·5	6	80·2	44	69·1	152	71·8	145
1951 % voting left	50·0	78	31·2	145	48·5	92	52·7	61	56·5	38	48·4	94	49·1	86	50·2	77
1955 % voting left	50·5	71	31·2	141	45·6	98	52·0	58	55·6	31	46·4	95	47·5	87	48·6	80
Local elections 1956–58:																
% voting in contested elections	56	1	41	80	42	71	44	53	52	7	44	53	36	116	34	130
% uncontested seats	48	22	0	132	0	132	0	132	27	45	0	132	2	107	0	132
Votes as % of total electorate	31	99	41	40	42	34	44	19	38	59	44	19	35	74	34	82
HEALTH																
Infant mortality rate, 1950–52	32	49	33	42	34	36	43	5	37	22	29	67	35	30	35	30
Infant mortality rate, 1955–57	27	50	26	57	25	64	28	41	27	50	28	41	27	50	29	27
Expect. of life at year One, 1950–52	68·1	146	68·1	146	67·9	151	68·6	133	67·9	151	68·3	139	67·8	153	68·0	149
T.B. notification rate, 1957	78	99	60	121	93	69	121	38	96	66	36	152	166	7	133	22
Mortality rate 1957—lung cancer	121	63	115	80	134	41	228	2	141	31	108	95	160	15	158	19
Mortality rate 1957—other cancer	115	36	117	31	118	27	104	94	128	10	108	72	112	51	115	36
Mortality rate 1957—bronchitis	143	41	114	68	136	49	153	30	145	39	133	53	167	18	212	4
EDUCATION																
% with terminal edn. age under 15	74·5	43	62·4	103	75·5	36	75·5	36	75·1	40	72·9	47	75·2	39	72·4	51
% aged 15–24 in full-time education	8·0	82	13·3	27	7·0	110	6·2	123	6·4	119	6·3	121	6·3	121	6·5	116

Lancashire

	OLDHAM		PRESTON		ROCHDALE		ST. HELENS		SALFORD		SOUTHPORT		WARRINGTON		WIGAN	
	Value	*Rank*	*Value*	*Rank*	*Value*	*Rank*	*Value*	*Rank*	*Value*	*Rank*	*Value*	*Rank*	*Value*	*Rank*	*Value*	*Rank*
POPULATION SIZE AND STRUCTURE																
Population ('000)	121	42	119	46	88	72	110.	55	178	25	84	78	81	85	85	77
% of population aged 0-14	21·2	98	22·2	67	19·6	138	24·6	23	23·6	40	16·7	154	23·9	35	22·9	53
% of population aged 15-64	67·7	53	67·6	58	68·5	28	67·2	82	67·0	90	65·8	125	67·4	70	67·7	57
% of population aged 65 or over	11·1	64	10·2	90	11·9	44	8·2	144	9·4	111	17·5	7	8·7	134	9·4	111
Females per 1000 males	1124	60	1118	66	1132	50	1036	141	1104	81	1332	6	1054	121	1074	106
Females per 1000 males, age 25-44	1054	67	993	132	1034	87	1021	103	1019	107	1248	4	987	136	1056	65
% of females 20-24 ever married	55·2	11	50·1	53	52·2	29	42·4	132	50·1	53	37·4	149	48·8	69	45·4	112
POPULATION CHANGE																
1931-51—total (%)	-13·6	149	-0·3	115	-7·4	139	2·6	104	-20·2	154	6·5	94	-1·1	121	-0·9	117
1931-51—births and deaths (%)	-0·3	144	5·9	114	-2·0	148	14·6	39	5·5	118	-7·8	155	11·1	63	8·5	86
1931-51—balance of change (%)	-13·3	136	-6·2	112	-5·4	107	-12·0	132	-25·7	153	14·3	52	-12·2	135	-9·4	124
1951-58 (%)	-2·4	110	-3·5	125	-4·0	135	0·3	72	-8·2	154	-2·7	113	-1·5	96	-3·8	132
Birth rate ratio, 1950-52	100	62	108	33	96	81	113	20	111	25	72	152	111	25	103	48
Birth rate ratio, 1955-57	97	69	102	44	97	69	103	41	104	37	84	119	102	44	94	83
% illegitimate births, 1950-52	5·5	55	5·3	63	6·5	24	3·6	131	7·1	9	5·7	41	5·6	49	2·7	154
% illegitimate births, 1955-57	5·7	39	5·8	35	6·0	31	3·1	143	5·9	33	6·1	29	5·1	64	2·0	157
HOUSEHOLDS AND HOUSING																
% persons in private h/hlds	97·7	70	97·8	62	98·5	29	97·7	70	97·7	70	94·2	136	97·8	62	98·7	20
% one-person h/hlds	12·4	35	11·5	45	14·3	16	5·9	148	12·0	39	15·1	8	8·0	111	7·6	119
% six- or more person h/hlds	5·6	127	7·6	70	4·9	150	15·1	3	8·3	52	5·0	148	10·5	17	10·7	15
% 1-3-room dwellings	23·3	20	15·9	37	23·7	19	10·5	83	15·2	41	9·5	94	14·1	50	14·4	46
Persons per room	0·76	57	0·76	57	0·72	94	0·87	8	0·78	40	0·64	150	0·83	16	0·83	16
% overcrowded h/hlds (composite)	6·3	70	6·4	67	6·2	73	10·0	20	7·9	38	5·1	108	7·6	41	8·5	30
% h/hlds at over 1½ persons per room	5·3	50	5·1	59	4·7	67	8·8	12	6·4	33	3·7	103	6·3	34	7·1	24
% h/hlds in shared dwellings	3·8	148	8·3	110	4·3	144	6·8	129	11·1	89	22·7	29	6·4	133	7·4	124
% h/hlds with piped water	95	52	93	95	94	76	98	2	97	10	96	27	95	52	96	27
% h/hlds with W.C.	86	147	98	39	86	147	98	39	98	39	95	110	69	156	98	39
% h/hlds with 5 amenities	37	154	49	139	39	153	51	134	43	151	73	51	49	139	45	147
% h/hlds with 5, or bath missing	80	141	92	67	80	141	96	9	91	80	92	67	66	152	91	80
New-housing rate 1945-58—total	31	126	34	116	39	102	48	80	16	152	22	145	43	93	36	111
New-housing rate 1945-58—L.A.s	27	100	30	87	35	69	36	66	13	144	13	144	37	65	32	80
% L.A. of total houses 1945-58	84·7	33	87·0	18	89·6	13	75·3	68	81·3	46	56·3	122	87·2	17	87·5	16

	A		B		C		D		E		F		G		H	
ECONOMIC CHARACTER																
Occupied as % of total population	69·1	1	66·9	7	68·6	3	62·0	62	68·5	4	53·3	147	66·0	20	63·4	45
% of women in labour force	40·3	4	38·0	15	40·5	11	30·7	108	38·3	11	36·9	25	33·9	54	34·1	52
% in manufacture etc.	60·6	19	48·5	60	66·7	11	62·3	15	51·8	50	24·5	129	59·0	30	48·5	60
% in all service industries	28·3	124	34·9	95	23·5	143	26·0	138	26·8	134	59·6	19	26·8	134	36·3	84
% in retail	9·0	105	9·6	96	7·5	134	8·3	124	6·9	141	16·6	9	8·6	117	12·8	36
% in finance, etc.	1·3	96	1·5	71	0·9	140	1·1	119	0·8	145	2·2	34	1·2	106	1·9	48
% in professional services	6·1	93	6·2	90	3·6	147	6·0	97	5·2	122	9·2	40	4·6	133	5·9	102
Job ratio	89	100	113	29	105	58	97	83	92	94	88	102	118	19	88	102
Commuting ratio	51	79	45	86	33	111	36	101	70	55	27	131	51	79	63	66
Per capita retail sales, 1950	125	80	164	35	124	85	95	13	92	132	165	33	148	56	146	60
SOCIAL CLASS																
% in social classes I + II	12·0	130	12·1	128	14·0	108	8·5	153	11·2	139	30·6	18	7·8	156	10·8	143
% in social classes IV + V	32·4	35	32·2	38	32·3	37	41·6	4	36·6	15	18·9	128	38·9	10	39·2	9
Social class index	73	131	74	128	79	114	55	155	66	144	152	23	55	155	63	148
Social Survey J-index, 1954	1·49	145	5·36	81	2·20	127	1·07	151	3·34	107	8·37	42	1·01	152	2·41	121
VOTING																
General elections—1951 poll	83·9	74	87·1	13	85·7	36	79·7	143	81·4	127	77·7	149	82·8	103	87·0	15
1955 poll	77·9	80	81·7	24	82·8	11	73·5	136	72·3	142	68·8	154	73·9	132	80·3	42
1951 % voting left	49·1	86	49·5	81	49·6	79	63·3	15	55·1	44	24·8	156	57·8	31	66·9	9
1955 % voting left	48·8	79	48·0	84	48·5	82	64·3	11	51·6	60	29·8	145	57·1	24	67·8	8
Local elections 1956-58:																
% voting in contested elections	44	53	49	19	49	19	36	116	36	116	47	31	38	102	19	157
% uncontested seats	23	50	8	87	22	54	47	23	2	107	9	84	26	47	90	2
Votes as % of total electorate	34	82	42	34	39	53	16	148	35	74	43	26	25	118	4	156
HEALTH																
Infant mortality rate, 1950-52	39	14	33	42	47	1	38	18	37	22	32	49	37	22	42	7
Infant mortality rate, 1955-57	28	41	31	11	26	57	30	17	29	27	29	27	33	4	31	11
Expect. of life at year One, 1950-52	68·1	146	68·2	143	68·5	133	69·0	122	67·6	156	69·0	122	68·9	127	67·8	153
T.B. notification rate, 1957	38	150	70	111	65	115	84	89	85	86	53	135	58	127	112	47
Mortality rate 1957—lung cancer	120	68	140	35	128	47	109	93	190	3	93	125	163	13	133	42
Mortality rate 1957—other cancer	135	3	113	47	110	61	106	81	133	6	104	94	120	20	91	139
Mortality rate 1957—bronchitis	221	3	164	22	149	33	178	13	277	1	80	120	202	6	196	7
EDUCATION																
% with terminal edn. age under 15	80·8	11	77·8	21	73·4	45	82·1	10	83·3	6	59·0	117	83·6	4	82·7	7
% aged 15-24 in full-time education	5·7	135	5·7	135	7·2	104	6·1	126	4·6	152	14·5	22	4·9	149	6·4	119

| | Lancashire | | | | | | | | Leicestershire | | Lincolnshire | | | | | |
| | CROSBY | | HUYTON WITH ROBY | | LANCASTER | | STRETFORD | | LEICESTER | | GRIMSBY | | LINCOLN | | SCUNTHORPE | |
	Value	Rank	Value	Rank	Value	Rank	Value	Rank	Value	Rank	Value	Rank	Value	Rank	Value	Rank
POPULATION SIZE AND STRUCTURE																
Population ('000)	58	133	56	141	52	152	62	125	285	12	95	70	69	104	54	143
% of population aged 0-14	21.8	80	31.1	1	20.3	121	21.5	93	22.1	72	24.9	16	20.8	108	25.5	9
% of population aged 15-64	65.8	125	63.4	152	67.9	47	68.9	21	67.1	86	64.8	143	67.0	90	67.4	70
% of population aged 65 or over	12.4	26	5.5	156	11.8	46	9.6	106	10.8	70	10.3	85	12.2	34	7.1	151
Females per 1000 males	1254	10	1086	95	1139	41	1091	91	1117	68	1050	126	1040	138	967	155
Females per 1000 males, age 25-44	1220	9	1126	27	1056	65	1013	111	1034	87	973	144	993	132	935	155
% of females 20-24 ever married	34.0	154	40.3	139	48.4	74	49.5	63	52.6	26	55.5	10	52.7	25	59.1	1
POPULATION CHANGE																
1931-51—total (%)	15.5	68	973.2	1	18.4	57	8.9	86	10.7	81	2.3	106	4.8	99	60.7	21
1931-51—births and deaths (%)	6.4	111	170.4	1	7.2	103	7.0	104	8.8	81	12.7	50	5.1	123	27.1	12
1931-51—balance of change (%)	9.1	66	802.8	1	11.2	59	1.9	81	1.9	81	-10.4	128	-0.3	91	33.6	30
1951-58 (%)	0.2	74	9.7	18	-4.9	143	-0.2	79	-2.6	112	1.9	58	4.1	37	11.9	11
Birth rate ratio, 1950-52	101	58	114	19	103	48	102	54	103	48	121	9	96	81	119	10
Birth rate ratio, 1955-57	104	37	137	1	94	83	98	64	98	64	122	7	99	58	110	16
% illegitimate births, 1950-52	4.6	89	3.9	113	5.5	55	5.7	41	5.5	55	6.7	18	6.7	18	4.8	84
% illegitimate births, 1955-57	3.8	110	3.5	124	6.7	13	6.1	29	6.4	21	5.7	39	6.2	27	4.2	96
HOUSEHOLDS AND HOUSING																
% persons in private h/hlds	98.2	44	98.9	16	89.3	152	98.4	33	97.2	89	95.3	125	95.4	124	98.0	49
% one-person h/hlds	10.6	60	5.2	153	9.2	89	10.4	63	10.6	60	9.1	91	9.8	81	4.5	155
% six- or more person h/hlds	8.9	36	17.4	1	8.4	49	6.9	93	7.0	88	9.4	26	7.5	73	10.0	19
% 1-3-room dwellings	6.1	146	9.0	104	14.3	47	5.5	150	5.1	153	6.5	142	8.6	110	5.0	155
Persons per room	0.65	145	0.90	4	0.74	76	0.68	128	0.68	128	0.71	106	0.69	120	0.76	57
% overcrowded h/hlds (composite)	4.9	112	11.1	11	5.6	91	5.9	80	5.2	105	5.9	80	4.6	119	4.8	115
% h/hlds at over 1½ persons per room	3.6	110	10.3	4	4.3	79	4.1	86	3.6	110	4.3	79	3.7	103	3.7	103
% h/hlds in shared dwellings	17.1	54	7.6	118	10.0	99	18.6	45	12.6	75	11.1	89	7.6	118	7.7	116
% h/hlds with piped water	96	27	97	10	95	52	96	27	91	119	79	156	89	137	92	108
% h/hlds with W.C.	98	39	99	8	99	8	98	39	91	135	98	39	96	94	99	8
% h/hlds with 5 amenities	81	33	94	3	67	73	86	24	57	116	59	108	55	125	79	39
% h/hlds with 5, or bath missing	95	18	97	3	94	34	95	18	85	126	78	144	87	114	90	91
New-housing rate 1945-58—total	33	119	57	61	29	131	33	119	57	61	62	47	74	22	113	2
New-housing rate 1945-58—L.A.s	21	125	35	69	23	115	26	106	43	50	43	50	56	18	90	1
% L.A. of total houses 1945-58	63.7	109	61.4	116	79.9	53	76.6	61	74.8	71	68.2	97	75.2	69	79.3	55

128

ECONOMIC CHARACTER																
Occupied as % of total population	55·9	131	63·3	46	55·1	139	65·6	23	66·5	13	57·0	118	57·3	113	59·7	79
% of women in labour force	34·4	51	31·9	89	33·1	69	34·5	49	38·3	11	25·1	148	27·0	137	21·6	156
% in manufacture etc.	12·1	154	12·8	153	46·5	65	73·1	4	58·2	31	36·4	98	46·1	66	63·5	14
% in all service industries	66·4	9	69·3	5	37·4	79	15·9	156	29·9	110	40·3	70	37·7	77	22·2	148
% in retail	23·9	1	12·6	39	9·9	89	3·7	156	8·8	115	10·9	63	10·5	75	7·8	131
% in finance, etc.	1·9	48	0·8	145	1·6	64	0·6	152	1·4	83	1·6	64	1·6	64	0·9	140
% in professional services	8·8	48	10·7	23	11·1	19	2·0	157	5·9	102	5·8	108	6·8	77	4·2	140
Job ratio	54	144	28	157	111	38	166	2	114	25	110	43	111	38	125	9
Commuting ratio	79	47	90	28	35	104	175	2	25	137	35	104	27	131	33	111
Per capita retail sales, 1950	186	16	38	157	154	47	102	124	163	37	141	64	178	23	139	66
SOCIAL CLASS																
% in social classes I + II	29·0	22	12·9	120	14·7	95	19·7	51	15·7	81	14·1	107	15·8	78	10·9	142
% in social classes IV + V	21·6	120	33·6	30	35·9	18	22·2	111	23·2	102	42·9	2	25·9	81	34·3	25
Social class index	139	28	74	128	76	124	112	48	99	64	69	136	93	82	68	139
Social Survey J-index, 1954	11·24	26	4·57	89	2·11	133	10·11	34	2·12	132	2·13	130	6·83	58	12·74	15
VOTING																
General elections—1951 poll	79·8	141	84·8	53	86·1	32	83·4	88	83·7	79	82·0	118	87·7	6	82·4	110
1955 poll	73·7	133	78·5	71	80·3	42	76·1	107	78·0	78	73·3	139	85·1	1	74·7	122
1951 % voting left	29·1	150	51·3	71	46·8	100	42·0	116	54·2	50	56·6	37	54·1	51	57·5	33
1955 % voting left	32·0	138	52·7	53	43·5	105	39·1	117	50·5	70	53·8	39	56·2	29	55·0	32
Local elections 1956-58:																
% voting in contested elections	46	40	35	124	50	14	41	80	38	102	36	116	51	10	45	47
% uncontested seats	58	11	21	58	0	132	0	132	4	99	40	30	0	132	54	17
Votes as % of total electorate	19	139	28	109	50	3	41	40	37	64	22	123	51	1	19	139
HEALTH																
Infant mortality rate, 1950-52	32	49	33	42	43	5	23	112	26	90	32	49	29	67	30	63
Infant mortality rate, 1955-57	22	88	31	11	30	17	29	27	20	110	29	27	26	57	28	41
Expect. of life at year One, 1950-52	69·4	107	70·1	78	70·5	58	69·0	122	69·9	90	70·0	84	70·7	45	71·2	27
T.B. notification rate, 1957	152	11	141	16	71	110	60	121	85	86	60	121	143	14	109	51
Mortality rate 1957—lung cancer	147	24	184	4	105	100	175	7	102	108	119	74	106	96	141	31
Mortality rate 1957—other cancer	109	67	122	17	88	144	92	138	105	86	120	20	85	147	114	42
Mortality rate 1957—bronchitis	136	49	165	20	92	99	131	58	96	92	106	78	75	129	108	73
EDUCATION																
% with terminal edn. age under 15	51·0	139	76·0	32	72·5	50	64·7	96	74·7	42	79·6	15	66·0	88	72·1	52
% aged 15-24 in full-time education	15·5	13	6·5	116	7·7	91	8·2	77	7·9	84	5·6	139	7·3	100	7·3	100

	London		Middlesex													
	LONDON A.C.		ACTON		BRENTFORD & CHISWICK		EALING		EDMONTON		ENFIELD		FINCHLEY		HARROW	
	Value	Rank	Value	Rank	Value	Rank	Value	Rank	Value	Rank	Value	Rank	Value	Rank	Value	Rank
POPULATION SIZE AND STRUCTURE																
Population ('000)	3348	1	67	112	59	131	187	20	104	64	110	53	70	101	219	18
% of population aged 0-14	19·6	138	18·8	146	19·3	144	20·2	124	21·0	104	23·2	47	19·9	130	21·1	101
% of population aged 15-64	69·3	17	69·8	8	69·1	20	69·8	8	69·7	11	67·4	70	68·6	27	70·1	6
% of population aged 65 or over	11·1	64	11·4	55	11·6	51	10·0	98	9·3	116	9·4	111	12·5	24	8·8	132
Females per 1000 males	1138	42	1113	73	1152	35	1137	44	1083	98	1095	68	1245	13	1126	56
Females per 1000 males, age 25-44	1031	91	1031	91	1069	51	1104	33	1038	82	1079	46	1191	11	1146	22
% of females 20-24 ever married	44·5	118	48·0	82	48·0	82	44·3	121	46·9	97	48·4	74	33·8	156	38·9	146
POPULATION CHANGE																
1931-51—total (%)	-23·9	156	-3·6	131	-6·1	138	60·5	22	34·3	40	63·1	20	18·4	57	127·1	11
1931-51—births and deaths (%)	3·9	131	7·0	104	5·8	115	15·0	34	16·5	30	19·5	22	6·0	112	28·4	9
1931-51—balance of change (%)	-27·8	156	-10·6	129	-11·9	131	45·5	24	17·8	47	43·6	25	12·4	57	98·7	11
1951-58 (%)	-3·7	129	-3·1	118	-3·7	129	-2·3	109	-8·7	156	-1·6	90	-1·3	93	-2·4	110
Birth rate ratio, 1950-52	93	96	90	108	89	112	79	138	82	126	85	121	81	130	79	138
Birth rate ratio, 1955-57	89	107	81	132	83	123	83	123	79	136	82	127	80	135	84	119
% illegitimate births, 1950-52	7·0	12	5·6	49	5·6	49	5·1	72	4·0	108	3·1	146	4·0	108	3·7	123
% illegitimate births, 1955-57	8·4	2	6·3	24	7·0	11	5·0	66	3·5	124	3·8	110	3·9	105	4·1	99
HOUSEHOLDS AND HOUSING																
% persons in private h/hlds	94·4	134	98·4	33	98·7	20	98·3	38	98·3	38	98·3	38	98·0	49	98·6	24
% one-person h/hlds	19·7	2	13·0	22	15·0	9	10·1	73	8·3	107	7·5	122	12·8	27	6·6	138
% six- or more person h/hlds	5·5	131	5·5	131	5·5	131	6·1	113	6·4	105	7·2	80	6·3	108	6·6	101
% 1-3-room dwellings	31·3	10	12·1	67	19·7	24	13·9	52	7·7	121	8·8	106	12·1	67	8·6	110
Persons per room	0·83	16	0·77	48	0·77	48	0·74	76	0·75	66	0·74	76	0·69	120	0·71	106
% overcrowded h/hlds (composite)	11·1	11	7·5	44	8·3	34	6·5	65	7·0	53	5·5	96	5·5	96	4·9	112
% h/hlds at over 1½ persons per room	7·6	20	5·6	42	6·0	38	4·6	72	4·6	72	3·9	94	4·1	86	3·3	121
% h/hlds in shared dwellings	47·8	4	48·0	3	42·6	10	25·6	19	24·9	22	17·1	54	34·2	13	15·7	63
% h/hlds with piped water	85	148	90	130	89	137	95	52	92	108	95	52	94	76	96	27
% h/hlds with W.C.	89	141	95	110	95	110	98	39	96	94	98	39	97	72	98	39
% h/hlds with 5 amenities	57	116	71	61	63	91	86	24	69	67	76	48	86	24	92	6
% h/hlds with 5, or bath missing	80	141	88	107	87	114	94	34	91	80	94	34	93	52	95	18
New-housing rate 1945-58—total	46	85	28	133	24	141	28	133	29	131	38	106	26	136	22	145
New-housing rate 1945-58—L.A.s	42	53	23	115	18	132	19	128	27	100	24	110	13	144	12	147
% L.A. of total houses 1945-58	91·2	9	84·1	37	71·9	83	66·7	100	92·1	7	62·5	112	49·6	133	52·8	129

130

131

ECONOMIC CHARACTER																
Occupied as % of total population	66·1	18	66·8	9	64·8	32	63·5	43	65·2	28	62·7	54	59·6	83	61·4	68
% of women in labour force	38·6	7	37·1	23	37·3	20	35·2	39	34·5	49	32·8	73	36·9	25	32·7	75
% in manufacture etc.	30·9	112	67·1	10	54·5	43	43·8	73	59·6	29	60·7	18	24·5	129	31·4	110
% in all service industries	50·4	43	21·3	152	24·5	141	42·1	62	30·1	109	26·7	136	55·2	28	52·5	37
% in retail	8·1	128	4·1	154	5·5	152	11·6	49	8·9	109	7·4	137	15·0	18	12·4	42
% in finance, etc.	6·3	2	1·9	48	1·1	119	1·6	64	0·7	148	1·0	132	2·5	18	1·9	48
% in professional services	9·2	40	2·2	155	3·3	150	7·4	65	7·0	72	5·7	112	9·2	40	9·1	43
Job ratio	146	4	182	1	134	5	62	135	68	127	95	88	61	137	51	147
Commuting ratio	63	66	177	1	139	3	82	42	90	28	69	58	87	34	78	48
Per capita retail sales, 1950	196	6	116	107	129	75	122	94	90	133	111	114	155	45	104	121
SOCIAL CLASS																
% in social classes I+II	17·0	65	18·5	56	21·8	43	23·9	32	14·6	97	18·4	57	35·2	8	29·5	20
% in social classes IV+V	28·8	55	22·9	106	23·5	99	18·1	133	23·9	96	24·6	89	14·1	151	14·5	150
Social class index	92	84	107	54	115	47	137	30	94	78	103	60	188	6	170	15
Social Survey J-index, 1954	3·44	109	4·30	93	6·85	57	3·93	98	12·45	18	2·54	117	8·73	41	6·17	70
VOTING																
General elections—1951 poll	78·2	148	86·9	16	86·2	29	85·0	48	82·5	109	82·6	106	84·0	71	85·7	36
1955 poll	69·5	151	82·6	13	82·0	19	81·6	27	74·5	124	76·7	98	78·3	74	80·4	41
1951 % voting left	55·1	44	52·2	67	48·0	95	44·1	110	58·4	25	50·3	76	33·8	141	39·6	126
1955 % voting left	53·5	44	50·6	67	47·0	91	38·9	119	56·6	27	47·2	90	31·4	140	38·3	120
Local elections 1956-58:																
% voting in contested elections	31	144	47	31	48	24	43	61	21	155	32	141	41	80	39	94
% uncontested seats	7	90	0	132	0	132	0	132	0	132	0	132	0	132	21	58
Votes as % of total electorate	30	102	47	10	48	6	43	26	21	128	32	92	41	40	30	105
HEALTH																
Infant mortality rate, 1950-52	24	103	22	122	23	112	24	103	21	133	21	133	17	153	19	146
Infant mortality rate, 1955-57	22	88	21	102	16	150	18	137	18	137	17	144	17	144	17	144
Expect. of life at year One, 1950-52	69·6	100	70·3	69	70·3	69	71·1	31	70·3	69	71·2	27	70·6	51	71·1	31
T.B. notification rate, 1957	148	13	77	101	125	31	89	76	101	58	27	155	53	135	90	73
Mortality rate 1957—lung cancer	143	28	161	14	139	39	146	25	159	17	102	108	96	120	126	53
Mortality rate 1957—other cancer	109	67	107	76	106	81	113	47	105	86	96	125	111	56	114	42
Mortality rate 1957—bronchitis	138	45	139	43	148	35	107	74	96	92	85	113	76	128	72	134
EDUCATION																
% with terminal edn. age under 15	61·8	107	60·7	112	58·8	118	55·4	128	67·6	80	64·7	96	44·6	152	49·3	144
% aged 15-24 in full-time education	9·0	60	8·9	63	9·6	55	11·7	40	8·1	80	9·8	52	16·8	7	15·1	18

Middlesex

	HAYES & HARLINGTON		HENDON		HESTON & ISLEWORTH		HORNSEY		RUISLIP-NORTHWOOD		SOUTHALL		SOUTHGATE		TOTTENHAM	
	Value	Rank	Value	Rank	Value	Rank	Value	Rank	Value	Rank	Value	Rank	Value	Rank	Value	Rank
POPULATION SIZE AND STRUCTURE																
Population ('000)	66	117	156	31	107	56	98	69	68	107	56	140	73	96	127	41
% of population aged 0-14	24·7	20	19·5	141	19·6	138	19·0	145	24·0	32	20·6	113	17·3	152	20·6	113
% of population aged 15-64	69·5	13	70·3	4	70·5	3	68·2	36	67·7	53	69·8	8	67·9	47	68·4	30
% of population aged 65 or over	5·8	155	10·2	90	9·9	100	12·8	20	8·3	141	9·6	106	14·8	13	11·0	67
Females per 1000 males	1032	143	1169	28	1100	84	1225	17	1113	73	1079	101	1239	15	1108	79
Females per 1000 males, age 25-44	1030	93	1132	25	1063	57	1094	38	1123	29	1026	99	1178	12	1013	111
% of females 20-24 ever married	50·3	48	35·2	153	40·8	137	45·2	114	39·5	145	48·4	74	36·1	152	48·3	77
POPULATION CHANGE																
1931-51—total (%)	185·6	5	34·8	38	40·1	35	2·9	103	325·9	2	43·9	32	30·9	43	-19·5	153
1931-51—births and deaths (%)	51·0	3	11·7	57	13·1	46	5·0	124	53·4	2	18·7	24	4·2	129	6·6	110
1931-51—balance of change (%)	134·6	6	23·1	43	27·0	36	-2·1	98	272·5	2	25·2	40	26·7	37	-26·1	154
1951-58 (%)	3·3	44	-2·8	115	-1·6	99	-1·5	96	9·7	18	-5·5	148	-3·3	121	-7·3	153
Birth rate ratio, 1950-52	91	103	81	130	72	152	86	120	79	138	82	126	71	155	82	126
Birth rate ratio, 1955-57	92	94	78	141	75	147	90	104	86	115	89	107	77	145	81	132
% illegitimate births, 1950-52	3·8	116	5·7	41	4·2	102	4·9	79	3·6	131	4·0	108	2·7	154	4·7	86
% illegitimate births, 1955-57	3·5	124	4·6	84	3·8	110	6·6	15	3·4	129	4·5	88	3·3	133	5·3	58
HOUSEHOLDS AND HOUSING																
% persons in private h/hlds	99·5	9	96·9	103	96·6	111	97·9	54	97·3	86	95·2	126	98·6	24	99·1	13
% one-person h/hlds	4·2	156	9·5	84	7·6	119	17·1	4	5·6	150	7·0	131	11·4	46	11·8	41
% six- or more person h/hlds	8·7	41	7·3	77	7·2	80	4·5	155	5·8	120	7·4	75	4·0	157	6·8	97
% 1-3-room dwellings	8·5	113	14·3	47	9·3	99	10·5	83	12·6	65	8·7	108	7·0	134	14·5	45
Persons per room	0·81	25	0·73	85	0·74	76	0·73	85	0·72	94	0·78	40	0·64	150	0·81	25
% overcrowded h/hlds (composite)	7·1	51	6·5	65	5·9	80	6·8	57	3·3	145	7·9	38	3·0	150	9·1	28
% h/hlds at over 1½ persons per room	5·2	55	5·1	59	4·2	83	4·7	67	2·1	140	5·5	44	2·1	150	6·7	28
% h/hlds in shared dwellings	12·4	77	23·2	28	19·1	42	63·5	1	6·1	136	23·7	25	29·5	16	43·9	7
% h/hlds with piped water	95	52	95	52	94	76	91	119	97	10	95	52	95	52	85	148
% h/hlds with W.C.	97	72	98	39	98	39	97	72	99	8	99	8	98	39	91	135
% h/hlds with 5 amenities	90	12	91	9	82	31	81	33	96	1	79	39	89	13	49	139
% h/hlds with 5, or bath missing	94	34	94	34	93	52	89	100	97	3	94	34	94	34	80	141
New-housing rate 1945-58—total	52	70	26	136	30	128	17	150	60	55	24	141	21	147	13	154
New-housing rate 1945-58—L.A.s	29	92	17	137	15	141	10	151	28	95	18	132	7	156	12	147
% L.A. of total houses 1945-58	56·7	121	66·3	102	50·7	132	59·2	118	46·0	140	73·9	73	32·7	153	91·2	9

132

Economic character																
Occupied as % of total population	67·7	5	61·8	64	62·7	54	62·4	57	59·6	83	62·4	57	56·4	126	65·6	23
% of women in labour force	32·7	75	35·6	32	33·1	69	38·6	7	30·6	111	33·8	55	34·6	46	35·9	30
% in manufacture etc.	59·9	27	33·9	104	43·7	74	19·1	138	14·3	148	50·6	55	24·4	131	56·1	42
% in all service industries	16·2	155	48·0	46	41·4	64	52·6	36	55·0	30	28·5	118	52·5	37	28·5	118
% in retail	4·0	155	10·3	79	8·9	109	12·5	41	8·9	109	8·5	120	15·7	11	8·2	126
% in finance, etc.	0·4	156	2·0	41	1·4	83	2·2	34	1·2	106	0·9	140	2·7	11	1·1	119
% in professional services	2·3	154	10·9	22	9·4	37	12·0	15	8·6	50	6·6	81	11·0	21	5·1	125
Job ratio	121	14	74	123	75	122	42	154	70	126	86	107	53	146	85	110
Commuting ratio	107	8	90	28	87	34	94	19	97	15	92	24	100	11	95	18
Per capita retail sales, 1950	79	146	143	62	115	109	88	134	111	114	120	99	138	68	118	104
Social class																
% in social classes I + II	13·3	115	32·5	13	21·7	44	27·2	26	32·6	11	14·2	103	40·0	3	11·6	136
% in social classes IV + V	22·4	108	15·8	145	19·6	126	15·9	143	12·1	154	25·8	84	10·1	157	25·8	84
Social class index	95	73	171	14	126	34	156	20	197	5	89	91	238	1	82	108
Social Survey J-index, 1954	0·26	157	9·76	38	8·78	40	6·39	68	4·88	83	1·25	148	10·88	30	1·78	139
Voting																
General elections—1951 poll	82·2	113	84·0	71	83·8	76	82·6	106	84·5	59	84·0	71	84·1	68	79·9	139
1955 poll	76·6	100	76·9	94	78·9	65	76·3	106	79·8	49	76·5	102	77·1	90	70·2	149
1951 % voting left	64·9	12	38·9	127	45·9	103	41·3	119	36·4	134	57·9	30	22·6	157	62·4	17
1955 % voting left	60·4	18	39·2	116	42·7	109	39·8	115	34·8	131	57·2	23	20·0	157	60·0	19
Local elections 1956-58:																
% voting in contested elections	27	150	36	116	47	31	40	87	43	61	37	107	28	148	25	152
% uncontested seats	4	99	6	93	0	132	0	132	0	132	0	132	0	132	0	132
Votes as % of total electorate	26	115	35	74	47	10	40	46	43	26	37	64	28	109	25	118
Health																
Infant mortality rate, 1950-52	17	153	20	142	20	142	21	133	28	76	22	122	17	153	23	112
Infant mortality rate, 1955-57	16	150	20	116	22	88	19	127	21	102	19	127	18	137	22	88
Expect. of life at year One, 1950-52	70·6	51	70·6	51	70·5	58	71·2	27	73·1	2	71·5	17	70·9	38	69·6	100
T.B. notification rate, 1957	111	49	110	50	51	138	132	24	97	64	197	1	102	56	102	56
Mortality rate 1957—lung cancer	181	5	121	63	100	111	106	96	98	116	119	74	131	44	170	9
Mortality rate 1957—other cancer	130	7	112	51	104	94	101	108	107	76	81	153	111	56	116	33
Mortality rate 1957—bronchitis	161	25	100	90	85	113	129	60	50	150	104	85	80	120	132	55
Education																
% with terminal edn. age under 15	70·5	57	49·1	145	51·8	136	48·0	146	44·4	153	65·6	91	36·0	155	67·3	82
% aged 15-24 in full-time education	7·8	88	16·5	9	11·8	37	13·2	28	15·5	13	7·6	93	19·3	3	6·5	116

	TWICKENHAM		UXBRIDGE		WEMBLEY		WILLESDEN		WOOD GREEN		GREAT YARMOUTH		NORWICH		NORTHAMPTON	
	Value	Rank	Value	Rank	Value	Rank	Value	Rank	Value	Rank	Value	Rank	Value	Rank	Value	Rank
POPULATION SIZE AND STRUCTURE																
Population ('000)	106	59	56	139	131	39	180	23	52	151	51	156	121	43	104	63
% of population aged 0-14	20·1	127	22·5	61	19·5	141	20·7	110	19·4	143	23·0	50	21·8	80	21·2	98
% of population aged 15-64	68·1	39	69·2	19	71·3	1	69·3	17	68·3	33	64·0	149	66·0	121	66·6	106
% of population aged 65 or over	11·8	46	8·3	141	9·2	121	10·0	98	12·3	30	13·0	18	12·2	34	12·2	34
Females per 1000 males	1150	37	1055	119	1120	64	1126	56	1149	39	1146	40	1130	53	1121	63
Females per 1000 males, age 25-44	1095	37	1059	61	1098	35	1049	73	1079	46	1065	52	1036	84	1021	103
% of females 20-24 ever married	43·2	125	45·2	114	39·9	142	43·3	124	45·7	109	50·0	56	50·9	41	50·3	48
POPULATION CHANGE																
1931-51—total (%)	33·2	41	75·5	18	99·7	14	-2·9	130	-3·8	132	-10·0	147	-4·0	133	8·2	88
1931-51—births and deaths (%)	9·6	74	22·1	17	25·0	15	11·2	61	4·2	129	3·8	132	5·7	116	5·7	116
1931-51—balance of change (%)	23·6	42	53·4	19	74·7	15	-14·1	139	-8·0	116	-13·8	137	-9·7	126	2·5	78
1951-58 (%)	-2·0	106	12·8	9	-3·5	125	-3·7	129	-6·0	150	0·6	68	-2·0	106	-3·6	127
Birth rate ratio, 1950-52	79	138	95	87	71	155	87	117	77	145	94	91	101	58	93	96
Birth rate ratio, 1955-57	83	123	103	41	73	153	91	100	78	141	92	94	94	83	91	100
% illegitimate births, 1950-52	4·8	84	4·3	98	3·0	148	7·0	12	3·7	123	5·4	60	6·4	26	5·7	41
% illegitimate births, 1955-57	4·3	94	3·5	124	3·3	133	8·8	1	3·7	115	7·9	4	6·0	31	6·3	24
HOUSEHOLDS AND HOUSING																
% persons in private h/hlds	97·6	74	92·7	143	99·7	2	97·9	52	99·6	5	95·0	130	97·0	98	96·5	113
% one-person h/hlds	10·8	55	6·0	147	7·1	129	12·8	27	13·1	20	11·8	41	11·3	48	10·3	65
% six- or more person h/hlds	5·7	124	7·9	62	5·4	135	7·0	88	5·0	148	7·0	88	8·0	60	6·2	111
% 1-3-room dwellings	14·2	49	7·6	123	11·5	71	16·9	33	11·4	73	7·3	129	10·2	88	12·2	66
Persons per room	0·71	106	0·74	76	0·72	94	0·85	11	0·75	66	0·60	156	0·68	128	0·68	128
% overcrowded h/hlds (composite)	5·1	108	5·4	100	5·8	83	12·4	6	6·0	76	2·6	153	4·1	128	4·5	121
% h/hlds at over 1½ persons per room	3·6	110	4·1	86	3·4	117	9·9	7	4·2	83	2·1	150	3·1	126	3·3	121
% h/hlds in shared dwellings	20·4	38	10·1	95	21·0	34	57·8	2	43·2	8	6·0	137	6·5	132	11·9	83
% h/hlds with piped water	94	76	94	76	97	10	89	137	90	130	92	108	94	76	95	52
% h/hlds with W.C.	98	39	97	72	98	39	94	119	94	119	98	39	95	110	97	72
% h/hlds with 5 amenities	77	45	85	28	95	2	72	55	68	71	47	142	56	120	61	95
% h/hlds with 5, or bath missing	92	67	93	52	96	136	86	121	87	114	90	91	91	80	93	52
New-housing rate 1945-58—total	30	128	89	6	26	136	8	157	14	153	79	15	71	27	48	80
New-housing rate 1945-58—L.A.s	16	139	48	36	14	142	4	157	9	153	62	8	58	14	33	76
% L.A. of total houses 1945-58	54·8	125	53·7	127	54·0	126	46·5	138	65·0	107	78·6	56	81·0	47	68·3	96

	1	2	3	4	5	6	7	8	9	10	11	12	13	14	15	16
ECONOMIC CHARACTER																
Occupied as % of total population	54	62·7	94	58·9	143	54·6	60	62·2	11	66·6	50	62·9	37	64·1	89	59·3
% of women in labour force	39	35·2	66	33·2	114	30·4	36	35·4	23	37·1	57	33·7	101	31·2	75	32·7
% in manufacture etc.	53	51·5	78	42·1	101	35·4	54	32·1	47	53·5	25	60·2	114	29·3	122	27·7
% in all service industries	100	33·8	73	39·4	60	42·7	54	43·8	129	27·6	126	28·0	40	52·2	33	53·4
% in retail	84	10·0	72	10·6	34	13·0	11	15·7	143	6·8	130	7·9	122	8·4	63	10·9
% in finance, etc.	59	1·7	3	4·0	83	1·4	55	1·8	119	1·1	119	1·1	119	1·1	41	2·0
% in professional services	70	7·2	74	6·9	90	6·2	127	4·9	144	5·2	146	3·7	16	11·8	56	7·9
Job ratio	58	105	14	121	51	106	133	63	92	93	114	81	114	81	139	60
Commuting ratio	135	26	101	36	153	18	5	110	16	96	5	110	51	76	46	80
Per capita retail sales, 1950	42	158	20	183	50	152	25	177	107	116	97	121	75	129	131	94
SOCIAL CLASS																
% in social classes I + II	78	15·8	88	15·2	61	17·7	51	19·7	68	16·7	19	29·6	48	20·1	23	28·1
% in social classes IV + V	124	20·1	89	24·6	35	32·4	129	18·7	87	24·8	152	13·3	122	21·3	140	17·0
Social class index	51	108	73	95	93	88	36	124	67	98	7	179	46	116	21	153
Social Survey J-index, 1954	46	7·89	48	7·75	104	3·65	78	5·53	106	3·54	46	7·89	53	7·21	61	6·68
VOTING																
General elections—1951 poll	23	86·5	65	84·2	93	83·3	125	81·7	112	82·3	20	86·6	56	84·7	128	81·3
1955 poll	13	82·6	94	76·9	54	79·6	121	75·1	119	75·2	30	81·5	24	81·7	92	77·0
1951 % voting left	54	53·7	46	55·0	89	48·8	41	55·8	28	58·2	124	39·9	84	49·2	129	37·9
1955 % voting left	53	52·7	42	53·6	78	48·9	38	53·9	28	56·3	128	36·2	63	51·0	144	30·2
Local elections 1956-58:																
% voting in contested elections	14	50	24	48	5	53	124	35	146	29	71	42	87	40	107	37
% uncontested seats	54	22	45	27	63	19	132	0	132	0	132	0	77	11	95	5
Votes as % of total electorate	34	42	59	38	46	40	74	35	107	29	34	42	64	37	68	36
HEALTH																
Infant mortality rate, 1950-52	112	23	112	23	96	25	90	26	96	25	133	21	133	21	122	22
Infant mortality rate, 1955-57	116	20	150	16	57	26	127	19	116	20	137	18	137	18	144	17
Expect. of life at year One, 1950-52	69	70·3	64	70·4	95	69·8	84	70·0	64	70·4	12	71·6	22	71·3	58	70·5
T.B. notification rate, 1957	114	66	64	97	156	20	73	90	35	122	135	53	109	72	94	82
Mortality rate 1957—lung cancer	116	98	139	82	35	140	78	116	10	169	28	143	19	158	53	126
Mortality rate 1957—other cancer	114	99	135	93	56	111	94	104	14	124	42	114	110	100	125	96
Mortality rate 1957—bronchitis	99	92	115	84	124	78	99	92	58	131	111	86	82	105	145	57
EDUCATION																
% with terminal edn. age under 15	62	70·1	67	69·3	38	75·4	131	54·2	106	62·0	149	46·8	100	63·6	136	51·8
% aged 15-24 in full-time education	112	6·9	94	7·5	84	7·9	49	10·0	74	8·4	20	14·9	80	8·1	25	13·8

	Northumberland				Nottinghamshire				Oxfordshire		Soke of Peterborough		Somerset		Hampshire	
	NEWCASTLE UPON TYNE		TYNEMOUTH		NOTTINGHAM		MANSFIELD		OXFORD		PETER-BOROUGH		BATH		BOURNE-MOUTH	
	Value	Rank	Value	Rank	Value	Rank	Value	Rank	Value	Rank	Value	Rank	Value	Rank	Value	Rank
POPULATION SIZE AND STRUCTURE																
Population ('000)	292	11	67	115	306	8	51	155	99	67	53	147	79	87	145	35
% of population aged 0-14	22.7	57	24.1	29	23.2	47	22.6	59	20.5	116	20.7	110	20.0	128	17.2	153
% of population aged 15-64	67.5	63	65.8	125	66.9	94	67.2	82	68.3	33	68.0	43	65.6	131	63.9	150
% of population aged 65 or over	9.8	102	10.1	95	9.9	100	10.2	90	11.2	61	11.3	58	14.4	14	18.9	3
Females per 1000 males	1099	85	1092	90	1104	81	1053	123	1125	58	1048	130	1223	18	1396	3
Females per 1000 males, age 25-44	1034	87	1042	79	1020	105	987	136	1007	116	968	146	1118	31	1257	3
% of females 20-24 ever married	45.4	112	49.9	59	55.6	9	57.6	6	43.1	127	50.8	42	47.1	95	42.8	129
POPULATION CHANGE																
1931-51—total (%)	1.9	107	1.0	111	10.8	80	11.5	77	22.5	53	22.7	52	15.2	71	24.0	51
1931-51—births and deaths (%)	8.5	86	10.1	70	9.6	74	11.9	56	12.0	54	7.9	94	-0.7	146	-5.7	152
1931-51—balance of change (%)	-6.6	113	-9.1	121	1.2	86	-0.4	92	10.5	60	14.8	51	15.9	48	29.7	32
1951-58 (%)	-6.6	151	3.2	46	2.3	52	1.9	58	5.5	32	4.4	34	1.4	64	-0.9	87
Birth rate ratio, 1950-52	106	38	117	12	107	36	102	54	91	103	96	81	92	99	76	147
Birth rate ratio, 1955-57	109	20	108	25	101	48	97	69	84	119	113	11	89	107	82	127
% illegitimate births, 1950-52	4.5	93	4.9	79	7.3	6	5.5	55	7.0	12	6.6	21	4.6	89	7.4	4
% illegitimate births, 1955-57	4.4	92	4.0	102	7.7	8	4.9	70	8.0	3	5.5	46	4.8	75	7.9	5
HOUSEHOLDS AND HOUSING																
% persons in private h/hlds	97.2	89	96.9	103	96.9	103	97.5	78	92.8	141	96.9	103	94.8	131	88.7	154
% one-person h/hlds	11.7	43	11.1	51	11.7	43	7.8	115	11.3	48	9.1	103	14.3	16	16.5	5
% six- or more person h/hlds	8.6	44	8.5	46	8.2	56	7.7	67	8.1	58	7.0	88	5.8	120	5.6	127
% 1-3-room dwellings	40.6	5	35.9	8	9.0	104	10.7	78	8.0	119	7.0	43	12.9	61	17.5	29
Persons per room	0.89	6	0.84	13	0.73	85	0.73	85	0.71	106	0.67	135	0.71	106	0.66	140
% overcrowded h/hlds (composite)	16.3	3	11.1	11	6.6	61	5.2	105	5.7	86	4.2	125	6.0	76	6.0	76
% h/hlds at over 1½ persons per room	12.9	3	8.6	13	5.3	50	3.9	94	4.0	90	3.2	124	3.8	98	4.5	75
% h/hlds in shared dwellings	12.1	80	9.4	102	11.5	86	8.5	108	18.7	43	10.1	95	30.0	15	19.8	40
% h/hlds with piped water	90	130	87	144	96	27	96	27	94	76	90	130	92	108	89	137
% h/hlds with W.C.	92	129	91	135	98	39	98	39	98	39	94	119	96	94	92	129
% h/hlds with 5 amenities	65	81	68	71	54	129	70	63	72	55	58	112	65	81	77	45
% h/hlds with 5, or bath missing	85	126	82	135	94	34	94	34	93	52	87	114	89	100	86	121
New-housing rate 1945-58—total	50	76	66	38	51	73	66	38	46	85	78	17	48	80	49	77
New-housing rate 1945-58—L.A.s	44	46	49	31	39	57	52	24	38	61	55	20	27	100	23	115
% L.A. of total houses 1945-58	88.1	15	73.5	74	77.3	60	78.5	58	82.6	42	70.6	87	56.2	123	46.1	139

ECONOMIC CHARACTER																
Occupied as % of total population	59·8	77	57·3	113	65·3	26	58·7	96	59·2	91	58·5	101	56·2	128	49·4	154
% of women in labour force	31·2	101	28·3	128	36·2	29	27·9	132	33·4	61	26·5	139	33·5	60	37·2	22
% in manufacture etc.	36·5	99	39·8	84	50·6	55	45·1	69	39·4	87	43·4	75	24·9	128	15·8	145
% in all service industries	45·8	50	36·1	85	35·7	88	37·3	81	47·1	48	33·3	102	57·1	24	65·6	11
% in retail	11·6	49	11·2	56	9·9	89	13·1	33	10·1	83	10·7	67	14·0	22	17·6	5
% in finance, etc.	2·5	18	1·5	71	2·0	41	1·8	55	1·5	71	1·4	83	1·7	59	3·6	5
% in professional services	7·8	57	6·5	84	6·8	77	8·0	55	17·4	5	5·5	117	12·4	12	9·5	36
Job ratio	133	6	86	107	113	29	100	75	132	7	119	17	99	79	106	51
Commuting ratio	63	66	51	79	43	89	78	48	42	90	39	95	30	120	30	120
Per capita retail sales, 1950	192	9	96	129	168	30	185	17	202	3	183	20	183	20	236	2
SOCIAL CLASS																
% in social classes I+II	14·9	91	14·9	91	13·3	115	12·5	125	19·3	53	17·9	59	23·0	37	29·1	21
% in social classes IV+V	28·4	58	32·9	33	33·4	32	32·7	34	27·2	66	23·2	102	22·3	110	17·6	134
Social class index	87	95	80	110	75	125	74	128	100	62	105	58	121	39	153	21
Social Survey J-index, 1954	5·70	74	6·96	56	4·84	84	1·86	138	4·04	96	1·64	141	4·64	86	11·56	24
VOTING																
General elections—1951 poll	85·1	44	84·5	59	83·1	97	83·3	93	82·0	118	86·8	17	85·6	38	79·2	146
1955 poll	77·4	85	79·3	61	76·8	96	78·3	74	78·2	77	83·0	10	82·5	15	73·5	136
1951 % voting left	53·1	58	43·6	112	53·9	53	69·9	5	44·0	111	47·3	98	44·7	108	30·0	147
1955 % voting left	52·7	53	35·8	129	50·8	65	68·5	7	37·6	124	46·7	93	37·4	125	27·9	147
Local elections 1956–58:																
% voting in contested elections	34	128	35	124	36	116	31	144	40	87	46	40	50	14	35	124
% uncontested seats	40	30	56	14	7	90	33	37	25	48	12	73	38	33	20	61
Votes as % of total electorate	21	125	16	148	35	74	20	133	36	68	39	53	31	99	28	109
HEALTH																
Infant mortality rate, 1950–52	32	49	41	9	30	63	33	42	21	133	23	112	24	103	28	76
Infant mortality rate, 1955–57	27	50	30	17	24	71	30	17	20	116	27	50	20	116	21	102
Expect. of life at year One, 1950–52	68·1	146	69·4	107	69·9	90	70·2	74	71·5	17	70·0	84	70·6	51	70·7	45
T.B. notification rate, 1957	158	10	171	3	131	26	54	132	129	27	83	91	48	143	121	38
Mortality rate 1957—lung cancer	140	35	120	68	127	50	73	146	109	93	122	62	98	116	76	145
Mortality rate 1957—other cancer	125	12	124	14	104	94	103	102	84	150	98	118	90	141	99	114
Mortality rate 1957—bronchitis	137	47	80	120	149	33	104	85	81	117	69	136	57	145	66	142
EDUCATION																
% with terminal edn. age under 15	70·5	57	76·8	26	79·6	15	79·0	17	58·8	118	71·1	56	52·3	134	61·1	111
% aged 15–24 in full-time education	7·4	97	6·1	126	5·3	147	6·9	112	15·6	12	8·8	66	11·8	37	14·3	23

Hampshire · Staffordshire

	PORTSMOUTH		SOUTHAMPTON		GOSPORT		SMETHWICK		STOKE-ON-TRENT		WALSALL		WEST BROMWICH		WOLVER-HAMPTON	
	Value	Rank	Value	Rank	Value	Rank	Value	Rank	Value	Rank	Value	Rank	Value	Rank	Value	Rank
POPULATION SIZE AND STRUCTURE																
Population ('000)	234	17	178	24	58	134	76	89	275	13	115	49	88	74	163	28
% of population aged 0-14	22·2	67	23·7	38	25·2	14	22·3	63	24·1	29	25·3	11	24·8	18	23·9	35
% of population aged 15-64	66·4	114	65·6	131	66·4	114	67·3	77	67·4	70	65·6	131	66·9	94	66·8	99
% of population aged 65 or over	11·4	55	10·7	72	8·4	138	10·4	80	8·5	137	9·1	125	8·3	141	9·3	116
Females per 1000 males	1025	48	1071	108	939	157	1086	95	1068	110	1071	108	1036	141	1055	119
Females per 1000 males, age 25-44	1000	124	1009	113	1021	103	1000	124	994	128	1027	97	957	149	987	136
% of females 20-24 ever married	56·0	7	52·3	28	58·7	3	51·2	38	52·6	26	50·1	53	51·1	40	49·5	63
POPULATION CHANGE																
1931-51—total (%)	-7·5	140	1·3	110	51·6	27	-9·5	146	-0·6	116	11·1	78	8·2	88	17·3	63
1931-51—births and deaths (%)	8·4	89	10·5	67	21·6	19	9·0	78	11·5	60	15·5	31	14·2	41	13·3	43
1931-51—balance of change (%)	-15·9	144	-9·2	122	30·0	31	-18·5	148	-12·1	133	-4·4	103	-6·0	110	-4·0	75
1951-58 (%)	-4·6	142	11·8	13	11·9	11	-4·9	143	-1·5	96	0·4	70	6·1	29	-9·1	157
Birth rate ratio, 1950-52	101	58	110	28	116	14	96	81	103	48	115	17	111	25	105	41
Birth rate ratio, 1955-57	101	48	109	20	109	20	81	132	94	83	103	41	101	48	94	83
% illegitimate births, 1950-52	6·3	27	6·6	21	4·6	89	3·8	116	3·7	123	4·2	102	3·3	143	4·5	93
% illegitimate births, 1955-57	6·2	27	5·7	39	4·1	99	6·4	21	3·5	124	4·2	96	3·7	115	6·3	24
HOUSEHOLDS AND HOUSING																
% persons in private h/hlds	91·7	147	96·8	108	89·4	150	99·6	5	98·3	37	98·8	18	98·2	44	97·7	70
% one-person h/hlds	11·3	48	10·2	69	8·2	108	8·9	94	7·3	126	8·0	111	7·1	129	8·0	111
% six- or more person h/hlds	7·9	62	8·7	41	7·6	70	8·0	60	9·8	21	11·4	9	11·5	8	9·3	28
% 1-3-room dwellings	8·5	113	9·3	99	9·3	99	6·4	143	9·4	97	7·4	127	14·1	50	8·0	119
Persons per room	0·70	115	0·75	66	0·72	94	0·74	76	0·84	13	0·80	30	0·84	13	0·75	66
% overcrowded h/hlds (composite)	5·6	91	7·6	41	3·8	136	7·4	48	9·5	25	7·5	44	11·0	13	6·3	70
% h/hlds at over 1½ persons per room	3·6	110	5·3	50	2·6	143	4·7	67	7·1	24	6·2	35	8·6	13	4·7	67
% h/hlds in shared dwellings	20·6	36	23·9	24	9·2	104	16·3	58	12·2	78	8·5	108	13·1	72	11·8	84
% h/hlds with piped water	93	95	93	95	95	51	92	108	93	95	90	130	81	154	90	130
% h/hlds with W.C.	97	72	97	72	98	39	95	110	97	72	93	125	85	149	96	94
% h/hlds with 5 amenities	64	87	69	68	74	49	44	150	46	144	56	120	57	116	66	76
% h/hlds with 5, or bath missing	92	67	92	67	93	52	88	107	89	100	86	121	76	146	89	100
New-housing rate 1945-58—total	60	55	72	25	68	33	19	148	65	42	65	42	84	11	53	69
New-housing rate 1945-58—L.A.s	50	28	48	36	42	53	18	132	58	14	57	16	59	11	44	46
% L.A. of total houses 1945-58	82·7	41	66·3	102	61·8	114	96·8	2	90·4	12	86·9	20	69·8	90	82·5	43

ECONOMIC CHARACTER

	1	2	3	4	5	6	7	8
Occupied as % of total population	55.9 (131)	56.8 (120)	58.1 (104)	66.2 (17)	68.7 (2)	64.1 (37)	66.6 (11)	64.1 (37)
% of women in labour force	25.2 (147)	26.2 (142)	20.9 (157)	35.2 (39)	37.3 (20)	32.6 (78)	33.0 (7)	32.0 (86)
% in manufacture etc.	29.0 (116)	30.9 (112)	16.3 (143)	75.1 (154)	65.2 (13)	56.9 (37)	68.1 (149)	56.7 (38)
% in all service industries	56.6 (25)	41.3 (65)	74.6 (2)	17.9 (149)	22.9 (145)	28.4 (122)	22.1 (146)	28.6 (115)
% in retail	10.6 (72)	11.5 (51)	7.0 (139)	6.1	7.6 (133)	10.6 (72)	6.5	8.9 (109)
% in finance, etc.	1.4 (83)	2.3 (27)	0.7 (148)	0.6 (152)	1.0 (132)	1.0 (132)	0.9 (140)	1.3 (96)
% in professional services	6.6 (81)	7.0 (72)	3.5 (149)	2.6 (153)	4.8 (129)	5.1 (125)	3.9 (143)	5.7 (112)
Job ratio	105 (58)	106 (51)	95 (88)	121 (14)	110 (43)	90 (98)	97 (83)	115 (23)
Commuting ratio	21 (147)	33 (111)	38 (98)	96 (16)	29 (123)	48 (82)	64 (63)	45 (86)
Per capita retail sales, 1950	123 (90)	143 (62)	80 (144)	119 (102)	122 (94)	124 (85)	106 (118)	168 (30)

SOCIAL CLASS

	1	2	3	4	5	6	7	8
% in social classes I + II	14.2 (103)	17.9 (59)	12.9 (120)	11.0 (140)	9.7 (151)	12.6 (124)	10.6 (144)	15.3 (86)
% in social classes IV + V	23.2 (102)	26.6 (71)	22.1 (113)	27.1 (68)	35.6 (20)	29.7 (50)	30.3 (47)	27.6 (63)
Social class index	95 (73)	98 (67)	94 (78)	78 (118)	63 (148)	78 (118)	72 (133)	89 (91)
Social Survey J-index, 1954	7.74 (49)	9.20 (39)	16.64 (8)	1.18 (150)	0.72 (155)	2.10 (134)	1.64 (141)	2.44 (119)

VOTING

	1	2	3	4	5	6	7	8
General elections—1951 poll	82.0 (118)	83.6 (81)	80.9 (133)	83.5 (83)	83.4 (88)	83.1 (97)	80.5 (135)	83.4 (88)
1955 poll	74.2 (127)	78.5 (71)	74.2 (127)	75.5 (116)	73.4 (138)	78.7 (66)	70.2 (149)	74.6 (123)
1951 % voting left	40.8 (122)	52.3 (65)	39.8 (125)	60.6 (20)	67.3 (8)	52.3 (65)	64.2 (13)	54.8 (48)
1955 % voting left	38.1 (121)	49.7 (74)	37.3 (126)	58.2 (21)	64.7 (10)	54.7 (35)	61.8 (13)	50.5 (70)
Local elections 1956-58:								
% voting in contested elections	41 (80)	48 (24)	46 (40)	38 (102)	32 (141)	36 (116)	33 (136)	34 (130)
% uncontested seats	0 (132)	0 (132)	16 (67)	0 (132)	29 (42)	6 (93)	14 (70)	40 (30)
Votes as % of total electorate	42 (34)	48 (6)	40 (46)	38 (59)	22 (123)	34 (82)	28 (109)	22 (123)

HEALTH

	1	2	3	4	5	6	7	8
Infant mortality rate, 1950-52	27 (84)	28 (76)	23 (112)	31 (57)	34 (36)	34 (36)	32 (49)	36 (25)
Infant mortality rate, 1955-57	23 (78)	32 (6)	19 (127)	24 (71)	29 (27)	24 (27)	24 (71)	29 (27)
Expect. of life at year One, 1950-52	70.2 (74)	70.0 (84)	70.7 (45)	69.8 (95)	67.9 (151)	69.2 (116)	68.8 (130)	69.9 (90)
T.B. notification rate, 1957	84 (89)	120 (40)	103 (55)	140 (18)	89 (76)	140 (18)	91 (72)	127 (29)
Mortality rate 1957—lung cancer	94 (124)	110 (91)	96 (120)	88 (130)	120 (68)	124 (59)	123 (61)	120 (68)
Mortality rate 1957—other cancer	109 (67)	100 (110)	98 (118)	100 (110)	121 (18)	119 (23)	104 (94)	112 (51)
Mortality rate 1957—bronchitis	87 (108)	102 (87)	68 (139)	161 (25)	149 (33)	118 (65)	205 (5)	137 (47)

EDUCATION

	1	2	3	4	5	6	7	8
% with terminal edn. age under 15	65.5 (92)	69.2 (69)	64.6 (98)	76.6 (27)	86.2 (1)	79.8 (13)	79.9 (12)	78.5 (20)
% aged 15-24 in full-time education	7.4 (97)	9.0 (60)	5.8 (131)	5.3 (147)	4.6 (152)	5.8 (131)	4.4 (154)	6.1 (126)

	Staffordshire		Suffolk		Surrey												
	NEWCASTLE UNDER LYME		IPSWICH		CROYDON		CARSHALTON		COULSDON & PURLEY		EPSOM & EWELL		ESHER		MERTON & MORDEN	
	Value	Rank	Value	Rank	Value	Rank	Value	Rank	Value	Rank	Value	Rank	Value	Rank	Value	Rank
POPULATION SIZE AND STRUCTURE																
Population ('000)	70	99	105	62	250	15	63	123	64	120	68	108	51	154	75	94
% of population aged 0-14	23·6	40	22·8	55	21·3	95	22·1	72	19·9	130	18·7	148	21·7	84	19·6	138
% of population aged 15-64	67·3	77	65·6	131	66·5	110	70·2	5	67·5	63	68·9	21	66·4	114	70·9	2
% of population aged 65 or over	9·1	125	11·6	51	12·2	34	7·7	149	12·6	22	12·4	26	11·9	44	9·5	108
Females per 1000 males	1077	103	1099	85	1166	30	1134	48	1238	16	1169	28	1197	21	1118	66
Females per 1000 males, age 25-44	1006	120	1063	57	1090	40	1153	16	1227	8	1149	19	1174	13	1099	34
% of females 20-24 ever married	51·5	37	52·9	24	46·4	104	36·5	151	31·3	157	33·9	155	38·4	147	39·9	142
POPULATION CHANGE																
1931-51—total (%)	27·9	45	19·7	56	7·2	91	119·4	12	60·3	23	93·2	16	58·7	24	81·3	17
1931-51—births and deaths (%)	14·8	36	10·8	66	7·6	97	25·1	14	11·2	61	15·5	31	12·4	52	18·9	23
1931-51—balance of change (%)	13·1	55	8·9	67	-0·4	92	94·3	12	49·1	21	77·7	14	46·3	22	62·4	17
1951-58 (%)	5·9	30	8·2	23	-0·2	79	-3·9	134	7·5	24	-0·7	85	10·2	16	-5·2	146
Birth rate ratio, 1950-52	99	68	110	28	90	108	78	143	79	138	70	157	84	122	73	149
Birth rate ratio, 1955-57	108	25	108	25	89	107	74	150	94	83	72	155	91	100	71	157
% illegitimate births, 1950-52	4·1	104	5·3	63	5·2	67	3·6	131	2·6	156	3·6	131	3·3	143	2·9	149
% illegitimate births, 1955-57	3·0	144	7·1	10	4·9	70	3·3	133	2·3	155	3·4	129	3·2	138	3·8	110
HOUSEHOLDS AND HOUSING																
% persons in private h/hlds	99·0	15	97·2	89	97·4	83	96·1	120	92·2	145	86·2	156	97·5	78	99·6	5
% one-person h/hlds	7·0	131	9·3	87	10·7	58	6·1	145	6·7	137	6·9	133	8·0	111	7·1	129
% six- or more person h/hlds	8·5	44	6·9	93	6·2	111	9·1	33	5·1	144	5·4	135	6·9	93	5·4	135
% 1-3-room dwellings	9·0	104	7·1	131	8·5	113	19·9	22	5·1	153	7·0	134	10·6	80	15·6	38
Persons per room	0·77	48	0·68	128	0·69	120	0·80	38	0·62	155	0·67	135	0·65	145	0·74	76
% overcrowded h/hlds (composite)	5·7	86	3·6	139	5·0	110	7·9	38	1·7	155	2·9	152	3·2	147	5·0	110
% h/hlds at over 1½ persons per room	4·2	83	2·3	146	3·4	117	6·8	27	1·2	157	2·2	148	2·3	146	3·6	110
% h/hlds in shared dwellings	7·7	116	9·2	104	22·7	29	10·2	92	8·2	112	7·8	115	7·4	124	13·9	69
% h/hlds with piped water	96	27	97	10	94	76	96	27	98	2	97	10	93	95	96	27
% h/hlds with W.C.	98	39	98	39	98	39	99	8	99	8	99	8	96	94	99	8
% h/hlds with 5 amenities	66	76	66	76	74	49	92	6	93	4	88	16	79	39	91	9
% h/hlds with 5, or bath missing	94	34	96	9	93	52	96	9	97	3	97	3	92	67	96	9
New-housing rate 1945-58—total	86	8	74	22	34	116	17	150	67	36	39	102	84	11	22	145
New-housing rate 1945-58—L.A.s	63	7	49	31	22	122	11	149	22	122	17	137	30	87	17	137
% L.A. of total houses 1945-58	73·1	78	66·6	101	66·0	104	63·0	110	33·2	151	41·9	146	35·5	149	76·2	62

141

ECONOMIC CHARACTER																
Occupied as % of total population	63·0	49	56·1	129	58·9	94	63·7	42	49·7	152	49·6	153	56·4	126	62·1	61
% of women in labour force	32·6	78	28·3	81	33·3	63	35·6	32	30·6	111	31·8	91	32·3	81	33·0	71
% in manufacture etc.	54·0	46	40·5	81	36·6	97	15·0	146	13·7	151	13·8	150	28·4	119	66·5	12
% in all service industries	33·9	99	40·3	70	43·5	57	71·6	3	65·1	12	71·2	4	59·7	17	26·0	138
% in retail	11·4	53	12·0	48	13·4	29	14·0	22	12·2	43	13·3	31	7·5	134	7·0	139
% in finance, etc.	1·2	106	2·2	34	2·3	27	1·0	132	1·8	55	2·2	34	2·6	15	1·0	132
% in professional services	5·9	102	7·6	62	8·2	53	35·0	1	21·7	3	29·7	2	12·4	12	4·3	138
Job ratio	92	94	104	65	78	120	30	155	47	151	54	144	82	112	67	129
Commuting ratio	69	58	25	137	64	63	88	31	86	37	72	54	81	44	114	4
Per capita retail sales, 1950	100	125	158	42	150	52	66	153	70	150	103	122	106	118	80	144
SOCIAL CLASS																
% in social classes I+II	16·3	73	16·1	76	24·8	30	22·4	41	45·4	1	35·6	6	37·4	4	23·9	32
% in social classes IV+V	31·8	40	27·2	66	18·4	131	22·0	115	11·5	155	16·8	141	17·2	139	15·4	146
Social class index	85	100	92	84	138	29	120	42	237	2	175	12	178	9	150	24
Social Survey J-index, 1954	3·13	110	2·69	116	9·89	36	14·26	14	20·16	1	17·23	4	16·82	7	17·67	3
VOTING																
General elections—1951 poll	87·5	8	85·1	44	83·5	83	85·1	44	81·3	128	81·9	122	83·4	88	86·7	19
1955 poll	80·7	36	80·5	39	77·5	84	80·7	36	76·5	102	77·6	83	79·3	61	81·6	27
1951 % voting left	58·0	29	53·4	55	41·5	118	41·2	120	27·0	153	31·2	145	28·5	151	45·4	105
1955 % voting left	56·8	25	52·9	50	37·9	122	34·6	132	25·2	154	28·6	146	24·8	155	42·8	108
Local elections 1956-58:																
% voting in contested elections	39	94	36	116	39	94	38	102	33	136	40	87	36	116	41	80
% uncontested seats	22	54	29	42	0	132	4	99	42	27	63	7	17	65	0	132
Votes as % of total electorate	32	92	26	115	39	53	37	64	19	139	13	152	30	105	40	46
HEALTH																
Infant mortality rate, 1950-52	38	18	27	84	21	133	28	76	21	133	21	133	20	142	15	157
Infant mortality rate, 1955-57	28	41	22	88	19	127	20	116	17	144	20	116	22	88	15	154
Expect. of life at year One, 1950-52	69·6	100	71·0	34	70·9	38	71·5	17	72·5	4	73·0	3	71·1	31	70·4	64
T.B. notification rate, 1957	88	79	49	142	97	64	59	124	93	69	95	67	58	127	64	117
Mortality rate 1957—lung cancer	66	150	87	131	114	82	124	59	47	157	62	152	139	39	160	15
Mortality rate 1957—other cancer	119	23	93	135	90	141	105	86	79	155	76	156	103	102	114	42
Mortality rate 1957—bronchitis	86	111	65	143	111	69	145	39	50	150	35	156	23	157	132	55
EDUCATION																
% with terminal edn. age under 15	77·5	23	70·4	59	55·6	127	67·9	77	34·4	156	45·7	151	51·8	136	62·9	102
% aged 15-24 in full-time education	8·7	69	7·3	100	11·8	37	10·0	49	25·0	1	17·6	5	18·7	4	11·7	40

		Surrey								Sussex						
		MITCHAM		SURBITON		SUTTON & CHEAM		WIMBLEDON		BRIGHTON		EASTBOURNE		HASTINGS		HOVE	
		Value	Rank	Value	Rank	Value	Rank	Value	Rank	Value	Rank	Value	Rank	Value	Rank	Value	Rank
POPULATION SIZE AND STRUCTURE																	
Population ('000)		67	114	61	128	81	86	58	135	156	30	58	136	66	118	70	102
% of population aged 0-14		21·7	84	21·6	89	19·7	135	18·8	146	19·8	133	17·8	151	19·6	138	15·8	157
% of population aged 15-64		69·4	15	68·1	39	68·8	23	66·8	99	64·8	143	63·2	153	60·7	156	62·9	154
% of population aged 65 or over		8·9	129	10·3	85	11·5	53	14·4	14	15·4	13	19·0	4	19·7	3	21·3	2
Females per 1000 males		1077	103	1136	45	1188	24	1263	9	1245	13	1385	5	1391	4	1481	2
Females per 1000 males, age 25-44		1038	82	1092	39	1156	15	1132	25	1148	20	1246	5	1232	7	1264	2
% of females 20-24 ever married		47·7	86	41·1	135	37·2	150	40·1	140	46·0	106	40·9	136	49·6	62	40·1	140
POPULATION CHANGE																	
1931-51—total (%)		18·3	59	101·7	13	66·8	19	-2·3	125	6·1	95	-1·2	122	-1·0	119	26·4	47
1931-51—births and deaths (%)		15·0	34	19·9	21	15·0	34	0·9	140	-0·2	143	-2·7	150	-6·0	153	-13·2	157
1931-51—balance of change (%)		3·3	76	81·8	13	51·8	20	-3·2	100	6·3	72	1·5	84	5·0	73	39·6	26
1951-58 (%)		-3·8	132	4·4	34	-1·8	102	-1·1	90	2·1	54	-0·2	79	-2·0	106	0·4	70
Birth rate ratio, 1950-52		81	130	83	123	73	149	82	126	88	113	77	154	87	117	71	155
Birth rate ratio, 1955-57		83	123	78	141	78	141	85	116	88	110	73	153	82	127	77	145
% illegitimate births, 1950-52		3·5	136	4·2	102	3·5	136	4·3	98	8·3	1	7·0	12	7·1	9	8·1	2
% illegitimate births, 1955-57		3·6	119	4·3	94	3·3	133	4·6	84	7·8	7	5·4	52	5·6	43	6·6	15
HOUSEHOLDS AND HOUSING																	
% persons in private h/hlds		99·5	9	97·8	62	97·3	86	97·0	98	94·6	133	89·4	150	91·3	148	94·4	134
% one-person h/hlds		7·4	124	9·4	85	8·4	105	14·9	10	16·2	6	14·7	12	17·5	3	20·3	1
% six- or more person h/hlds		6·0	115	5·8	120	5·8	120	5·8	120	6·8	97	6·0	115	5·5	131	4·4	156
% 1-3-room dwellings		13·4	56	13·3	58	7·0	134	15·6	38	23·8	18	9·3	99	18·5	26	28·6	12
Persons per room		0·76	57	0·72	94	0·68	128	0·68	128	0·74	76	0·63	153	0·65	145	0·64	150
% overcrowded h/hlds (composite)		5·7	86	5·4	100	4·8	115	5·7	86	7·5	44	3·3	145	4·3	124	4·8	115
% h/hlds at over 1½ persons per room		4·0	90	3·9	94	3·4	117	4·1	86	5·4	45	2·6	143	3·0	129	3·4	117
% h/hlds in shared dwellings		18·7	43	14·6	65	18·0	49	29·2	17	22·5	31	22·1	32	18·3	47	17·2	52
% h/hlds with piped water		94	76	94	76	97	10	91	119	90	130	96	27	90	130	87	144
% h/hlds with W.C.		98	39	96	94	99	8	96	94	95	110	98	39	95	110	90	139
% h/hlds with 5 amenities		80	35	86	24	88	16	69	67	64	87	70	63	61	95	72	55
% h/hlds with 5, or bath missing		94	34	93	52	96	9	88	107	88	107	94	34	87	114	82	135
New-housing rate 1945-58—total		45	88	41	97	32	123	18	149	60	55	51	73	32	123	43	93
New-housing rate 1945-58—L.A.s		35	69	16	139	9	153	9	153	38	61	30	88	20	126	18	132
% L.A. of total houses 1945-58		77·4	59	38·7	147	28·3	154	51·3	130	64·1	108	58·2	119	61·6	115	43·0	145

142

	1	2	3	4	5	6	7	8
ECONOMIC CHARACTER								
Occupied as % of total population	64·4 (34)	59·8 (77)	58·0 (106)	59·3 (89)	54·5 (144)	51·7 (150)	48·2 (156)	48·4 (155)
% of women in labour force	33·2 (66)	32·1 (84)	33·2 (66)	38·1 (13)	34·9 (41)	38·7 (5)	35·4 (36)	38·1 (13)
% in manufacture etc.	59·8 (25)	28·3 (118)	15·2 (147)	20·7 (135)	23·7 (132)	11·4 (156)	11·8 (155)	25·9 (126)
% in all service industries	24·5 (141)	55·2 (28)	58·8 (21)	52·2 (40)	55·5 (27)	67·8 (6)	67·1 (5)	59·7 (17)
% in retail	6·6 (145)	8·6 (117)	18·9 (3)	12·7 (37)	14·6 (20)	15·5 (13)	16·8 (8)	13·5 (27)
% in finance, etc.	0·6 (152)	1·5 (71)	2·7 (11)	2·3 (27)	3·9 (4)	2·4 (21)	2·3 (27)	2·4 (21)
% in professional services	4·2 (140)	6·9 (74)	12·6 (11)	9·7 (35)	10·3 (30)	15·0 (7)	13·5 (9)	10·6 (26)
Job ratio	67 (129)	72 (125)	55 (143)	80 (116)	100 (75)	104 (65)	94 (91)	86 (107)
Commuting ratio	99 (13)	93 (20)	86 (37)	108 (7)	39 (95)	18 (153)	16 (156)	76 (51)
Per capita retail sales, 1950	68 (151)	100 (125)	153 (49)	164 (35)	171 (27)	200 (5)	149 (53)	133 (72)
SOCIAL CLASS								
% in social classes I+II	16·0 (77)	32·5 (13)	31·8 (16)	30·7 (17)	21·0 (46)	26·7 (27)	23·6 (34)	35·3 (7)
% in social classes IV+V	21·8 (117)	14·6 (149)	15·2 (147)	17·4 (137)	24·1 (94)	22·4 (108)	24·5 (91)	15·9 (143)
Social class index	104 (59)	178 (9)	172 (13)	159 (19)	111 (49)	131 (31)	117 (45)	178 (9)
Social Survey J-index, 1954	14·88 (12)	17·87 (2)	14·58 (13)	10·64 (31)	11·60 (23)	11·14 (28)	11·67 (20)	11·05 (29)
VOTING								
General elections—1951 poll	84·6 (58)	81·1 (131)	81·7 (125)	82·6 (106)	76·3 (156)	81·9 (122)	77·4 (151)	77·4 (151)
1955 poll	80·5 (39)	79·6 (54)	76·4 (104)	78·3 (74)	68·7 (155)	76·8 (110)	75·7 (112)	71·0 (148)
1951 % voting left	45·3 (106)	36·4 (135)	37·2 (131)	33·6 (142)	38·2 (128)	32·9 (143)	36·3 (137)	25·8 (154)
1955 % voting left	43·5 (105)	35·1 (130)	34·0 (136)	34·5 (133)	37·9 (122)	34·3 (135)	32·5 (137)	25·8 (152)
Local elections 1956-58:								
% voting in contested elections	46 (40)	39 (94)	45 (47)	41 (80)	43 (61)	55 (2)	45 (47)	42 (71)
% uncontested seats	10 (81)	0 (132)	31 (38)	31 (38)	56 (14)	20 (61)	63 (7)	81 (3)
Votes as % of total electorate	41 (40)	39 (53)	32 (92)	31 (99)	20 (133)	43 (26)	16 (148)	9 (155)
HEALTH								
Infant mortality rate, 1950-52	25 (96)	21 (133)	19 (146)	17 (153)	31 (57)	17 (153)	23 (112)	19 (146)
Infant mortality rate, 1955-57	14 (156)	17 (144)	21 (102)	12 (157)	21 (102)	17 (144)	20 (116)	16 (150)
Expect. of life at year One, 1950-52	70·8 (41)	71·5 (17)	70·9 (38)	70·8 (41)	70·6 (51)	70·0 (84)	70·4 (64)	70·5 (58)
T.B. notification rate, 1957	36 (152)	62 (119)	81 (96)	165 (9)	78 (99)	45 (146)	51 (138)	78 (99)
Mortality rate 1957—lung cancer	179 (6)	91 (127)	112 (89)	100 (111)	98 (116)	103 (105)	95 (122)	84 (136)
Mortality rate 1957—other cancer	107 (76)	103 (102)	117 (31)	81 (153)	112 (51)	106 (81)	87 (145)	107 (76)
Mortality rate 1957—bronchitis	106 (78)	68 (139)	73 (133)	79 (123)	87 (108)	37 (154)	71 (135)	39 (153)
EDUCATION								
% with terminal edn. age under 15	68·7 (73)	46·4 (150)	49·4 (143)	47·2 (148)	62·1 (104)	60·0 (114)	60·7 (112)	51·4 (138)
% aged 15-24 in full-time education	8·6 (71)	14·7 (21)	16·6 (7)	15·2 (16)	10·4 (47)	13·5 (26)	10·7 (45)	16·2 (10)

| | Sussex | | Warwickshire | | | | | | | | Wiltshire | | Worcestershire | | | |
| | WORTHING | | BIRMINGHAM | | COVENTRY | | NUNEATON | | SOLIHULL | | SWINDON | | DUDLEY | | WORCESTER | |
	Value	Rank	Value	Rank	Value	Rank	Value	Rank	Value	Rank	Value	Rank	Value	Rank	Value	Rank
POPULATION SIZE AND STRUCTURE																
Population ('000)	69	103	1,113	2	258	14	54	142	68	109	69	105	63	124	60	130
% of population aged 0-14	16·6	155	23·8	37	24·0	32	24·7	20	24·6	23	21·8	80	23·9	35	21·6	89
% of population aged 15-64	58·8	157	66·9	94	68·0	43	66·5	110	66·3	117	66·7	102	67·3	77	66·8	99
% of population aged 65 or over	24·6	1	9·3	116	8·0	147	8·8	132	9·1	125	11·5	53	8·8	132	11·6	51
Females per 1000 males	1507	1	1084	97	995	153	1009	150	1098	87	1048	130	1049	127	1125	58
Females per 1000 males, age 25-44	1306	1	1006	120	931	156	950	153	1096	36	993	132	980	139	1062	59
% of females 20-24 ever married	43·1	127	48·0	82	53·8	19	58·9	2	42·2	132	53·6	21	48·4	74	46·7	101
POPULATION CHANGE																
1931-51—total (%)	49·1	28	11·0	79	45·0	31	17·0	64	167·9	7	10·5	82	4·9	97	15·5	68
1931-51—births and deaths (%)	-12·3	156	13·0	48	18·7	24	17·1	28	37·7	4	8·2	91	13·2	45	7·4	99
1931-51—balance of change (%)	61·4	18	-2·0	96	26·3	38	-0·1	90	130·2	2	2·3	80	-8·2	117	8·1	68
1951-58 (%)	7·3	25	-1·6	99	8·8	21	3·7	42	25·2	3	16·4	5	3·2	46	7·1	27
Birth rate ratio, 1950-52	72	152	105	41	103	48	104	43	88	113	100	62	102	54	99	68
Birth rate ratio, 1955-57	81	132	100	53	103	41	99	58	103	41	115	10	92	94	94	83
% illegitimate births, 1950-52	5·7	41	5·4	60	6·1	29	3·7	123	3·3	143	5·1	72	2·8	152	5·6	49
% illegitimate births, 1955-57	5·0	66	6·6	15	5·7	39	3·6	119	2·7	151	4·7	80	2·6	153	4·5	88
HOUSEHOLDS AND HOUSING																
% persons in private h/hlds	94·0	138	96·8	108	96·8	108	97·8	62	98·6	24	99·1	13	99·3	12	96·4	116
% one-person h/hlds	15·8	7	9·0	92	7·6	119	5·9	148	5·5	151	7·8	115	6·8	135	10·1	73
% six- or more person h/hlds	5·1	144	9·5	23	7·5	73	10·2	18	6·1	113	7·5	73	11·6	7	8·2	56
% 1-3-room dwellings	11·0	76	14·6	43	8·2	117	6·1	147	4·7	156	5·4	151	15·5	40	11·2	74
Persons per room	0·60	156	0·76	57	0·76	57	0·75	66	0·65	145	0·71	106	0·83	16	0·73	85
% overcrowded h/hlds (composite)	2·5	155	8·8	29	7·5	44	5·6	91	2·6	153	4·1	128	10·4	18	6·3	70
% h/hlds at over 1½ persons per room	1·9	153	6·9	26	5·3	50	3·8	98	1·8	155	2·7	140	8·2	18	4·6	71
% h/hlds in shared dwellings	12·9	73	14·0	68	13·9	69	10·2	92	5·9	138	10·0	99	9·8	101	11·5	86
% h/hlds with piped water	95	52	93	95	94	76	93	95	94	76	91	119	84	152	89	137
% h/hlds with W.C.	97	72	87	144	95	110	95	110	94	119	97	72	87	144	93	125
% h/hlds with 5 amenities	83	30	59	108	72	55	56	120	87	20	59	108	62	92	60	101
% h/hlds with 5, or bath missing	94	34	82	135	92	67	89	100	91	80	90	91	78	144	85	126
New-housing rate 1945-58—total	83	13	36	111	86	8	77	20	129	1	101	5	62	47	70	28
New-housing rate 1945-58—L.A.s	23	115	27	100	49	31	58	14	32	80	82	2	53	22	51	26
% L.A. of total houses 1945-58	27·9	155	75·7	66	57·0	120	75·2	69	24·7	156	80·5	51	85·0	30	72·5	81

144

	1	2	3	4	5	6	7	8	9	10	11	12	13	14	15	16
ECONOMIC CHARACTER																
Occupied as % of total population	43·6	157	66·5	13	65·0	30	63·2	47	59·2	91	57·2	115	65·1	29	62·4	57
% of women in labour force	31·6	93	35·5	34	28·8	125	29·6	117	29·2	120	26·8	138	32·0	86	34·6	46
% in manufacture etc.	16·4	142	60·3	22	69·4	5	54·2	45	46·8	64	49·3	58	54·4	44	40·6	80
% in all service industries	65·9	10	28·5	118	21·6	151	31·2	107	40·7	68	28·9	114	34·7	96	43·6	56
% in retail	17·8	4	7·4	137	6·3	148	11·1	58	9·5	99	10·8	65	10·0	84	13·3	31
% in finance, etc.	2·6	15	1·8	55	0·9	140	1·4	83	1·1	119	1·1	119	1·3	96	1·4	83
% in professional services	10·7	23	5·8	108	4·0	142	6·0	97	8·7	49	4·6	133	5·8	108	7·6	62
Job ratio	96	85	112	34	113	29	78	120	51	147	110	43	86	107	113	29
Commuting ratio	30	120	23	144	30	120	49	81	81	44	32	115	76	51	30	120
Per capita retail sales, 1950	171	27	135	69	122	94	134	71	86	138	159	40	125	80	244	1
SOCIAL CLASS																
% in social classes I+II	32·7	10	13·7	111	13·2	117	10·5	146	32·6	11	11·9	132	12·3	126	16·8	67
% in social classes IV+V	17·5	135	27·3	66	26·2	76	35·1	23	15·0	148	26·0	78	31·4	41	24·7	88
Social class index	164	18	85	100	86	97	66	144	176	11	83	106	75	125	99	64
Social Survey J-index, 1954	10·41	33	2·44	119	4·62	87	2·17	128	11·21	27	4·20	95	1·56	143	7·48	52
VOTING																
General elections—1951 poll	80·0	137	79·8	141	86·2	29	85·0	48	83·2	95	84·8	53	83·7	79	82·1	115
1955 poll	72·7	141	71·5	147	81·6	27	79·7	52	78·3	74	80·0	46	79·8	49	77·8	82
1951 % voting left	25·4	155	52·4	64	59·0	23	60·0	21	29·7	148	57·0	35	58·4	25	44·5	109
1955 % voting left	22·9	156	50·1	73	53·7	40	55·8	30	27·8	148	54·9	33	54·9	33	43·2	107
Local elections 1956-58:																
% voting in contested elections	37	107	36	116	46	40	41	80	43	61	27	150	40	87	47	31
% uncontested seats	58	11	0	132	0	132	8	87	60	9	11	77	0	132	54	17
Votes as % of total electorate	16	148	36	68	46	13	38	59	18	143	24	120	40	46	21	128
HEALTH																
Infant mortality rate, 1950-52	24	103	28	76	33	42	28	76	28	76	22	122	35	30	26	90
Infant mortality rate, 1955-57	24	71	24	71	28	41	23	78	15	154	23	78	29	27	25	64
Expect. of life at year One, 1950-52	71·2	27	69·8	95	70·1	78	70·2	74	71·9	8	70·2	74	69·0	122	70·0	84
T.B. notification rate, 1957	51	137	119	41	133	22	88	79	73	108	82	94	142	15	47	144
Mortality rate 1957—lung cancer	84	136	125	56	113	86	95	122	119	74	49	155	113	86	127	50
Mortality rate 1957—other cancer	98	118	110	61	102	106	104	94	124	14	95	127	118	27	110	61
Mortality rate 1957—bronchitis	37	154	140	42	87	108	146	37	68	139	93	96	185	11	118	65
EDUCATION																
% with terminal edn. age under 15	55·7	126	75·8	34	70·2	61	86·1	2	55·2	129	72·7	49	83·5	5	69·2	69
% aged 15-24 in full-time education	15·9	11	5·8	131	7·1	107	4·8	150	14·1	24	5·5	144	4·0	156	7·1	107

| | Worcestershire | | Yorkshire | | | | | | | | | | | | | | |
| | OLDBURY | | KINGSTON UPON HULL | | MIDDLES-BROUGH | | BARNSLEY | | BRADFORD | | DEWSBURY | | DONCASTER | | HALIFAX | |
	Value	Rank	Value	Rank	Value	Rank	Value	Rank	Value	Rank	Value	Rank	Value	Rank	Value	Rank
POPULATION SIZE AND STRUCTURE																
Population ('000)	54	145	299	9	147	33	76	90	292	10	53	146	82	83	98	68
% of population aged 0-14	24·0	32	25·5	9	26·4	4	24·9	16	21·0	104	23·1	49	21·9	76	20·6	113
% of population aged 15-64	68·4	30	65·3	135	65·2	137	66·4	114	67·3	77	65·8	125	68·7	25	67·1	86
% of population aged 65 or over	7·6	150	9·2	121	8·4	138	8·7	134	11·7	48	11·1	64	9·4	111	12·3	30
Females per 1000 males	1031	45	1090	93	1041	136	997	152	1150	37	1109	77	1038	140	1164	31
Females per 1000 males, age 25-44	957	149	1027	97	973	144	917	157	1028	95	1014	108	1007	116	1028	95
% of females 20-24 ever married	49·0	66	53·4	22	49·9	59	58·6	4	51·2	38	53·8	19	55·0	13	50·3	48
POPULATION CHANGE																
1931-51—total (%)	47·1	30	-4·6	134	6·0	96	2·4	105	-2·1	124	-1·5	123	26·8	46	0·3	114
1931-51—births and deaths (%)	22·1	17	12·0	54	14·6	39	13·3	43	1·2	140	4·2	130	11·4	59	-0·3	145
1931-51—balance of change (%)	25·0	41	-16·6	145	-8·6	119	-10·9	130	-3·3	101	-5·7	109	15·4	49	0·6	89
1951-58 (%)	2·2	53	0·6	68	3·6	43	-0·1	77	-1·6	99	-0·3	82	2·6	49	-3·2	120
Birth rate ratio, 1950-52	91	103	122	7	137	1	122	7	106	38	115	17	102	54	99	68
Birth rate ratio, 1955-57	87	113	113	11	133	3	111	13	107	30	109	20	98	64	101	48
% illegitimate births, 1950-52	4·0	108	5·6	49	6·0	33	4·9	79	6·7	18	5·7	41	5·9	35	7·4	4
% illegitimate births, 1955-57	2·8	148	5·6	43	5·4	52	3·2	138	6·5	18	4·7	80	5·3	58	6·6	15
HOUSEHOLDS AND HOUSING																
% persons in private h/hlds	98·3	38	97·4	83	97·5	78	97·5	78	97·4	83	97·8	62	96·0	122	97·1	94
% one-person h/hlds	6·2	142	11·1	51	7·8	115	8·0	111	14·3	16	12·8	27	7·5	122	14·6	13
% six- or more person h/hlds	9·9	20	18·4	36	12·7	6	10·7	15	6·4	105	7·1	84	8·1	58	5·1	144
% 1-3-room dwellings	7·5	125			16·4	35	18·8	25	36·1	7	43·4	4	3·6	157	44·7	2
Persons per room	0·79	35	0·77	48	0·82	21	0·82	21	0·77	48	0·81	25	0·68	128	0·80	30
% overcrowded h/hlds (composite)	9·2	26	6·6	61	9·7	23	8·3	34	9·2	26	10·8	15	4·5	121	9·6	24
% h/hlds at over 1½ persons per room	6·5	31	5·7	39	8·3	16	7·3	22	7·3	22	7·4	21	3·6	110	6·5	31
% h/hlds in shared dwellings	14·3	66	6·7	130	7·1	127	4·1	145	5·6	140	1·5	157	7·3	126	2·9	154
% h/hlds with piped water	88	141	83	153	91	119	93	95	95	52	94	76	94	76	95	52
% h/hlds with W.C.	92	129	99	8	99	8	74	152	87	144	66	157	98	39	78	151
% h/hlds with 5 amenities	69	67	59	108	55	125	48	141	55	125	47	142	72	55	50	136
% h/hlds with 5, or bath missing	85	126	81	139	91	80	68	151	82	135	61	157	93	52	74	147
New-housing rate 1945-58—total	41	97	36	111	61	50	54	67	37	108	56	65	72	25	35	114
New-housing rate 1945-58—L.A.s	29	92	30	87	53	22	48	36	28	95	46	41	59	11	30	87
% L.A. of total houses 1945-58	71·9	83	84·4	35	86·8	21	89·1	14	76·0	64	82·9	40	80·9	48	86·3	24

	1	2	3	4	5	6	7	8	9	10	11	12	13	14	15	16
ECONOMIC CHARACTER																
Occupied as % of total population	66·3	15	57·7	109	59·6	86	59·7	79	65·0	30	61·4	68	58·1	104	63·2	47
% of women in labour force	31·9	89	27·9	132	27·2	134	25·7	145	38·6	7	33·8	55	26·3	141	37·4	19
% in manufacture etc.	78·4	1	38·6	92	43·1	76	49·9	57	56·0	40	49·2	59	47·6	63	60·5	21
% in all service industries	14·4	157	35·5	90	35·7	88	36·0	87	32·6	105	35·5	90	33·0	103	29·4	112
% in retail	3·7	156	10·2	81	12·2	43	13·3	31	8·8	114	8·4	122	11·1	58	8·9	109
% in finance, etc.	0·4	156	1·5	71	1·6	64	1·4	83	1·9	48	1·3	96	1·5	71	1·6	64
% in professional services	2·1	156	6·1	93	7·3	67	6·5	84	5·5	117	6·4	87	5·9	102	5·9	102
Job ratio	101	72	105	58	92	94	98	82	108	47	99	79	126	8	105	58
Commuting ratio	92	24	18	153	41	91	54	76	24	141	54	76	60	70	27	131
Per capita retail sales, 1950	63	155	118	104	123	90	154	47	159	40	127	77	193	7	148	56
SOCIAL CLASS																
% in social classes I + II	13·0	119	12·7	123	12·2	127	9·8	150	15·7	81	14·2	103	15·0	90	16·3	73
% in social classes IV + V	30·6	45	38·9	10	40·0	7	40·4	5	29·3	52	33·5	31	28·5	57	28·0	59
Social class index	78	118	68	139	66	144	59	151	87	95	78	118	87	95	91	87
Social Survey J-index, 1954	5·67	75	1·32	147	4·35	92	1·25	148	2·41	121	2·26	125	8·17	44	6·59	63
VOTING																
General elections—1951 poll	83·3	93	81·8	124	83·5	83	77·2	153	85·4	41	85·8	35	86·2	29	84·2	65
1955 poll	78·6	68	74·4	125	77·3	87	78·6	68	76·8	96	80·8	34	81·8	22	80·2	44
1951 % voting left	55·7	42	52·1	69	57·1	34	69·7	6	54·0	52	53·3	56	49·6	79	50·6	74
1955 % voting left	46·1	96	53·5	44	52·0	58	72·8	5	52·9	50	52·1	57	48·3	83	48·6	80
Local elections 1956-58: % voting in contested elections	34	130	34	130	38	102	53	5	43	61	51	10	51	10	46	40
% uncontested seats	10	81	13	72	49	21	60	9	0	132	11	77	19	63	52	19
Votes as % of total electorate	31	99	31	99	20	133	17	145	43	26	46	13	43	26	21	128
HEALTH																
Infant mortality rate, 1950-52	26	90	40	10	35	30	35	30	38	18	31	57	33	42	31	57
Infant mortality rate, 1955-57	21	102	28	41	33	4	31	11	29	27	29	27	31	11	22	88
Expect. of life at year One, 1950-52	69·4	107	69·5	103	68·3	139	68·9	127	68·5	133	68·2	143	69·2	116	68·5	133
T.B. notification rate, 1957	88	79	105	53	141	16	84	89	136	20	19	157	151	12	98	61
Mortality rate 1957—lung cancer	165	12	157	21	114	82	73	146	104	103	99	113	120	68	87	131
Mortality rate 1957—other cancer	104	94	115	36	103	102	99	114	108	72	114	42	121	18	124	14
Mortality rate 1957—bronchitis	165	20	153	30	101	88	167	18	146	37	195	8	176	14	126	62
EDUCATION																
% with terminal edn. age under 15	78·7	19	76·0	32	71·3	55	79·6	15	66·2	85	72·9	47	59·4	116	67·9	77
% aged 15-24 in full-time education	6·1	126	5·6	139	6·4	119	6·1	126	7·9	84	6·1	126	8·7	69	7·8	88

Yorkshire

	HUDDERSFIELD		LEEDS		ROTHERHAM		SHEFFIELD		WAKEFIELD		HARROGATE		KEIGHLEY		YORK	
	Value	Rank	Value	Rank	Value	Rank	Value	Rank	Value	Rank	Value	Rank	Value	Rank	Value	Rank
POPULATION SIZE AND STRUCTURE																
Population ('000)	129	40	505	6	82	81	513	5	60	129	50	157	57	138	105	61
% of population aged 0-14	20·0	128	21·8	80	24·6	23	22·1	72	21·7	84	17·9	149	20·2	124	22·0	75
% of population aged 15-64	68·1	39	68·1	39	66·0	121	67·5	63	67·8	49	66·1	119	67·7	53	67·6	58
% of population aged 65 or over	11·9	44	10·1	95	9·4	111	10·4	80	10·5	76	16·0	8	12·1	38	10·4	80
Females per 1000 males	1118	66	1131	51	1029	46	1079	101	1059	118	1352	6	1186	25	1090	93
Females per 1000 males, age 25-44	1007	116	1047	77	974	142	1026	99	961	148	1208	10	1064	55	1076	49
% of females 20-24 ever married	50·1	53	50·4	46	58·6	4	53·4	22	51·9	34	42·8	129	52·0	32	46·4	104
POPULATION CHANGE																
1931-51—total (%)	4·9	97	4·6	100	9·5	84	-1·0	119	1·8	109	15·3	70	0·7	113	12·0	75
1931-51—births and deaths (%)	0·4	142	5·4	121	14·8	36	7·7	96	7·3	101	2·6	136	0·0	143	10·4	68
1931-51—balance of change (%)	4·5	74	-0·8	94	-5·3	106	-8·7	120	-5·5	108	12·7	56	0·7	88	1·6	83
1951-58 (%)	-0·7	85	1·3	68	2·1	54	-2·7	113	-1·0	88	3·9	41	-3·0	116	0·2	74
Birth rate ratio, 1950-52	96	81	99	68	110	28	90	108	103	48	80	133	94	91	97	74
Birth rate ratio, 1955-57	100	53	99	58	106	34	92	94	98	64	91	100	96	74	93	90
% illegitimate births, 1950-52	5·2	67	6·7	18	3·9	113	3·6	131	5·2	67	6·1	29	4·6	89	5·5	55
% illegitimate births, 1955-57	5·4	52	6·4	21	3·2	138	3·8	110	3·9	105	6·5	18	4·6	84	5·2	61
HOUSEHOLDS AND HOUSING																
% persons in private h/hlds	97·1	94	97·5	78	97·9	54	98·1	47	92·8	141	93·5	140	97·8	62	95·1	128
% one-person h/hlds	12·9	24	12·5	33	7·3	126	9·8	81	10·3	65	14·9	10	12·5	33	10·4	63
% six- or more person h/hlds	5·3	139	6·6	101	9·8	21	7·1	84	7·8	65	5·1	144	5·5	131	7·0	88
% 1-3-room dwellings	36·5	6	29·0	11	6·7	139	17·6	28	20·7	21	13·4	56	27·5	13	13·8	53
Persons per room	0·77	48	0·76	57	0·78	40	0·75	66	0·77	48	0·64	150	0·72	94	0·72	94
% overcrowded h/hlds (composite)	7·2	50	7·4	48	6·8	57	6·7	59	6·5	65	3·9	133	5·6	91	4·2	125
% h/hlds at over 1½ persons per room	5·6	42	5·7	39	5·3	50	5·3	50	5·1	59	2·9	133	4·3	78	3·3	121
% h/hlds in shared dwellings	3·5	151	5·8	139	7·5	121	7·4	124	3·6	150	16·2	59	2·3	156	8·3	110
% h/hlds with piped water	97	10	94	76	98	2	95	52	98	2	95	52	97	10	95	52
% h/hlds with W.C.	74	152	71	154	96	94	93	125	85	149	96	94	91	135	97	72
% h/hlds with 5 amenities	54	129	60	101	58	112	53	132	64	87	80	35	50	136	65	81
% h/hlds with 5, or bath missing	72	149	66	152	93	52	89	100	83	130	92	67	87	114	92	67
New-housing rate 1945-58—total	44	91	46	85	61	50	44	91	60	55	58	58	34	116	58	58
New-housing rate 1945-58—L.A.s	31	84	32	80	45	43	33	76	50	28	26	106	26	106	38	61
% L.A. of total houses 1945-58	69·7	91	69·3	93	73·3	76	75·9	65	84·3	36	44·7	141	78·6	56	65·2	106

148

ECONOMIC CHARACTER																
Occupied as % of total population	62·8	52	64·0	39	58·2	102	61·9	63	56·6	122	55·1	139	64·0	39	60·0	75
% of women in labour force	34·6	46	36·6	27	24·9	149	31·3	98	30·6	111	38·0	15	38·4	10	32·3	81
% in manufacture etc.	61·8	16	51·6	51	57·7	32	57·0	37	39·7	86	14·0	149	68·1	7	38·0	94
% in all service industries	26·6	137	35·0	94	29·4	112	29·6	111	44·1	53	64·5	13	23·3	144	39·2	74
% in retail	8·1	128	9·2	101	9·7	93	9·0	105	8·9	109	15·0	18	6·9	141	9·9	89
% in finance, etc.	1·2	106	2·2	34	1·4	83	1·3	96	1·2	106	7·1	1	1·0	132	1·8	55
% in professional services	4·8	129	6·5	84	5·9	102	6·2	90	12·1	144	10·6	26	4·6	133	7·5	64
Job ratio	114	25	106	57	110	43	106	51	122	11	103	68	104	65	112	34
Commuting ratio	34	107	20	149	62	68	16	156	69	58	28	126	20	149	27	131
Per capita retail sales, 1950	140	53	147	58	133	72	124	85	151	51	132	74	120	99	154	47
SOCIAL CLASS																
% in social classes I + II	16·3	73	16·2	75	11·0	140	14·2	103	14·7	95	27·8	24	16·6	70	15·2	88
% in social classes IV + V	27·8	61	26·3	75	35·3	22	29·8	49	30·0	48	18·5	130	26·8	70	27·0	69
Social class index	91	87	94	78	67	141	83	106	84	103	146	25	94	78	90	90
Social Survey J-index, 1954	5·52	79	3·82	102	1·71	140	3·00	111	3·63	105	7·00	55	2·53	118	2·22	126
VOTING																
General elections—1951 poll	86·3	26	82·0	118	84·2	65	82·6	106	85·3	42	78·7	147	87·5	8	86·4	25
1955 poll	79·7	52	74·0	130	77·4	85	73·2	140	77·9	80	71·9	144	83·9	4	83·5	6
1951 % voting left	48·5	92	53·2	57	65·6	10	58·9	24	58·3	27	29·4	149	52·7	61	49·3	82
1955 % voting left	47·7	86	51·4	62	63·3	12	56·8	25	60·5	17	27·7	149	46·5	94	49·1	77
Local elections 1956–58:																
% voting in contested elections	46	40	35	124	40	87	29	146	46	40	39	94	47	31	53	5
% uncontested seats	22	54	0	132	64	6	17	65	3	104	44	26	10	81	3	104
Votes as % of total electorate	35	74	35	74	15	151	24	120	45	16	21	128	42	34	51	1
HEALTH																
Infant mortality rate, 1950–52	25	96	30	63	36	24	27	84	35	30	32	49	32	49	23	112
Infant mortality rate, 1955–57	22	88	26	57	25	64	23	78	30	17	24	71	28	41	19	127
Expect. of life at year One, 1950–52	68·4	136	68·3	139	69·9	90	69·0	122	70·4	64	69·9	90	68·2	143	69·4	107
T.B. notification rate, 1957	74	106	87	82	50	140	119	41	64	117	56	130	105	53	59	124
Mortality rate 1957—lung cancer	119	74	129	45	112	89	141	31	78	143	65	151	81	141	85	133
Mortality rate 1957—other cancer	111	56	114	42	114	42	111	56	99	114	106	81	109	67	96	125
Mortality rate 1957—bronchitis	109	71	160	27	138	45	153	30	175	15	54	147	160	27	106	78
EDUCATION																
% with terminal edn. age under 15	70·4	59	75·7	35	78·8	18	76·9	25	69·1	71	54·2	131	75·1	40	65·4	93
% aged 15–24 in full-time education	8·9	63	7·7	91	5·8	131	7·4	97	9·0	60	12·6	31	8·4	74	8·9	63

	Glamorganshire								Monmouthshire	
	CARDIFF		MERTHYR TYDFIL		SWANSEA		RHONDDA		NEWPORT	
	Value	*Rank*	*Value*	*Rank*	*Value*	*Rank*	*Value*	*Rank*	*Value*	*Rank*
POPULATION SIZE AND STRUCTURE										
Population ('000)	244	16	61	127	161	29	111	51	106	60
% of population aged 0-14	23·6	40	22·6	59	22·1	72	23·2	47	23·4	43
% of population aged 15-64	66·6	106	66·7	102	67·6	58	66·6	106	67·1	86
% of population aged 65 or over	9·8	102	10·7	72	10·3	85	10·2	90	9·4	111
Females per 1000 males	1110	76	1048	130	1064	115	1048	130	1054	121
Females per 1000 males, age 25-44	1048	75	1028	95	1007	116	1035	85	1007	116
% of females 20-24 ever married	45·8	108	49·9	59	47·6	88	52·2	29	48·1	77
POPULATION CHANGE										
1931-51—total (%)	7·4	90	-14·0	150	-2·3	125	-21·2	155	7·2	91
1931-51—births and deaths (%)	9·4	77	2·8	135	7·3	101	5·2	123	11·0	64
1931-51—balance of change (%)	-2·0	96	-16·8	146	-9·6	125	-26·4	155	-3·8	102
1951-58 (%)	4·0	39	-3·0	116	1·4	64	-4·5	139	-1·3	93
Birth rate ratio, 1950-52	113	20	110	28	100	62	103	48	109	30
Birth rate ratio, 1955-57	107	30	98	64	99	58	92	94	96	74
% illegitimate births, 1950-52	5·2	67	3·4	139	3·4	139	3·4	139	3·7	123
% illegitimate births, 1955-57	4·9	70	2·7	151	3·2	138	2·9	146	4·0	102
HOUSEHOLDS AND HOUSING										
% persons in private h/hlds	97·2	89	98·5	29	96·8	108	99·5	9	97·5	78
% one-person h/hlds	10·1	73	9·4	85	8·6	100	8·4	105	8·7	97
% six- or more person h/hlds	9·0	34	9·2	31	8·7	41	9·4	26	9·2	31
% 1-3-room dwellings	7·6	123	10·5	83	7·1	131	5·6	148	12·7	63
Persons per room	0·77	48	0·72	94	0·76	57	0·71	106	0·78	40
% overcrowded h/hlds (composite)	10·0	20	6·4	67	7·8	40	8·3	34	10·9	14
% h/hlds at over 1½ persons per room	6·1	37	4·6	71	4·9	62	5·2	55	6·6	29
% h/hlds in shared dwellings	36·5	11	7·5	121	20·5	37	23·5	27	25·5	20
% h/hlds with piped water	93	95	91	119	85	148	85	148	85	148
% h/hlds with W.C.	97	72	92	129	91	135	94	119	89	141
% h/hlds with 5 amenities	71	60	30	156	60	101	20	157	59	108
% h/hlds with 5, or bath missing	92	67	64	154	74	147	63	156	82	135
New-housing rate 1945-58—total	57	61	33	119	48	80	13	154	46	85
New-housing rate 1945-58—L.A.s	40	56	32	80	39	57	12	147	38	61
% L.A. of total houses 1945-58	70·6	87	94·5	4	80·1	52	95·5	3	81·8	45

ECONOMIC CHARACTER										
Occupied as % of total population	57·6	111	54·0	145	55·3	137	53·4	146	57·7	109
% of women in labour force	29·5	118	24·1	151	25·3	146	22·8	154	26·1	143
% in manufacture etc.	33·6	106	51·6	51	39·6	87	61·1	17	38·8	91
% in all service industries	44·7	52	34·3	97	37·1	83	28·4	122	36·1	85
% in retail	10·2	81	10·7	67	10·6	72	10·7	67	9·9	89
% in finance, etc.	2·4	21	1·2	106	1·8	55	1·0	132	1·5	71
% in professional services	7·7	59	7·6	62	8·2	53	6·1	93	6·8	77
Job ratio	116	22	83	111	95	88	82	112	104	65
Commuting ratio	28	126	31	116	24	141	25	137	28	126
Per capita retail sales, 1950	143	62	82	141	112	113	73	149	134	70
SOCIAL CLASS										
% in social classes I+II	17·5	63	10·4	147	15·4	85	8·4	154	14·7	95
% in social classes IV+V	28·0	59	40·4	5	34·2	26	39·8	8	33·7	29
Social class index	94	78	61	150	80	111	56	153	79	114
Social Survey J-index, 1954	5·82	73	0·80	154	3·90	100	0·49	156	5·63	76
VOTING										
General elections—1951 poll	85·0	48	84·4	61	83·9	74	85·9	34	86·2	29
1955 poll	79·0	64	77·3	87	73·7	133	78·6	68	81·6	27
1951 % voting left	51·0	72	79·6	2	62·2	18	85·5	1	52·8	60
1955 % voting left	49·7	74	77·2	2	61·1	15	80·9	1	53·7	40
Local elections 1956-58:										
% voting in contested elections	44	53	42	71	39	94	43	61	51	10
% uncontested seats	0	132	92	1	65	5	52	19	23	50
Votes as % of total electorate	44	19	3	157	12	153	20	133	41	40
HEALTH										
Infant mortality rate, 1950-52	29	67	43	5	33	42	45	2	34	36
Infant mortality rate, 1955-57	28	41	35	2	29	27	29	27	31	11
Expect. of life at year One, 1950-52	69·3	112	68·3	139	69·0	122	67·7	155	69·6	100
T.B. notification rate, 1957	133	22	76	104	123	34	68	112	167	6
Mortality rate 1957—lung cancer	124	58	82	139	129	45	69	149	98	116
Mortality rate 1957—other cancer	99	114	110	61	110	61	126	11	117	31
Mortality rate 1957—bronchitis	109	71	135	51	125	63	231	2	133	53
EDUCATION										
% with terminal edn. age under 15	66·5	84	57·4	122	65·7	90	69·3	67	66·1	86
% aged 15-24 in full-time education	9·3	58	9·9	51	9·7	53	10·0	49	8·8	66

151

APPENDIX C

The Scottish Towns—A Comparison

THERE were in 1951 seven Scottish towns with populations of 50,000 or over: Edinburgh, Glasgow, Aberdeen, Dundee, Motherwell & Wishaw, Greenock and Paisley. They were excluded from the main analysis because the Scottish statistics are in part different from those for England and Wales. It seemed a pity, however, to omit the Scottish towns entirely, and the available data are assembled in this Appendix. The missing series are the two education variables, the J-index, the job ratio, the commuting ratio and one of the household arrangements series. The remaining variables are listed in Table 32, together with the ranks. The sources of the data are set out in a note at the end of the Appendix.

The Scottish ranks are based on the rank order of the 157 English and Welsh towns. For example, Aberdeen, with 5·5 per cent. illegitimate births in the period 1950-52, equalled six English towns (Colchester, Oldham, Lancaster, Leicester, Mansfield and York) which had the same illegitimacy rate and occupied rank 55. The same rank was therefore allocated to Aberdeen. When there was no equivalent English value, the nearest value was taken instead. Rank 1, for example, means equal to or exceeding the highest English value. Table 32 makes it possible to compare the Scottish with the English and Welsh towns for 54 of the variables.

It is at once evident that, as a group, the Scottish towns differ radically from the English and Welsh towns with respect to housing. Unlike the housing of many of the industrial towns of northern England, with their small and primitive terraced cottages put up by the jerry builders of the Victorian era, the Scottish tenement has its roots further back in history. Trevelyan[1] writes of Edinburgh at the beginning of the eighteenth century:

> Edinburgh indeed was an extreme example of the French type of town, kept within its ancient limits for reason of safety and defence, and therefore forced to find room for growth by pushing its tenement flats high in air—in contrast to the ground plan of the easy-going peaceful towns of England. . . .

The lack of water closets, according to Trevelyan, also roused much comment among the English travellers:

> . . . while far overhead the windows opened, six or ten storeys in the air, and the close stools of Edinburgh discharged the collected filth of the last twenty-four hours into the street. It was good manners for those above to cry 'Gardy-loo' (gardez l'eau) before throwing.

[1] Trevelyan, G. M., *English Social History*, Longmans Green, London, 1944.

152

Almost a century and a half later Edwin Chadwick[1] wrote:

The prisons were formerly distinguished for their filth and bad ventilation; but the descriptions given by Howard of the worst prisons he visited in England . . . were exceeded in every wynd in Edinburgh and Glasgow inspected by Dr Arnott and myself. . . .

Chadwick also wrote disparagingly of many large English towns but the 1911 Census revealed that there were proportionately as many people living at over 4 persons to the room in Scotland (8·6 per cent.) as there were over 2 persons to the room in England. No fewer than 45 per cent. of the Scottish population lived at a density of more than 2 persons per room. In 1951 the average (median) percentage of dwellings with 1-3 rooms for the 157 towns in England and Wales was 10·6 per cent. The percentages for the seven Scottish towns varied from 60·4 per cent. to 79·5. This inevitably implies overcrowding of the worst type. Among the 157 towns of England and Wales, the average percentage of households living at over $1\frac{1}{2}$ persons per room in England and Wales in 1951 was 4·3. In Scotland the percentage varies from $4\frac{1}{2}$ times that figure in Paisley to over $7\frac{1}{2}$ times in Glasgow, where one third of the households lived at this abominably low standard. The Scottish towns exceed by a considerable margin even the low level of housing of the Durham towns.

Nor are the Scottish houses better provided as regards household amenities (more properly called household necessities); most of the Scottish towns are near the bottom of the list with respect to internal supply of piped water; all except one (Edinburgh, which is in 150th position) have relatively fewer water closets than the worst of the English and Welsh towns. All except Edinburgh are also near the bottom of the scale with respect to the five arrangements combined.

Housing is the Scottish lament and the significance of all other differences dwindles by comparison. But, as might be expected, infant mortality rates are higher on average in the Scottish towns, which also has substantially higher tuberculosis rates. There are, on average, fewer people in social classes I + II and more in IV + V than in England and Wales; birth rates are higher. There are fewer deaths due to bronchitis.

These Scottish towns are not of course alike in all respects. Overcrowding is lower in Edinburgh and Paisley than in the other Scottish towns; it is highest in Glasgow and Motherwell & Wishaw. In terms of social class, Edinburgh leads, followed a long way behind by Aberdeen, Dundee, Glasgow, Paisley, Motherwell & Wishaw and Greenock, in that order, if we take the percentage in social classes I + II as a criterion. The order is only slightly different for the other social class variables.

In terms of population change between 1931 and 1951, all Scottish towns, except Paisley, lost population through migration, the biggest losses

[1] Quoted by Trevelyan, *op. cit.*

TABLE 32

Scottish towns with populations in 1951 of 50,000 or over—basic data and ranks

(For explanation of ranks see text)

Variable	Aberdeenshire		Angus		Lanarkshire				Midlothian		Renfrewshire			
	ABERDEEN		DUNDEE		GLASGOW		MOTHERWELL & WISHAW		EDINBURGH		GREENOCK		PAISLEY	
	Value	Rank	Value	Rank	Value	Rank	Value	Rank	Value	Rank	Value	Rank	Value	Rank
POPULATION SIZE AND STRUCTURE														
1. Population ('000)	183	21	177	25	1090	2	68	108	467	7	76	92	94	70
2. % of population aged 0-14	23·2	47	24·2	27	24·8	18	26·5	4	21·8	80	26·7	4	24·8	18
3. % of population aged 15-64	66·8	99	65·4	134	66·6	106	65·1	139	66·8	99	64·5	146	66·1	119
4. % of population aged 65 or over	10·0	98	10·4	80	8·6	136	8·4	138	11·3	58	8·8	132	9·0	127
5. Females per 1000 males	1185	26	1186	25	1100	84	1057	118	1183	28	1066	111	1129	54
6. Females per 1000 males, age 25-44	1142	24	1130	26	1074	49	1067	51	1125	28	1033	90	1095	37
7. % of females aged 20-24 married[1]	39·5	145	41·4	134	38·0	148	37·4	149	36·7	151	42·0	133	40·8	137
POPULATION CHANGE														
8. 1931-51—total (%)	7·6	90	0·1	114	-0·3	115	3·9	101	6·3	94	-3·4	131	6·0	96
9. 1931-51—births and deaths (%)	11·1	63	8·8	81	12·3	52	17·4	28	6·5	110	15·0	34	12·9	49
10. 1931-51—balance of change (%)	-3·4	101	-8·7	120	-12·6	135	-13·5	136	-0·1	90	-18·4	148	-6·8	113
11. 1951-58 (%)	2·0	56	1·6	63	-1·0	88	5·9	30	0·1	76	2·2	53	3·0	48
12. Birth rate ratio, 1950-52	101	59	109	32	118	11	114	19	102	55	122	7	106	39
13. Birth rate ratio, 1955-57	106	34	115	10	128	4	126	5	106	34	129	4	119	9
14. % illegitimate births, 1950-52	5·5	55	6·6	21	5·2	67	3·5	136	5·4	60	4·5	93	3·9	113
15. % illegitimate births, 1955-57	5·2	61	5·3	58	4·7	80	2·9	146	5·0	66	4·3	94	3·9	105
HOUSEHOLDS AND HOUSING														
16. % persons in private h/hlds	95·3	125	97·3	86	96·7	110	99·2	12	94·5	133	96·6	111	97·1	94
17. % one-person h/hlds	11·9	40	15·1	8	11·4	46	9·2	89	14·2	18	9·8	81	12·0	39
18. % six- or more person h/hlds	8·6	44	8·8	39	12·1	7	12·0	7	7·9	62	13·4	4	11·2	10
19. % 1-3-room dwellings	63·8	1	77·8	1	75·5	1	72·7	1	60·4	1	74·7	1	79·5	1
20. Persons per room	1·04	1	1·13	1	1·27	1	1·28	1	0·94	3	1·25	1	1·24	1
21. % overcrowded h/hlds (composite)	31·3	1	35·0	1	42·1	1	42·2	1	25·3	1	42·9	1	38·7	1
22. % h/hlds at over 1½ persons per room	23·2	69	24·8	1	33·4	1	32·6	1	19·4	1			29·1	1
23. % h/hlds in shared dwellings	13·9	69	4·5	143	7·1	127	10·1	95	9·4	102	12·0	81	3·3	152
24. % h/hlds with piped water	81	154	95	51	92	107	90	129	90	129	88	141	97	10
25. % h/hlds with W.C.	42	157	57	157	62	157	54	157	80	151	66	157	51	157
26. % h/hlds with 5 amenities	39	153	38	153	44	150	45	147	60	101	46	144	46	144
27. % h/hlds with all 5, or only bath missing					Not available		Not available		60	101				
28. New-housing rate 1945-58—total	61	49	69	30	49	76	76	21	42	95	61	49	72	25
29. New-housing rate 1945-58—L.A.s	46	40	50	27	43	49	67	4	29	92	40	56	67	4
30. % L.A. of total houses 1945-58	75·5	67	72·8	79	87·4	16	88·6	14	69·0	94	65·9	104	94·0	5

154

ECONOMIC CHARACTER														
31. Occupied as % of total population	57·2	115	64·3	35	62·6	55	59·1	93	59·1	93	60·1	74	64·0	39
32. % of women in labour force	32·3	81	39·3	5	33·1	69	27·5	134	34·6	46	28·4	126	35·5	34
33. % in manufacture	33·0	109	51·6	51	43·5	74	56·1	41	33·3	108	49·2	59	54·7	43
34. % in all service industries	46·2	49	33·8	100	38·1	76	25·9	139	47·7	47	33·4	101	34·1	98
35. % in retail	12·1	46	10·0	84	10·3	79	9·3	100	10·7	67	10·5	75	10·7	67
36. % in finance, etc.	2·0	41	1·6	64	2·1	38	1·2	106	3·0	7	1·1	119	1·0	132
37. % in professional services	10·7	23	7·6	62	8·3	52	5·1	125	11·2	18	6·7	79	7·6	62
38. Job ratio	Not available													
39. Commuting ratio	Not available													
40. Per capita retail sales, 1950 (£)	162	37	139	66	138	68	109	116	153	49	99	127	124	85
SOCIAL CLASS														
41. % in social classes I + II	15·6	83	13·7	111	12·1	128	10·8	143	19·0	55	10·4	147	11·4	138
42. % in social classes IV + V	31·3	42	33·2	32	31·8	40	34·7	24	24·9	87	35·5	20	34·5	24
43. Social class index	84	111	77	131	74	135	67	148	104	66	65	149	69	147
44. Social Survey J-index, 1954	Not available													
VOTING														
General elections:														
45. 1951 poll	82·8	103	87·0	15	80·5	135	84·7	56	81·9	122	83·0	99	84·4	61
46. 1955 poll	77·2	89	82·5	15	71·5	147	76·5	102	74·9	121	77·9	80	76·2	106
47. 1951 % voting left	53·3	56	54·1	51	53·4	55	57·3	33	43·1	115	57·1	34	55·4	43
48. 1955 % voting left	55·0	32	53·7	40	51·9	59	53·9	38	42·4	110	51·4	62	56·4	28
Local elections, 1956-58:														
49. % voting in contested elections	30·6	144	44·4	53	31·6	141	43·1	61	31·5	141	39·8	87	36·5	108
S.1 % uncontested seats	39	32	31	38	1	109	4	99	11	77	3	104	0	132
S.2 Votes as % of total electorate	19·4	139	31·9	92	31·5	92	41·6	34	28·2	109	38·2	59	36·5	64
HEALTH														
50. Infant mortality rate, 1950-52	28	76	40	10	44	3	36	25	28	76	40	10	43	5
51. Infant mortality rate, 1955-57	22	88	30	17	35	2	30	17	24	71	37	2	33	4
S.3 Expectation of life at year one, 1950-52	69·9	90	69·4	107	68·6	133	68·7	130	69·0	122	69·8	95	69·6	100
52. T.B. notification rate, 1956[2]	204	1	250	1	269	1	157	10	198	1	183	2	137	20
53. Mortality rate 1957—lung cancer	107	95	118	77	150	24	79	142	126	53	141	31	102	108
54. Mortality rate 1957—other cancer	108	72	119	23	114	42	110	61	111	56	104	94	100	110
55. Mortality rate 1957—bronchitis	51	151	64	143	109	71	64	143	75	129	59	144	87	108
EDUCATION														
56. % with terminal edn. age under 15	Not available													
57. % aged 15-24 in full-time education	Not available													

[1] No data were available for widowed, divorced or separated women for three of the towns. Figures are therefore given for married women and not, as in England and Wales, for women *ever* married. The difference, however, is small.

[2] The data for notifications of tuberculosis apply to 1956, instead of, as in England and Wales, to 1957. The 1957 Scottish data may have been affected by a national X-ray campaign, and 1956 data were preferred.

being in Greenock and Motherwell & Wishaw, but this was generally balanced by an increase due to births and deaths. The greatest increase of population between 1951 and 1958, as well as the greatest relative amount of new housing, occurred in Motherwell & Wishaw and Paisley, which also showed the largest figure for the share of total new building due to local authorities.

The data are best summarised by means of an analysis similar to that conducted for the 157 English and Welsh towns in Chapters V and VI. The Scottish towns were not included in that analysis; no doubt, if they had been, a few of the correlations and therefore the principal components would have been different, but the impact of seven towns on a hundred and fifty-seven would not be substantial.

The scores of the principal components for each of the seven Scottish towns were calculated by the method described in Chapter V, using the same weights as had been assigned to the 157 English and Welsh towns. Since the data were unobtainable for six out of the fifty-seven variables, the scores are only approximately comparable to the English and Welsh scores. In view of the substantial differences (see Table 33 below), there seemed no point in making corrections, especially as they would be little more than guesses.

We have in short attached the same relative importance to each of the primary variables in computing the Scottish scores as were used for English and Welsh towns. This makes possible a direct comparison between the Scottish and the English towns. Whether it is valid to interpret the Scottish data in this way is another question. The Scottish towns occupy a relatively low place in the hierarchy of towns, ranked according to social class, because of their poor housing conditions. Housing is an important part of the social status of an English town and overcrowding is highly correlated with low social status (see Chapter IV), but in Scotland different standards ought perhaps to be applied. A reasonably high social status is not incompatible with living in cramped quarters and sharing the toilet on the landing with the neighbours below. Only on the strict standards set by the English suburban five-room house, are the Scottish towns the poor cousins.

The relative position of the Scottish towns can be seen in Figure 4 (facing p. 158), which reproduces Figure 2 of Chapter VI with the Scottish towns superimposed. It is clear both from the tables and from the diagram that the Scottish towns differ considerably from the English ones, particularly with respect to components I and IV. The explanation is not far to seek. Both components I and IV, and especially the latter, are closely associated with housing density; in component I the association is by virtue of the correlation of social class with housing density. The very severe degree of overcrowding in the Scottish towns, as compared with England and Wales, is therefore responsible for the very high multiples shown in Table 33.

TABLE 33

SCOTTISH TOWNS WITH POPULATIONS IN 1951 OF 50,000 OR OVER. VALUES OF FOUR PRINCIPAL COMPONENTS EXPRESSED AS MULTIPLES OF THE STANDARD DEVIATION OF COMPONENT SCORES OF THE ENGLISH AND WELSH TOWNS

| Town | Principal component | | | |
	I	II	III	IV
Aberdeen	−1·46	1·27	−0·30	5·09
Dundee	−1·84	1·24	−0·35	4·65
Glasgow	−2·50	0·71	−1·11	6·79
Motherwell & Wishaw	−2·61	0·14	−0·14	6·09
Edinburgh	−0·64	0·97	−0·81	4·02
Greenock	−2·31	0·22	−0·02	5·53
Paisley	−2·10	0·59	−0·26	4·72
Mean values	−1·91	0·73	−0·43	5·27

(e.g. for component I, the standard deviation of the 157 English and Welsh towns was 0·409 and the mean was zero. The value of component I for Aberdeen was −0·596. The multiple, as given in table is therefore −0·596/0·409 = −1·46)

Edinburgh, the Scottish capital, with its administrative and professional offices, university and fine schools, occupies a place in the diagram akin to the old industrial and textile towns of Leeds, Bradford and Rochdale, at least with respect to the first two components (it has a much higher score on component IV than these English towns). Aberdeen, similarly, is not primarily an industrial town, though it is a centre of the fishing industry. Dundee, Paisley, Greenock and Motherwell & Wishaw are industrial towns, the former two being largely concerned with jute and cotton spinning respectively, Greenock with shipbuilding and Motherwell & Wishaw with iron and steel. Paisley and Motherwell & Wishaw are part of the Central Clydeside conurbation of which the chief town is Glasgow. The latter, with over 40 per cent. of the population working in the area employed in manufacturing industry, though not specialising in any one branch of it, may be compared in size and position with Birmingham.

It is clear, therefore, that the Scottish towns do not fit into any neat classification applied to the English and Welsh towns. Edinburgh is more like the non-industrial towns of groups 2 and 3 (see p. 84) than the Lancashire and Yorkshire textile towns, and similarly Aberdeen.

The reason for the displacement lies, of course, in the low Scottish housing standards and we might ask how the Scottish towns compare with those in England and Wales for characteristics other than housing conditions. This involves removing from the values of the components the fractions due to the six housing variables listed as numbers 19-22, 25 and 26 in Table 32. The revised positions are shown in Figure 4 in brackets, with the Scottish towns now more closely in line with the English ones. Edinburgh lies well up among the *non*-industrial towns while the other six are distributed among the various groups of industrial towns.

M

Sources of Data for the Seven Scottish Towns

Some of the Scottish data, like those for England and Wales, can be taken from several sources. We give below the publications from which the data were actually extracted:

A. General Registry Office, Edinburgh, Census 1951, Scotland, Volume III, *General Volume*, Edinburgh: H.M.S.O., 1954.

  items 1-6, 8-10, 17, 18, 20, 24-26

B. General Registry Office, Edinburgh, Census 1951, *Report on the Fifteenth Census of Scotland*, Volume I, Parts 1-4, 21, 27. Edinburgh: H.M.S.O., various years.

  items 7, 16, 19, 21-23

C. General Registry Office, Edinburgh, Census 1951, Scotland, Volume IV, *Occupations and Industries*, Edinburgh: H.M.S.O., 1956.

  items 31-37, 41-43

D. General Registry Office, Edinburgh, *Annual Report of the Registrar-General for Scotland*, reports for the years 1950-52 and 1955-57, Edinburgh: H.M.S.O., various years.

  items 12-15, 49-51, 53-55, S.1-S.3

E. The Registrar-General, Scotland, *Annual Estimates of the Population of Scotland 1958*, Edinburgh: H.M.S.O., 1958.

  item 11 (for 1958 populations)

F. Department of Health for Scotland, *Housing Return for Scotland, 30th June 1958*, Edinburgh: H.M.S.O., 1958.

  items 28-30

G. Board of Trade, *Census of Distribution and Other Services*, Volume I, London: H.M.S.O., 1953.

  item 40

H. *The Times Guide to the House of Commons 1951*, and *1955*, London: 1951 and 1955.

  items 45-48

I. Unpublished figures by courtesy of the Department of Health for Scotland.

  item 52

APPENDIX D

A Technique for Estimating the Expectation of Life at Age ONE for Local Authority Areas in England and Wales

by N. H. CARRIER

Population Investigation Committee and London School of Economics

1. *Introduction*

The problem set was the estimation of $\mathring{e}_1$ as a function of infant mortality and the sex-age-standardised ratio of local mortality to national mortality in England and Wales, 1951, i.e. in terms of columns 16 and 18 of *The Registrar-General's Statistical Review, Tables, Part I,* Table 12, or *Tables, Part II,* Table E.[1]

The procedure involved a number of isolated studies and their final integration into the completed result.

2. *The relationship between $\mathring{e}_1$, $\mathring{e}_0$ and q_0* (both sexes combined)[2]

First the relationship between q_0 and L_0/l_0 was studied from the post-war data of England and Wales.[3] The data fitted closely $1 - L_0/l_0 = 0.819q_0$. There is an exact relationship between $\mathring{e}_0$, $\mathring{e}_1$, L_0/l_0 and q_0. Substituting the above formula values for L_0/l_0

$$\mathring{e}_1(1 - q_0) = (\mathring{e}_0 - 1 + 0.819q_0). \qquad (1)$$

As a test of this formula, 1951 England and Wales values were substituted, namely $\mathring{e}_0 = 68.36$, $q_0 = 0.02954$. The formula gives $\mathring{e}_1 = 69.44$; the correct value is 69.42.

3. *The pattern of age-specific mortality in local areas* (both sexes combined)

Whilst the data are not published to permit the calculation of age-

---

[1] $\mathring{e}_x$ is the 'expectation of life', that is the average future lifetime, of persons aged exactly x, who were subject throughout their lives to the recorded age death rates of the period. The suffixes $_0$ and $_1$ indicate expectation of life at birth and at age One respectively.

[2] q_0 is the proportion of children who, at current rates, will not survive the first year of life.

[3] L_0 is the number of years lived by a cohort of children from birth to the first birthday. l_0 is the original number of children in the cohort at birth.

specific death rates for individual towns, *The Registrar-General's Statistical Review, Tables, Part I*, gives, in Tables 15 and 2, deaths and populations for regions by age (mainly in 10-year age-groups). A study was made of 1951 age-specific regional death rates, expressed as proportions of the corresponding national rates.

A tendency was found for the ratios of regional to national death rates at middle and older ages to be consistent, but there was no clear tendency for any particular pattern apart from this. For example, contrary to expectation, there was no clear tendency for the ratios at the older ages to be nearer unity than the ratios at middle ages. Ratios at younger ages were less consistent but, as death rates are so low at these ages, this is of little significance in the present context.

It was concluded that models of local mortality would best be provided by applying the same factor to the national death rate at each age.

4. $\mathring{e}_1$ for five models of local mortality (both sexes combined)

Using abridged life-table techniques, $\mathring{e}_1$ was calculated for five models of local mortality; the 1951 national age-specific death rates, and rates 15 per cent. and 30 per cent. below and above. These are values of $\mathring{e}_1$ appropriate to 'theoretical' towns with local death rate ratios (the column 16 reference in the introduction) of 0·70, 0·85, 1·00, 1·15 and 1·30. Values of $\mathring{e}_1$ for intermediate ratios were obtained by 5-point interpolation. Denote these values by $\mathring{e}_1(r)$, where r is the ratio.

5. Integration of isolated studies

Actual and 'theoretical' localities differ in that the ratio of the local to the national age-specific death rate is the same at all ages for the theoretical locality, but differs for the actual locality—column 16 gives the weighted average of the various ratios. Thus the model with a given ratio will only be expected to give approximately correct results, for areas with the same ratio in column 16, for indices summarising mortality at *all* ages, such as $\mathring{e}_0$.

Denote the infant mortality rate of an actual locality by i and the national rate by I, and denote by $\mathring{e}_1(i,r)$ the expectation of life at age One of the actual locality. It will be assumed that the expectation of life at birth of the actual locality, and a model with the same ratio, r, are the same, and can be denoted by the single symbol $\mathring{e}_0(r)$. The infant mortality rate of the model will be Ir.

Then from equation (1):

for the actual locality: $\mathring{e}_1(i,r)(1-i) = \mathring{e}_0(r)-1+0\cdot819$
and for the model: $\mathring{e}_1(r)(1-Ir) = \mathring{e}_0(r)-1+0\cdot819Ir$

Eliminating $\mathring{e}_0(r)$ and re-arranging, approximately:

$$\mathring{e}_1(i,r)-\mathring{e}_1(r) = [i-Ir][\mathring{e}_1(r)+0\cdot819]$$

The right hand side of this equation gives an expression for the 'correction' to be applied to the values of $\hat{e}_1(r)$ (calculated as described in paragraph 4 above) to give values of $\hat{e}_1(i,r)$ as required.

6. *Later modification*

Mainly because the records of smaller towns for single years were liable to chance fluctuation—but there is also the point that mortality in 1951 was abnormally high—it was decided to employ the average mortality of the selected towns for the years 1950-52. It was then necessary to determine the relationship between the average mortality of these towns in this period, and the mortality of England and Wales in 1951, to enter the table of $\hat{e}_1(i,r)$. (The average infant mortality rate for the period is also the appropriate value to enter for i.) The appropriate value for r was calculated as

$$\frac{\text{(Average value of column 16 for 1950-52)} \times \text{(Average C.M.I.}^1 \text{ for 1950-52)}}{\text{C.M.I. for 1951}}$$

---

[1] C.M.I. = Comparative Mortality Index, from *The Registrar-General's Statistical Review, Tables, Part I*, Table 3.

APPENDIX E

Notes on Related Research

A NUMBER of references to works of general importance in urban analysis are included in the text. An excellent annotated bibliography of urban sociology in Britain, covering items published up to 31st May 1955, is provided by Ruth Glass in Current Sociology Vol. 4, *Urban sociology*, Unesco, Paris, 1955. The purpose of this Appendix is to refer to previous research of *direct* relevance to the kind of multivariate analysis of urban characteristics that was attempted in Chapters V and VI.

The central idea of this was to unravel the relationships between a large number of urban characteristics, rather than to study in detail any single characteristic. The kind of unravelling we were concerned with did not even focus on any one variable or field. In this, the study was distinct from a much more common type of research which seeks to explain inter-town differences in some particular factor, such as infant mortality, in terms of other variables, say, social class, poverty and housing density. Examples are B. Woolf and J. Waterhouse, 'Studies on infant mortality, Part I. Influence of social conditions in county boroughs of England and Wales', *Journal of Hygiene*, XLIV, 2, 1945; and W. T. Martin, 'Ecological change in satellite rural areas', *American Sociological Review*, XXII, 2, 1957. Broadly similar, in different fields, are the publications by J. P. Martin, *Social Aspects of Prescribing*, Heinemann, London, 1957, who studies differences in rates of prescribing in different towns, and by B. Benjamin, 'Tuberculosis and social conditions in the metropolitan boroughs of London', *British Journal of Tuberculosis and Diseases of the Chest*, XLVII, 1953. A. B. Hill and W. J. Martin, 'Poliomyelitis and social environment', *British Medical Journal*, II, 1949, are concerned with polio incidence. W. George, 'Social conditions and the Labour vote in the county boroughs of England and Wales', *The British Journal of Sociology*, II, 3, 1951, uses multiple regression techniques to analyse the relationship between social conditions and voting in English cities. Methodologically the most far-reaching study of this type is that by D. J. Bogue and D. L. Harris, *Comparative population and urban research via multiple regression and covariance analysis*, Scripps Foundation for Research in Population Problems, Oxford, Ohio, 1954, which seeks to explain differences of growth and suburbanisation between metropolitan areas in the United States.

Mention should also be made of an ingenious multivariate analysis of individual settlements and contiguous areas in East Sussex by L. S. Jay and G. P. Hirsch: 'Comparative analysis of settlements' in *Sociologia Ruralis*, I, 1, 1960.

A different type of study, so far carried out mainly in the United States, aims at a classification of areas into types by means of a simultaneous analysis of a large number of variables. This is broadly what we have attempted. The published example that comes closest to our own approach appeared nearly twenty years ago, in a paper by D. O. Price, 'Factor analysis in the study of metropolitan centers', *Social Forces*, XX, 4, 1942. Price took 15 variables relating to the demographic, social and economic characteristics of the 93 American cities which, in 1930, had populations of 100,000 or more, and attempted to find a small number of fundamental factors which could adequately summarise the features of these towns. The method used was factor analysis, rather than that of component analysis which we employed. Price identified four fundamental factors, and ranked the cities according to a weighted combination of these.

The studies by E. Shevky and M. Williams, *The social areas of Los Angeles: analysis and typology*, University of California Press, Berkeley, 1949; and E. Shevky and W. Bell, *Social area analysis: theory, illustrative application and computational procedures*, Stanford Sociological Series, No. 1, Stanford University Press, 1955, summarise variations between Los Angeles census tracts by means of social status indices. These authors combine seven primary variables into three indices, of social rank, urbanisation and segregation, and classify tracts accordingly. W. Bell, 'The social areas of the San Francisco Bay region', *American Sociological Review*, XVIII, 1, 1953; and M. D. van Arsdol and others, 'The generality of urban social area indices', *American Sociological Review*, XXIII, 3, 1958, test the classification thus arrived at by factor analysis. This work in turn led to the more sophisticated approach used by C. F. Schmid in his later studies. In 1950 Schmid published an analysis of the characteristics of census tracts in 23 mainly medium-sized American cities, in a paper entitled 'Generalizations concerning the ecology of the American city', *American Sociological Review*, XV, 2. Twelve indices are used, based on 1940 statistics, most of them connected with social stratification: income, occupational status, employment, education, race and nationality, fertility, sex, and age. The aim is to see whether the patterns of variation between tracts differed much from one city to another. Two main 'dependent' variables are taken, first rent and then educational level, and correlations are calculated between each of these and the remaining indices. A combination of scale analysis and ranking techniques is then used to arrange the tracts within a city into types according to their pattern of characteristics.

The study was repeated on 1950 material, with only minor changes in design and coverage, in C. F. Schmid and others, 'The ecology of the

American city: further comparison and validation of generalizations', *American Sociological Review*, XXIII, 1958. The most recent publications by C. F. Schmid, 'Urban crime areas,' Part I and Part II, in *American Sociological Review*, XXV, 4, 1960, and XXV, 5, 1960, contain an elaborate and searching analysis of 1950 census data for a large number of variables and areas. Although this study is centred on the subject of crime, its multivariate techniques are of wide interest and applicability.

An interesting study by R. C. Tryon, *Identification of social areas by cluster analysis*, University of California Publications in Psychology, VIII, No. 1, 1955, analyses altogether 33 census characteristics relating to the 243 census tracts in San Francisco. Correlations are worked out, and an attempt is made to find patterns of correlation coefficients. Three major discriminating factors are arrived at, and used in classifying tracts.

Finally, one could mention a great number of studies which aim to combine series relating to various characteristics of urban life into single descriptive indices. An outstanding example is the work of E. J. Buckatzsch, 'An index of social conditions in 81 county boroughs', *Bulletin of the Oxford University Institute of Statistics*, VIII, 12, 1946, and 'The influence of social conditions on mortality rates', *Population Studies*, I, iii, 1947. In studying the influence of social conditions on mortality, Buckatzsch reduces a number of series relating to unemployment, social class, poor relief, local government, finance and overcrowding to two fundamental factors by means of component analysis. Another example is the study by L. T. Wilkins, 'Estimating the social class of towns', *Applied Statistics*, I, 1, 1952, which combines a series of data, using multiple regression analysis, into a social class index of British towns. Many other examples could be cited, especially from the American literature.

INDEX

This index does not include references to individual towns. Appendix B, which contains the complete data for each town, has its own index, on pages 110-111. The geographical position of the towns is indexed on pages 94-95 accompanying the map.

As regards the individual variables, the index does not give page references to Tables 2, 26-30, and Appendix B.

Age composition, 7, 12, 15, 23-24; definition of variables, 97; and population change, 47, 50; and population size, 46, 48; and principal components, 15, 16, 72, 73, 77, 79; and social class, 53, 54; correlation with other variables, 61; in Scotland, 154; regional differences, 43, 44
  of towns, 14, 15, 23, 42, 75, 76, 83, 89, 91, 92; *see also* population change

Bell, W., 163
Benjamin, B., 162
Birth rates, 26, 65, 98; definition of variables, 99; and population change, 47, 50; and population size, 46, 48; and principal components, 16, 71, 72, 73, 77, 79; and social class, 53, 54; in Scotland, 154; regional differences, 44
Board of Trade, 7, 104, 158
Bogue, D. J., 162
Bronchitis, deaths from, 37, 38; definition of variable, 107, 108; and population change, 51, 52; and population size, 47, 49; and principal components, 16; and social class, 53, 55; in Scotland, 153, 155; regional differences, 45
Buckatzsch, E. J., 164

Cancer, deaths from, 38; definition of variables, 107, 108; and population change, 51, 52; and population size, 47, 49; and principal components, 16; and social class, 55; in Scotland, 155; regional differences, 45
Carrier, N. H. (Author of Appendix D), 108, 159-161
Census of distribution, 7, 104, 158
  of population, 4, 5, 6, 7, 8, 19, 25n, 27, 28, 52, 97, 98, 99, 100, 101, 102, 103, 104, 105, 106, 107, 108, 109, 153, 158
Chadwick, Edwin, 153
Classification of towns, 17-19, 84-7, 156-7; according to function, 6, 80; and component analysis, 12-19, 75-6, 79,

80-93; general nature of, 16, 22, 93; homogeneity in, 83, 88-9; limitations of, 89, 93; *see also under* individual variables
Cluster analysis, 164
Commercial towns, in classification, 17, 84
Common factors in urban differentiation, 12-13, 42; *see under* principal components
Commuting ratio, 6, 31, 33; definition of variable, 103-4; and population change, 51, 52; and population size, 46, 49; and principal components, 72, 73; and social class, 53, 55; regional differences, 44
Component analysis, 3, 12, 42, 67-79, 163, 164; explanation of, 13-14, 67-9; limitations of, 15-16, 76; and classification of towns, 12-19, 75-6, 79, 80-93; for Scottish towns, 156; *see also* multivariate analysis
Components, *see* principal components
Component scores, 69, 80, 81, 82, 83; for English and Welsh towns, 84-8; for Scottish towns, 156; correlations with variables, 71-5
Constituencies, 7n, 106; *see also*, local authority areas, towns, voting
Conurbations, 5, 6, 25n, 33, 40, 87; *see also* local authority areas, towns
Correlation coefficients, 12, 19, 58-65; and component analysis, 67, 70; and logarithmic transformation, 59-60; and rank correlation, 59-60; between variables and principal components, 71-9; statistical significance of, 60; *see also* component analysis, principal components
  matrix, *see* correlation coefficients

Davis, B., 59n
Department of Health for Scotland, 158
Dependent variates, 66; *see also* component analysis, multivariate analysis
Duncan, O. D., 59n, 63n, 80n

165

CENTRE FOR URBAN STUDIES

Previous Publications

Statement of Evidence to Royal Commission on Local Government in Greater London, 1959

Centre for Urban Studies, Report No. 1

NEWCOMERS

The West Indians in London

RUTH GLASS

assisted by

HAROLD POLLINS

CENTRE FOR URBAN STUDIES

AND

GEORGE ALLEN AND UNWIN LTD., 1960

This report was published in the United States by the Harvard University Press, in 1961, under the title:

LONDON'S NEWCOMERS: The West Indian Migrants